The New

BIRDWATCHER'S POCKET GUIDE
to Britain and Europe

Peter Hayman & Rob Hume

Bounty
Books

First published in 2002 by Mitchell Beazley,
an imprint of Octopus Publishing Group Ltd

This paperback edition published in 2006 by Bounty Books,
a division of Octopus Publishing Group Ltd,
Endeavour House, 189 Shaftesbury Avenue, London WC2H 8JY
www.octopusbooks.co.uk
An Hachette UK Company
www.hachette.co.uk
Reprinted 2007 (twice), 2008, 2010, 2011, 2012, 2013
Copyright © Octopus Publishing Group Ltd

ISBN:978-0-753714-54-6

A CIP catalogue record for this book is available from
the British Library

Executive Editor: Lindsay Porter
Executive Art Editor: Christine Keilty
Project Editor: Chloë Garrow
Editor: John Woodward
Design: Alexa Brommer
Production: Alexandra McCulloch

Printed and bound in China

key to symbols

	not recorded in Britain
	rare vagrant in Britain
	resident in Britain
	rare, but annual, visitor to Britain
	summer visitor to Britain
	winter visitor to Britain
	passage migrant to Britain
	town and built-up areas
	freshwater marsh
	coast and sea
	farmland
	low scrub
	high scrub
	lakes and reservoirs
	mountains, moorlands, and crags
	rivers and streams
	cliffs and islands
	broadleaved woods
	pine woods
	mixed woods
♂	male
♀	female

ad	adult
juv	juvenile
imm	immature

Introduction

This book reveals our own fascination with birds while helping you to tell them apart. We hope it will open up new lines of thought for you, too, as you see the diversity and the complex relationships of Europe's birds. The book covers all the birds that breed regularly in Europe, as well as the regular visitors. In a book of this size, which we were determined would remain suitable for a shirt or jacket pocket, we could not include every bird from North Africa and the Middle East, nor the many rarities that visit Europe. Britain and Ireland alone have many more species that are seen just a handful of times each year, or maybe at intervals of several years. We have, however, given greater coverage to the birds that matter, the ones that you will see most often, at the expense of these irregular vagrants. We are also aware that habitat, distribution and time of year are critical elements of the identification process and can only be briefly indicated within a guide of this compact form. We decided, however, that the inclusion of more birds was a better service to the reader than fewer pictures but many more maps

We have tried to make the book both useful and interesting to experienced observers, who want a reminder of the more difficult identification challenges in Europe, as well as to beginners who are starting out on this enjoyable but challenging hobby, and feel in need of a helping hand. We recommend the companion volume, *The Complete Guide to the Birdlife of Britain & Europe*, which has more space devoted to the behaviour, distribution and biology of Europe's birds. It can be studied at leisure at home, while this little guide can be taken out to be consulted while you are actually watching the birds. Use it as an aide-mémoire in the field when you need the occasional prompt to ensure that you take note of the most critical features in identifying the species in front of you.

There is much to learn about even the most familiar birds. Much new information in this book comes from the artist's long hours of research in the collection of The Natural History Museum. However, such careful study, while informing us of many new discoveries about birds, can never replace familiarity with the living bird in the wild. Finding and identifying birds for yourself is a tremendously satisfying occupation: if this book helps, or sparks off new ideas, we will be delighted. If it also broadens the interest of readers who may not have considered the implications of, for example, the wear and bleaching of feathers, the regular moult cycles of birds and the changes in colour and pattern according to age and season, it will have succeeded.

Enjoy this book: but most of all enjoy the birds. When trying to identify them, do not be put off by seeming difficulties and problems: if you cannot always tell what a bird is, it doesn't much matter. It is still good fun, and is part of a lifetime of learning and improvement, and you will get there in the end with persistence and practice. Birds will always repay close attention, however expert, experienced or new to the pursuit you may be.

The parts of a bird

Throughout this book we have tried to avoid technical terms as far as possible, but some of the more precise details cannot be effectively described in any other way. So it is worth taking the time to study the basic anatomy of a typical bird, and becoming familiar with the names of all the main feather groups and facial markings. These terms are shown on the diagrams below, which will also provide a useful reference when reading the main species descriptions.

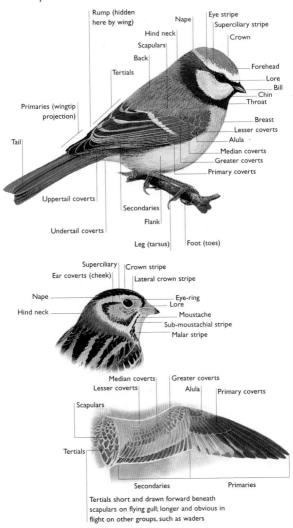

Tertials short and drawn forward beneath scapulars on flying gull; longer and obvious in flight on other groups, such as waders

Contents

Great Northern & White-billed Divers

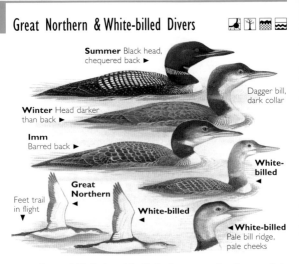

Summer Black head, chequered back ►

Dagger bill, dark collar

Winter Head darker than back ►

Imm Barred back ►

Feet trail in flight ▼

Great Northern ◄

White-billed ◄

White-billed ◄

◄**White-billed** Pale bill ridge, pale cheeks

Big, dagger-billed, broad-bodied divers, evenly chequered in summer with white-striped collar on black head and neck. Winter and immature brown above; Great Northern blacker on head with black half-collar and thick, pale bill with dark upper edge. Winter and immature White-billed browner on big head, with pale cheek, forehead bulge, bill pale on upper edge.

Black-throated Diver

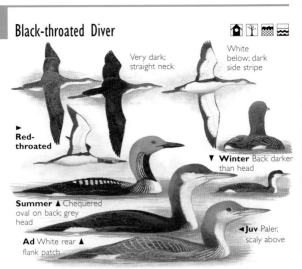

Very dark; straight neck

White below; dark side stripe

► **Red-throated**

▼ **Winter** Back darker than head

Summer ▲ Chequered oval on back; grey head

◄**Juv** Paler, scaly above

Ad White rear ▲ flank patch

Narrower-bodied, smaller-billed than Great Northern Diver. Summer adult has grey head, striped neck patch, discrete ovals of white bars on black back. Winter and immature grey-brown and white, with back darker than slightly greyer nape, white flank patch and hint of Z-shaped edge to dark hindneck. Bill straight, slim, blue-grey to yellowish with darker tip.

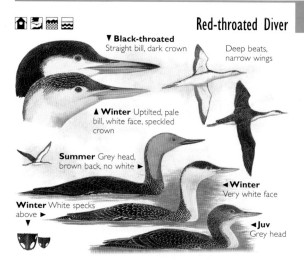

Red-throated Diver

▼ Black-throated
Straight bill, dark crown

Deep beats, narrow wings

▲ Winter Uptilted, pale bill, white face, speckled crown

Summer Grey head, brown back, no white ▶

◀Winter
Very white face

Winter White specks above ▶
▼

◀Juv
Grey head

The smallest diver. Bill tapers upwards and is held uptilted when swimming. In summer has grey head, striped neck sides, dark throat, no white on back. Winter and immature browner, with fine white speckling over upperside, pale face (palest of divers) with white extending above eye. Quickest diver in flight; flies with deepest wingbeats, slightly drooped head, trailing legs.

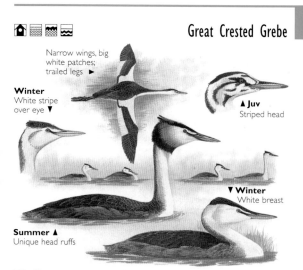

Great Crested Grebe

Narrow wings, big white patches; trailed legs ▶

Winter
White stripe over eye ▼

▲ Juv
Striped head

▼ Winter
White breast

Summer ▲
Unique head ruffs

Wholly aquatic, long-necked, spike-billed bird with gleaming white foreneck and breast. In summer has unique black crown with tufts, and white face with broad chestnut and black frill. Stark grey-brown and white in winter, with white line between black cap and eyestripe. Flies low and fast, feet trailed, head and neck stretched and drooped, showing big white wing patches.

Red-necked Grebe

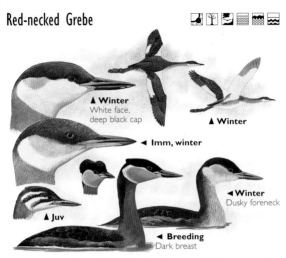

▲ Winter
White face,
deep black cap

▲ Winter

◄ Imm, winter

▲ Juv

◄Winter
Dusky foreneck

◄ Breeding
Dark breast

Big, stocky grebe; often looks dark and dull. In summer has black cap, dark red neck (brighter close up, fades paler), mid to dark grey face with whitish upper edge. Winter and immature birds blackish with dead white to greyish face below deep black cap, no white over eye, dusky foreneck, only breast clear white. Only grebe with stout yellow-and-black bill.

Slavonian Grebe

◄Winter
Straight bill, pale tip, small cap

◄Black-necked
Peaked cap, uptilted bill

Winter ►
Variations

Breeding
Yellow tufts,
red flanks ▼

▲ Winter
White cheeks almost
meet on nape

Medium-sized grebe with a small, straight, tapered bill. In summer has rufous neck and flanks (dark at distance), black head with wedge-shaped golden to buff tuft behind eye. Winter bird black and white with striking white foreneck, silvery flanks. Head flatter than Black-necked, cap sharper black against cleaner white face. Pale spot in front of eye, dark band near pale bill tip.

Little Grebe

▼ Breeding
Rufous face,
yellow gape

Winter ►
No white
on wing

▲ Winter
Dull brown, weak
cap, pale gape

Breeding
Dumpy, tailless,
dark greyish with
paler stern ▼

Winter ▼ ▲
Dull overall, weak face
pattern, dusky neck

Tiny, rotund, almost tailless aquatic bird. Dark in summer except for pale spot at base of bill; face deep rusty-red at close range. Browner in winter, with buffish face contrasting with darker crown and hindneck, but less so than Black-necked; no real white. Bill short, stubby, with pale gape mark. Only grebe with no white in wing. Frequent high, whinnying trill.

Black-necked Grebe

Winter ►
Variations in
head pattern

Uptilted
bill tip

Slavonian
Straight bill,
flatter cap ►

Slavonian
▼

Winter
Peaked cap, dusky
cheek ►

Breeding
Drooped yellow
tufts, red flank,
black neck ►

Small grebe, with a long neck that exaggerates size when alert. Slim all-dark bill with slight upturn. Dark in summer, with coppery flanks, sharply peaked black head and neck, and fan of gold or buff drooped from cheek. Black and dull white in winter, with more or less 'hooked' white ear patch that breaks smooth line of cap, typically dusky foreneck, peaked head.

9

Cory's Shearwater

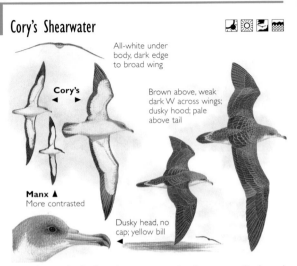

All-white under body, dark edge to broad wing

Cory's

Brown above, weak dark W across wings; dusky hood; pale above tail

Manx
More contrasted

Dusky head, no cap; yellow bill

Big, brown-backed inshore to oceanic shearwater. Back and wings mid-brown with faint darker W effect, large dusky head with no sharp cap, variable whitish patch above tail. Bill pale yellowish, hard to see against pale sea but obvious against dark water at long range. Lazy, rolling glide with slow wingbeats, soaring and banking in strong winds.

Manx Shearwater

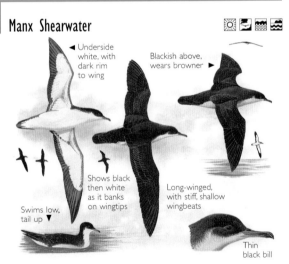

◄ Underside white, with dark rim to wing

Blackish above, wears browner ►

Shows black then white as it banks on wingtips

Long-winged, with stiff, shallow wingbeats

Swims low, tail up ▼

Thin black bill

Small, neat, contrasty shearwater, typically seen flying low over open sea with cross-shaped profile. Often shows black upperparts then white underside as it banks from wingtip to wingtip. Black above (fading to brown-black); gleaming white beneath. Thin black bill. Flies with flurries of quick, stiff, shallow beats, or just a quick downward flick between glides.

Levantine Shearwater

◀ Broad dark wingtip; variable diagonal band

Dark brown above; dusky cap and chest sides ◀

Short rear body, tail, toes ▼

White flank patch

▲ Variable amount of brown below

Palest form only slightly browner than Manx ▶

Small, dark-backed, white-bellied shearwater of the Mediterranean. Often seen not far offshore, low over the sea, flying in tight groups or singly, or swimming in 'rafts'. Dark black-brown above, pale beneath with a broad diagonal band across underwing and dark rim to underwing tips. Short rear body and only slightly protruding feet are hard to judge except in ideal conditions.

Balearic Shearwater

Balearic ▶ Long toes

Levantine ▶ Short toes, tail, rear body

Long rear body, tail, toes

Longer arm to wing ratio than Levantine

◀ Dark wing pit

Dark brown above, underside dusky; no pale flank patch

Dark ▲ vent

Balearic Shorter, two-tone bill

Levantine Long, dark bill

A long-winged, slim, dark shearwater of the Mediterranean, often moving out into the Atlantic and north to the English Channel and North Sea. The long rear body and protruding feet are distinctive if visible, best seen against a smooth, pale sea. Most are dusky below, paler ones having dark under the tail and dark wingpits, and a broad, dark rim around the tip and hindwing below.

Great & Sooty Shearwaters

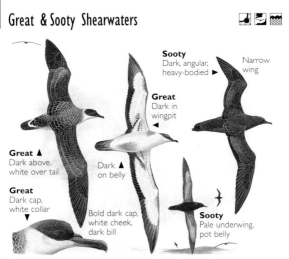

Sooty
Dark, angular;
heavy-bodied ►

Narrow
wing

Great
Dark in
wingpit
◄

Great ▲
Dark above,
white over tail

Dark ▲
on belly

Great
Dark cap,
white collar
▼

Bold dark cap,
white cheek,
dark bill

Sooty
Pale underwing,
pot belly

Large shearwaters, oceanic or off headlands. Great Shearwater
dark brown above, with prominent dark cap against white neck,
white above tail; white underside with dark smudges under wing
and on belly. Sooty more angular, pot-bellied, narrow-winged;
all dark except for characteristic silvery underwing panel. Both
bank onto wingtip over sea; both rise high in strong wind.

Leach's & Storm Petrels

▼ ♂ **Leach's**

Storm
Round tail,
big white
rump ►

♀ **Leach's** ▲
Notched tail,
pale wing panel

Storm
White line
beneath
wing ►

Dark
upperwing

◄ ▲ **Leach's**
Erratic, tern-like,
angular shape

Storm ▲ ►
Rounder wings,
Swallow-like action

Tiny seabirds. Storm Petrel highly oceanic, Leach's sometimes
blown inshore or inland in autumn. Storm very dark with bold
white rump, white bar under wing, broad round tail; flies with
wings curved back, rolling and gliding briefly. Leach's bigger,
obvious pale panel above, rump more V-shaped, tail notched;
flight more erratic on more angled wings, may patter over waves.

Gannet

Ad Gleaming white except for black wingtips, yellow-buff head ►

Juv Dusky, with underwing paler; pointed tail ►

Pointed bill and tail give sharp-ended look

Often flies with head tilted down

Ad ►

Juv ► Dark above, paler at base of tail

▲ **Imm** Immatures have variable piebald stages

Ads ▲ Brilliant white against dark sea at very long range

Imm ▲

Ad ►

Juv ▲

Biggest North Atlantic seabird; dagger bill and almost bulbous head and neck more prominent in flight than pointed tail. Wings long, angled, tapered to point. Adult gleaming white over dark sea, visible at great range; black wingtips. Yellow-buff head easy to see at reasonable range. Juvenile very dark with white specks, looks greyish over sea with little pattern; superficially like immature Great Black-backed Gull or big skua, but pointed bill and narrow tail unlike any gull's. Becomes piebald over next two to three years, with obvious yellowish head, large black wingtips. Patrols 20–30m above sea, looking down, half-turning before diving with steep plunge, often with eyecatching splash. Silent at sea; mechanical *arrah arrah* chorus at breeding colony.

Cormorant

Ad Long, broad wings, longer tail than geese ▼

Treetop colony ►

◄ **Shag** Narrower wings

▲ **Imm** White belly

Flight strong, fast, often very high

Often perches with open wings

Imm Variably white below ►

Race *sinensis* Europe, SE England ▼

Imm ►

Swims with bill uptilted

Adult has white throat ▼

Winter ◄

▼ **Imm** ▼

▲ **Breeding** White thigh patch

▲ **Juv**

Goose-sized, long-bodied, broad-tailed aquatic bird. Bill thick, hooked, forehead low and flat unlike Shag. Adult blackish, browner on back, with yellow gape, whitish chin. In spring head variably streaked white, bold white throat; yellow and brown facial skin and big white thigh patch distinctive. Immature browner, white below, becoming sharply contrasted, much more white than immature Shag. Swims low with head raised, bill uptilted; dives frequently from surface. Stands upright on buoys, posts, piers, trees, rocks; often perches with wings held open. Flies powerfully, flocks often in long lines or V-shapes high over sea or marsh. Breeds on sea cliff ledges or in trees inland, making large stick nests. Deep, grunting, croaking calls near nest.

Shag

Ad ▶ Yellow gape, dark throat

▼ Juv Dark below, white chin

▼ Sub-ad Thin bill, round forehead

▼ Imm Mediterranean

▲ Imm Fades pale on wing

▲ Breeding Curly crest

Uptilted bill, round head

Large, long-bodied, snaky-necked seabird, with slim, upstanding, curved crest in summer. Adult oily-green, looking black at long range, with bright yellow gape and chin patch. Juvenile dark brown, slightly paler below but white only on diffuse chin spot. Head rather round, making steep angle above slim, hooked bill. Tends to fly low over the sea; dives well, even in surging swell.

Pygmy Cormorant

Frequent short glides on bowed wings

Juv White belly ▶

Round head, short thick bill, long tail

Flight quick, angled neck, longish tail, arched wings

◀ Breeding

▲ Non-breeding

▲ Ad Some white on chin

Smaller, chunkier, thicker-necked than Cormorant, with shorter, stubby bill, dark, rounded head and noticeably long tail. Perches upright, often in trees, with tail length obvious. Flies quickly, at distance quite like heavy Glossy Ibis but thick neck and broad tail distinctive close up. Where common, often flies in long lines or shapeless groups, roosts in flocks and breeds colonially.

15

Bittern

▲ Thick dagger bill, black moustache

Broad, bowed wings with pale panel ◄

Heavily mottled golden-buff body

▲ Head withdrawn into thick neck

Stalks fish with forward lean ►

Large, thickset, heavy-necked, heron-like marshland bird. Stands hunched or upright with neck erect, flies with head somewhat extended and big feet trailing. Pale, warm brown plumage mottled with black, streaked along foreneck; in flight upperwing shows paler forewing band. Gives loud, deep, hollow, booming *whoomp* from reedbeds in spring.

Squacco Heron

Breeding Long plumes, bright pinkish-buff body ►

Imm Dark on back ►

Vivid white wings show in flight ►

▼ **Ad, winter** Duller plumage

Hunched, thick-necked, dagger-billed

▲ **Juv** Dark, streaky; white on wings

Small, squat heron, bright pinkish-buff in spring with long, pale head plumes draped over back. At other times dull, pale brown-buff, but reveals striking white wings in flight. Juveniles much darker on back, streaked on foreneck. Typically stands still, leaning forward, in thick waterside vegetation or on floating weed. Flies up in a flurry with flashing white wings.

Little Bittern

▲ **Juv**
Streaked

▲ Trailing feet

◄ ♀ **spring**

All plumages show big pale wing patch

▲ ♂ **spring**

Tiny heron, usually seen flying low and fast over reeds with trailing feet, but may stand in open or perch on open stem. Distinctive pale oval patch on upperwing. Male colourful, bright peachy-buff with green-black back and wingtips. Female streaked brown on neck, browner back. Juvenile browner still, more streaked, but tiny size and pale wing patch distinctive.

Night Heron

Ad Grey wings, black back ◄

Ad ▲   **Juv** ▲

▼ **Ad, spring** Black cap, white plumes

Juv ►

Imm ▼

◄ **Juv** Pale spots

Sub-ad ▲
Legs may be red in spring

Medium-large, squat, thick-billed heron with broad bow wings. Adult black and grey with all-pale grey wings; in spring has two long white plumes from black cap, face and breast flushed yellow-ochre, vivid yellow legs briefly orange-red. Juvenile brown with drop-shaped pale spots, later greyer with spots smaller and sparse. Frequent deep, hoarse *qwok* call at dusk.

Great White Egret

A giant egret, with angular shoulders and neck, and long dagger bill. All white, all year. Bill usually yellow; black in spring. Legs blackish to dull pale yellow (mostly above joint), briefly reddish in spring. Face colours brighter when breeding. Breeding plumes extend as broad, wispy fan over lower back. In flight coiled neck is deep, angular. Flies with slow wingbeats and trailing legs.

Little Egret

Medium-sized all-white heron with a long, slender neck, thin, dark, sharp bill, and grey face. Long, thin plumes from nape; in spring also wispy back plumes. Legs black with distinctive bright to dull yellow or greenish-yellow toes, striking in flight. Agile, active feeder on shorelines and wetland. Flight quick, on bowed wings, with less ponderous wingbeats than Great White.

Cattle Egret

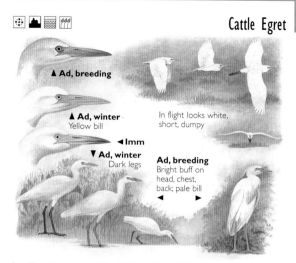

▲ Ad, breeding

▲ Ad, winter
Yellow bill

◄ Imm

▼ Ad, winter
Dark legs

In flight looks white,
short, dumpy

Ad, breeding
Bright buff on
head, chest,
back; pale bill
◄   ►

Small, white, heron-like bird with a thick, short bill. Rounded forehead and throat profile, rather short neck. Mostly white, but deep, bright golden-buff on back and chest in spring. Bill yellow; legs dull, dark, becoming redder in spring. Typically in small groups around animals or at refuse tips, gathering in larger flocks to fly to big roosts in trees. Flight quite quick, direct.

Spoonbill

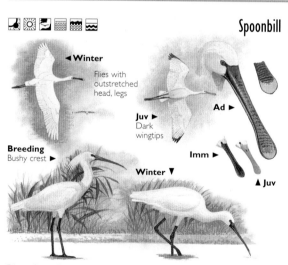

◄ Winter

Flies with
outstretched
head, legs

Juv ►
Dark
wingtips

Ad ►

Imm ►

▲ Juv

Breeding
Bushy crest ►

Winter ▼

Big, white, long-striding heron-like bird of shallow water, with unique bill. In spring has bushy crest, buff patch on upper chest. Bill long, flat, thin, slightly downcurved from side, broadening into wide, round tip; black with yellow tip on adult, pink on juvenile, all-black on immature. Young birds have thin black wingtips. Flies strongly with head outstretched, wings flat.

Purple Heron

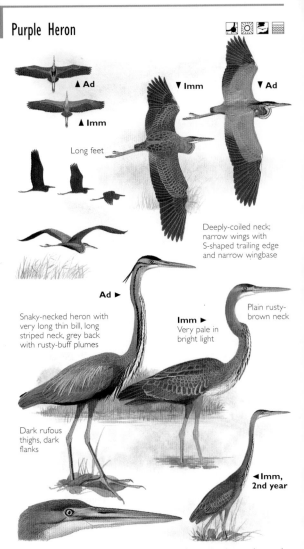

▲ Ad

▲ Imm

▼ Imm

▼ Ad

Long feet

Deeply-coiled neck; narrow wings with S-shaped trailing edge and narrow wingbase

Ad ▶

Snaky-necked heron with very long thin bill, long striped neck, grey back with rusty-buff plumes

Imm ▶
Very pale in bright light

Plain rusty-brown neck

Dark rufous thighs, dark flanks

◀ Imm, 2nd year

Large, dark, slim heron with long thin bill, slender snaky neck, long legs and toes. Often seen flying low over marsh before diving out of sight into reeds. Inconspicuous when feeding but may stand in the open at edge of marsh. Adult dark grey-brown with black-striped chestnut neck. Reddish on front edge of wing and underwing coverts, shows in flight; greyer on upperwing coverts but never so pale as Grey Heron. Immature duller, paler, buff-brown with paler neck streaks, much slimmer-necked than Bittern. Flies on arched wings, narrower at base than Grey's, bulging at rear, but action similar to slightly larger Grey; neck coils in deeper S-shape than Grey. Long toes obvious. Generally silent but occasional sharp, rasping note in flight.

Grey Heron

Ad, winter ▼

Shorter feet than Purple Heron ▼

Very broad wings, rounded neck bulge

White spots on leading edge of wing ◄

Slow beats, deeply arched wings

Nests in trees

◄**Ad, breeding** Long head plumes, white back plumes

Bill brightens in spring

Neck hunched or extended

▲ **Imm** Grey cap and hindneck, rather dull, plain face

◄**Ad, winter**

Big, pale heron with thick dagger-like bill and long neck, often withdrawn as it stands upright, but hunched. Often stands on dry land away from water, sometimes in groups. Adults immaculate pale grey, white, and grey-black, with white head crossed by black eyestripe and wispy crest. White neck and chest, spotted with black down foreneck; black flanks. Immature greyer, duller, with pale grey head. Bill yellowish to green, turns pink or orange in spring. Flight ponderous, with wings deeply bowed, head withdrawn, legs trailing, but occasionally flies short distance with head extended; more acrobatic when descending to big, stick nests in treetop colony. Loud, harsh *fraank* note in flight; bill clattering and other sounds from colony.

Crane

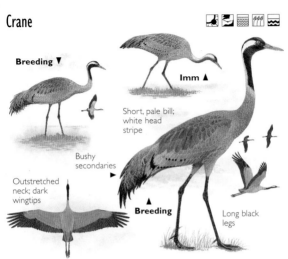

Breeding ▼

Imm ▲

Short, pale bill; white head stripe

Bushy secondaries ▶

Outstretched neck; dark wingtips

Breeding ▲

Long black legs

Huge grey bird of fields and wetlands, often in flocks. Small head and neck broaden into heavy body. Bushy 'tail' of secondaries. Adult head black with white stripe from eye onto nape, red crown (hard to see), square black throat. Small pale bill. Brown back in summer. Immature has ginger-brown, unmarked head. Flies with head and legs outstretched; loud, deep, clanging calls.

Demoiselle Crane

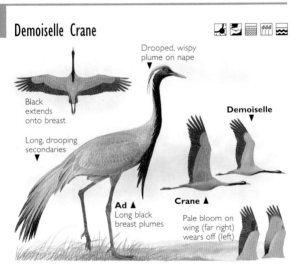

Drooped, wispy plume on nape ▼

Black extends onto breast

Demoiselle ▼

Long, drooping secondaries ▼

Ad ▲
Long black breast plumes

Crane ▲
Pale bloom on wing (far right) wears off (left)

Elegant crane with small bill, steep forehead (sometimes evident in flight) and elongated, pointed (not bushy) secondaries. Black on head, extending down to long, pointed black chest feathers; small, wispy white tuft behind eye. Immature has faint echo of head pattern, best identified by secondary points. In flight has slightly less sharp grey-black upperwing contrast than Crane.

White Stork

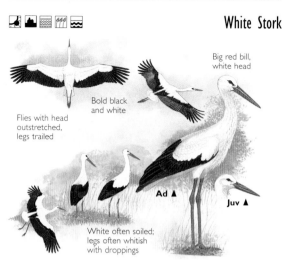

Big red bill, white head

Bold black and white

Flies with head outstretched, legs trailed

Ad ▲

Juv ▲

White often soiled; legs often whitish with droppings

Large, long-legged, dagger-billed terrestrial bird. White to soiled brown-grey, with black flight feathers, lined with greyish when fresh. Bright red bill, red legs (often soiled white by droppings). Immature has black bill. Majestic flier on long, flat, fingered wings, head outstretched; black on wings almost joins over lower back, underwings white with black flight feathers.

Black Stork

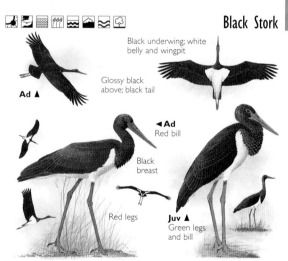

Black underwing; white belly and wingpit

Glossy black above; black tail

Ad ▲

◄ **Ad**
Red bill

Black breast

Red legs

Juv ▲
Green legs and bill

Large, slim, thin-necked stork with long, slender, deep red bill and long red legs. Adult glossy black on head, neck, chest and upperside; white belly and small white triangle under base of wing. Immature duller, dark olive-brown with greenish legs and bill. Flies on flat or arched wings, not bowed like heron, with steady, powerful beats, head outstretched, legs trailed.

Dalmatian Pelican

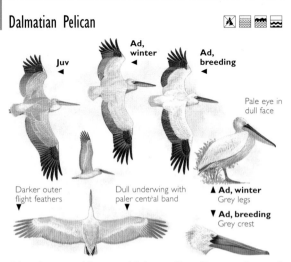

Juv

Ad, winter

Ad, breeding

Pale eye in dull face

Darker outer flight feathers

Dull underwing with paler central band

▲ Ad, winter
Grey legs

▼ Ad, breeding
Grey crest

Gigantic grey-white waterbird, usually solitary or in small groups. Dull, with pale eye inconspicuous in grey face; throat pouch reddish when breeding. Slight curly crest. Faint dull pinkish on chest but lacks bright pink on body. Underwing shows pale grey in flight with broad, paler central band. Flies powerfully, head withdrawn onto deep, angular chest.

White Pelican

Ad, breeding ▶
Dark eye in pink face

Ad ▲
Black and white underwing, pink legs

▲ Ad, winter
Dark eye

Juv ▶

Imm ▶

Juv ▲ Dark underwing with pale band

Juv ▶

Huge pink-white waterbird, often in flocks which look solid pink at distance on water, or on ground in spring. Adult clean white or rich pink. Dark eye obvious in pink face, throat pouch yellow. Underwing white with black flight feathers, recalling stork. Juvenile dull, browner on back, with pale-centred dark underwing. Powerful flier, flocks in coordinated lines and spirals.

Greater Flamingo

Neck and legs extended in flight

Unique long neck, long legs, downcurved bill

Ad, summer ►

Ad, winter ◄ ►

Imm ►

Ad, summer

◄ Ad, summer

◄ Imm

Juv ►

Remarkable long-legged, long-necked, small-headed wading bird of shallow water. May swim on deeper lagoons. Adult pale pink to whitish with black and crimson wings. Immature duller, sullied grey. Bill angled down, vivid pink with black tip. Legs all pink (escaped Chilean race has grey legs with pink joints). Flies with head and legs extended in extraordinary, long, thin shape.

Glossy Ibis

Blackish at distance; brown at closer range

Green, red and magenta show on wing in sunlight

▼ Winter

▲ Breeding

◄ Breeding

Long, thick, curved bill

▲ Juv

Large, slender waterbird with long neck, long legs, curved bill. Looks black at long range and in flight. Close views reveal coppery-brown colour, spotted white on head in winter. Sunshine picks out glossy green and magenta on wing. Bill dark, with blue-white lines at base to eye; legs dark. Feeds in close groups in marsh, flies in lines and V-shapes with head outstretched.

Mute Swan

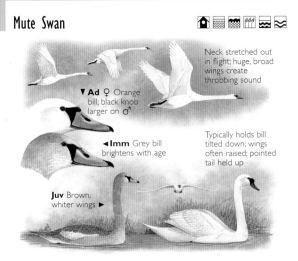

Neck stretched out in flight; huge, broad wings create throbbing sound

▼Ad ♀ Orange bill; black knob larger on ♂

◄Imm Grey bill brightens with age

Typically holds bill tilted down; wings often raised; pointed tail held up

Juv Brown, whiter wings ►

Huge white waterbird. Adult all-white except for black-tipped orange bill, black facial knob. Immature begins dull grey-brown, becoming patchy with grey bill, black facial patch. Swims with neck in S-shape, or raised with bill tilted down; tail pointed, often raised. Flies with head outstretched, wings slightly arched, with wings producing deep, musical throbbing sound.

Bewick's Swan

Ads ▲ Neck stocky or slim, head horizontal, short, square tail

Shorter-necked than other swans; no rhythmic throbbing from wings

Ad Small round yellow patch on bill ▼

Juv Dull, pale brownish-grey ►

Ad All white; shortish neck

▲ Juv Adult bill pattern in cream, pink, grey

Smallest swan, but still large, seen on water and often feeding on dry land, usually in flocks. Adult white except for black bill with yellow at base: yellow typically in rounded patch each side, but patches may join in variable pattern across top. Immature dull ash-grey; bill pale whitish, pink and grey with echo of adult pattern. Musical, bugling calls; no loud wing noise in flight.

Canada & Egyptian Geese

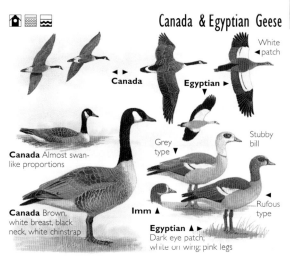

Canada Almost swan-like proportions

Canada Brown, white breast, black neck, white chinstrap

Canada ◀ ▶

Egyptian ▶

White ◀ patch

Grey type ▼

Stubby bill

Rufous ◀ type

Imm ▲

Egyptian ▲ ▶
Dark eye patch; white on wing; pink legs

Canada is large black, brown, and white goose with distinctive black neck, white chinstrap, white breast, and white stern. Often swims, grazes on dry land, and flies in flocks. Loud, deep, honking calls. Egyptian smaller, longer-legged, with small pink bill, brown patch on face, grey-brown to rufous back and big white forewing patch on otherwise black wings.

Whooper Swan

Whooper ▼

▼ **Bewick's**
Concave profile

▲ **Juv**
▼ **Imm**

Juv Dull grey-brown

▲ Long yellow bill patch

Ads
Long neck, horizontal bill, short tail

Large, straight-necked swan. Wings not raised over back as in Mute Swan; holds head horizontal. Short square tail. Bill longer, more wedge-shaped than Bewick's, black with yellow sides extending forward in longer, more pointed patch, usually joined across top at base. Immature ashy-grey with pale bill, gradually developing adult pattern. Loud, clanging, whooping calls.

27

Greylag Goose

Ad ▲

Tiny black marks below

Ad Pale grey-brown, barred white ▼

▲ Imm

Thick orange bill

Ads Pale grey upperwing and underwing patch, grey rump

Thick pink legs (rarely orange)

Big, pale goose, contrasty in strong sun but more uniform in even light. Big head, thick orange bill, pink (rarely orange) legs. Brown back with even rows of pale feather tips; white stern. Sometimes a little white on face and black dots on belly, but neither very obvious. In flight reveals very pale, blue-grey forewing, both above and below. Loud, rattling, honking calls.

Bean Goose

Wide grey tailband ◄

Ads Small-billed, short-necked form

◄   ►

▲ Small orange band

Long-necked form

Orange legs

▲ Wide orange band

Dark forewing

Dark, with crisp white bars ▼

▲ Ad Long-billed, long-necked form

Bill length and amount of orange variable

Large, handsome goose with complex variations. Adult basically dark brown, with even, narrow, striking lines of pale feather edges above. Head deep liver-brown; contrasts with paler breast, but less so than Pink-footed. Bill long, orange and black or black with narrow orange band; legs yellow-orange. Looks dark, long-necked, and powerful in flight. Deep two- or three-note calls.

White-fronted Goose

Greenland race: orange bill, dark plumage

▼ White forehead

▲ Russian race: pink bill

Upperwing dark, fine white bar

Ad ▲
White forehead, black belly bars, orange legs

▲ **Ad** Mid grey forewing, black on belly

Broad dark tailband

Juv ►
No white on head, no black

▲ **Juv**
No black on belly

Handsome, angular goose; adult has obvious white forehead blaze and bold black belly bars, immature plain. Russian race has pink bill, Greenland race (darker, more black below) has orange bill. Legs bright orange. In flight, forewing shows mid grey, less grey than Pink-footed. Loud, sharp, yodelling *kik-yik, lyo-lyok* calls; flock sound has fast, pack-of-hounds character.

Pink-footed Goose

▼ **Ad**
Dark head

Narrow grey tailband

▲ **Juv**

Blackish bill with thin pink band
▼

Grey
◄ wing

Pale chest

Ad ▲
Round, dark head, pale breast; pale bars on grey back

Pink legs

▲ **Juv**
Dull, browner than adult

Beautiful, round-headed, short-billed goose, with strong contrast between dark head/neck and pale chest. Upperparts variably brownish to pale grey with even, thin, white bars; bold white stern. Small black bill with pink band. Legs pale dingy pink to deep red-pink. Small dark head in flight, forewing mid grey. Deep honking calls mixed with sharp, high *wink-wink*.

29

Lesser White-fronted Goose

Juv Yellow eye-ring, tiny bill ►

Ad Yellow eye-ring, white blaze ▼

Tiny, vivid pink bill

▲ Juv

▲ Ad

Coverts and tertials almost plain ▼

Juv Gets white face before black bars ►

Orange legs

▲ **Ad** Dark back, narrow black belly bars

Small, neat, long-winged goose with round head, steep forehead, stubby bill, yellow eye-ring. Now very rare. Adult has white forehead blaze extending to crown, small black belly patches, rather dark, uniform upperside. Immature lacks white blaze and black belly; eye-ring and long wingtips best identification clues. High-pitched, fast, yapping calls.

Barnacle Goose

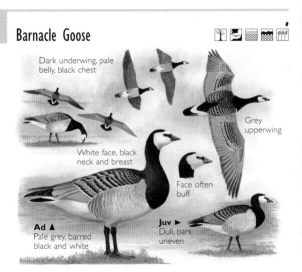

Dark underwing, pale belly, black chest

Grey upperwing

White face, black neck and breast

Face often buff

Ad ▲ Pale grey, barred black and white

Juv ► Dull, bars uneven

Highly social goose, feeding and flying in dense, irregular flocks. Bold black neck and chest; barred black, white, and grey back; silky white underside. Cream to white face extends around eye, unlike Canada Goose. Immature duller, with less even barring on upperparts. Bill and legs black. Loud, short, gruff barking *kaw* in flight creates quick-fire chorus from large flock.

Brent & Red-breasted Geese

Brent ►
Dark, plain wings, white stern

Brent, juv White bars on wing

Brent Pale-bellied ▼

Brent, juv
Pale-bellied; white bars ▼

Brent
Dark-bellied
◄ ▼

Brent, juv
Dark-bellied ▼

Brent Dark-bellied ▼

Juv lacks white on neck until midwinter

▲ **Brent, juv**
Dark-bellied

Brent
'Black Brant' ▼

Red-breasted Ad
▼

▼ **Juv**

Broad white collar, white flank, black belly ▲

Red-breasted ▲

1st winter some heads have no red patch

Brent is small, very dark goose with black head, neck and chest. Adult has small white patch on neck, juvenile has pale bars on wings. Bill and legs black. Dark-bellied has dark grey-brown back, belly slightly paler; pale-bellied has much paler belly; rare 'Black Brant' has blackish belly, broad white flash on flank, and broad white collar. Flocks give even, croaking, rhythmic chorus. Red-breasted is unique black, white, and red goose with tiny black bill. Hard to spot in tight flocks of other species, but forms huge flocks in eastern Europe. Adult has complex pattern of red patches surrounded by white on head, neck, and breast; immature has more open, less neat pattern. Bold white flank stripe. White bars on inner wing often more obvious than red patches. Sharp, loud *kik-wek* call.

Shelduck

Big, rounded, long-bodied, upstanding duck, with piebald plumage and red bill. Adult has black head, black stripe along back, black wingtip; broad rusty-orange band around foreparts. Immature white-faced, lacks orange, back browner. Bill of male vivid scarlet with large knob; female lacks knob. Legs pink. Loud rhythmic *ga-ga-ga-gah* and hissy, whistling notes.

Ruddy Shelduck

Typical shelduck form with rounded head, big body, and longish legs, but strong orange-buff colour overall, big white forewing patch in flight; bill and legs black. Male has cream head with narrow black collar, female lacks collar but has slight paler mask effect. Beware confusion with escaped relatives with grey, dark or whiter heads. Nasal, honking, goose-like calls in flight.

Wigeon

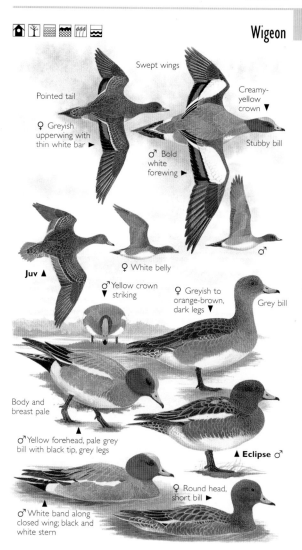

Swept wings

Pointed tail

Creamy-yellow crown ▼

♀ Greyish upperwing with thin white bar ►

Stubby bill

♂ Bold white forewing ►

White belly

♀

Juv ▲

♂

♂ Yellow crown striking ▼

♀ Greyish to orange-brown, dark legs ▼

Grey bill

Body and breast pale

♂ Yellow forehead, pale grey bill with black tip, grey legs ▲

▲ **Eclipse** ♂

♂ White band along closed wing; black and white stern

♀ Round head, short bill ►

Social duck that feeds and swims in dense flocks. Short grey bill, short dark legs, pointed tail, swept-back wings give distinctive character. Looks squat on ground but swift and elegant in flight. Winter male bright, blue-grey, looking paler than smaller Teal. Pink breast, white band along middle, chestnut head, pale yellowish forehead, white patch in front of black stern. Male in eclipse red-brown with dark reddish head. Adult male shows big white wing patch; first-winter male lacks white but otherwise shows adult pattern. Female rufous or greyer, more mottled, less streaked than bigger Mallard; white belly patch well defined; forewing greyish, hindwing dark with no obvious colour. Loud, explosive *whi-ooo* whistle from male, female has abrupt growl.

33

Mallard

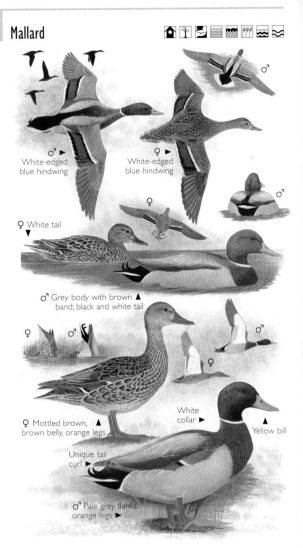

♂
♀

♂ ►
White-edged
blue hindwing

♀ ►
White-edged
blue hindwing

♂

♀ White tail
▼

♂ Grey body with brown ▲
band; black and white tail

♀   ♂

♂   ♀

♀ Mottled brown, ▲
brown belly, orange legs

White
collar ►

Yellow bill
▲

Unique tail
curl ►

♂ Pale grey flanks,
orange legs ►

Common, large duck with long bill and short, vivid orange legs.
Male grey with glossy green head, white collar, brown breast,
black and white stern; bill pale greeny-yellow. Darker in eclipse,
lacking green on more striped head. Female mottled and streaked
brown and cream, tail almost white; bill olive or brown with dull
orange marks. In flight reveals white underwing but dark belly
unlike Wigeon or Gadwall. All adults have purple-blue wing
patch edged white at front and back, giving two obvious white
bars on inner wing in flight. Some interbreeding with domestic
forms produces various patchy, brown or white birds, but these
retain basic character and often blue wing patch and curly tail of
males. Female gives loud, coarse, descending quacks; male whistles.

Gadwall

♂ White patch on hindwing, black stern ▶

♀ White patch on hindwing ▶

Juv ▲ Little white on wing

▲ ♂ White underwing

▲ ♀ White underwing, well-defined white belly

♂ White wing patch, grey body, black stern ▼

Blackish bill

♂ ♀

♀ Orange panels ▲ on bill

Steep forehead, long, slim bill

Juv ▲ White wing patch, orange legs

♂ ▶

Rather drab-looking duck, yet beautifully marked at close range. Generally rather scarce and local. Long, narrow bill and steep forehead give different character from Mallard. Male darker grey than Mallard or Wigeon, with paler, browner tertials and head, black stern without white; black bill. Female mottled and streaked buff-brown, with well-defined white belly; paler on face, bill dark with sharply-defined orange side panels. All have yellow-orange legs and small, square patch of white at base of hindwing, often showing as white square or diamond when swimming but sometimes hidden, obvious in flight and squarer than narrow streak on female Wigeon. Female quacks quietly; male gives nasal *eh-eh* in flight.

Shoveler

♂ Blue forewing, long black head and bill ◄

White breast

▲ ♀ White underwing, dark belly

◄ ♀ Grey forewing

♂ Blackish head, white breast, huge bill ▼

Juv ♀ ▲

♀ ▼

Orange legs

◄ ♂ Deep rufous sides, white rear flank

▼ ♀ Long bill, flat head

Swims low in water, long wingtips held up over pointed tail

Large, forward-leaning, big-headed, long-billed duck with vivid orange legs. Sometimes swims in dense feeding groups; often sits or stands on muddy shorelines. Male striking, with green-black head against white chest, yellow eyes, and long, broad-tipped black bill. Body blue-grey, white, and black with deep rusty-brown underside. In eclipse dark reddish-brown, with mottled whitish facial crescent between eye and bill. Female more Mallard-like with slightly more striped face; long, broad, orange-sided bill and quite short-tailed impression best clues on water; long wingtips evident when up-ending. In flight shows pale blue-grey forewings. Gives short *took-took* and quiet quacks; also quite loud, deep 'whoofing' noise from wings as it takes flight.

Pintail

♂ Long head, neck and tail; long wings with pale trailing edge ►

♀ Long shape, strong pale line along hindwing ►

♂ ▲ ▼

▲ ♀ Grey bill, pale head, slim neck

♀

♂ ▲ ▼
White stripe from breast to neck, grey body with yellowish patch on rear flank

Grey legs and bill

Elegant, long-necked duck with long tail, dark grey legs, and slim, grey bill. Mostly scarce except on a few traditional estuary and washland sites where large numbers spend the winter. Male has dark brown head with striking white breast, white extending into long point up neck side. Grey body, white belly, creamy patch in front of black stern, long, whippy tail spike. Similar Long-tailed Duck squatter, short-billed, dark-winged, much more marine. Female Pintail greyer than Mallard, with plainer face, greyish or buff, and contrasted dark bill. In flight reveals long, narrow, whitish trailing edge to inner wing (usually best plumage clue), long pointed tail, slender wings. A quiet bird: female quacks, male gives double whistle.

37

Teal

♂ Black patch broader than on ►

♀ White midwing bar, bright green hindwing patch ►

♂ Small, dark, with white midwing bar

Small, agile, flies in close pairs or tight flocks, almost wader-like

♀ White underwing band, grey forewing ▼

♂

♀

♂ Very dark head with green band ►

♀ Green wing patch, white streak beside tail ▼

Buff triangle under tail ▼

Short grey legs

♀ Grey bill ►

♂ White line along body; black-edged buff patch at rear ▼

Eclipse ♂ and juv like ♀

Small duck with dark bill and legs. Often flies in groups with agile, coordinated, almost wader-like flight. Male looks dark, less blue-grey than Wigeon; has dark brown head with broad, deep green band visible close up, grey body with narrow white and black horizontal stripes, black-edged triangular patch of pale creamy-buff in front of black stern. Female mottled grey-brown, distinctive pale streak beside tail. Both have bright green hindwing patch with broad pale stripe in front, narrow trailing edge (unlike two equal white bars on Garganey). Eclipse males and juveniles difficult in autumn, when may look dark-capped, pale-faced; wing patch, size, grey legs all help. Bright, metallic *crik crik* call of male rings across marsh; female has weak quack.

Garganey

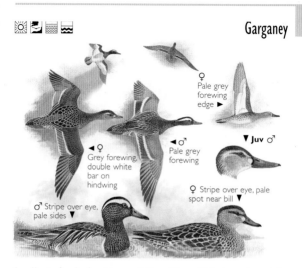

♀ Pale grey forewing edge ▶

♀ Grey forewing, double white bar on hindwing

◀♂ Pale grey forewing

▼ Juv ♂

♀ Stripe over eye, pale spot near bill ▼

♂ Stripe over eye, pale sides ▼

Small, stocky duck with grey bill and legs. Male in spring pink-brown and grey, with brown head and white crescent from above eye, pale blue-grey forewing. Female mottled like Teal but forewing grey, hindwing duller with two parallel pale bars but no vivid green. Female and eclipse male have whitish stripe over eye, pale line beneath, white spot near bill and chin.

Marbled Duck

♂ Pale hindwing, dark mask

Pale hindwing and tail

Whitish underwing

♂

♀

♂ Dark mask, drooped crest ▶

♀ Weak mask, dark bill ▼

A rare, threatened duck of southern Europe. Smallish, chunky, plain-looking at a distance, showing large, pale spots or mottles and barred chest when close up. Slim, blackish bill. Dark band behind eye, paler face, cap, and short droopy crest; pale area on tertials. In flight looks pale, with hindwing band palest area above, underwing whitish, pale tail.

39

Pochard

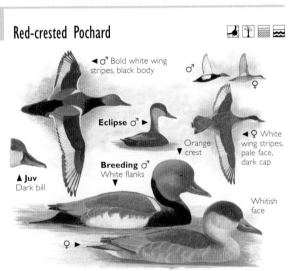

Grey
wingbar ▶ ♂

▲ ♀

Imm ♂ ▲
Pale face, dark cap

Grey bill
band ▼

♀ Grey bill
band, pale face
and throat ▼

♂ ▲
Red head, grey body
black at front and rear

Long-billed, round-headed, round-backed but long-bodied
diving duck, often inactive in daytime flocks. Male has deep
reddish head, red eye, pale grey body, black breast and stern.
Female echoes pattern but duller: liver-brown head with whitish
face and throat, pale line behind eye. Grey wingbar in flight.
Deep, growling call, wheezy notes and whistles from male.

Red-crested Pochard

◀ ♂ Bold white wing
stripes, black body

♂   ♀

Eclipse ♂ ▶

Orange
▼ crest

◀ ♀ White
wing stripes,
pale face,
dark cap

Breeding ♂
White flanks ▼

▲ **Juv**
Dark bill

Whitish
face

♀ ▶

Large, extravagant, big-headed duck, deep-bodied and broad-
winged. Male mid brown with white flank, black neck and
breast, rufous brown lower face, orange-buff crest fading paler,
red bill. Female mid brown with dark bill, brown cap and
hindneck, and dull whitish face. Both sexes have long, broad
white wingbar, and mostly white underwing.

Ferruginous Duck

White belly

Blurred belly

Bold white band along whole wing

Peaked head

White forewing edge

♂ Deep rufous, white undertail, white eye

White undertail

Neat, handsome diving duck with slim dark grey bill, sloping forehead, high crown, long, broad, vivid white wingbar. Male looks plain at distance, but close up shows deep mahogany red, with white patch under tail edged darker, eye white. Female duller, eye brown, but similar white patch under tail. Bill has black tip (larger on female) and diffuse pale band just behind tip.

White-headed Duck

Juv Bulbous grey bill, short head stripe

Imm ♂ May have black head

♀ Bulbous grey bill, bold head stripe

♂ Bulbous blue bill, pale body

Eclipse ♂

Strange, broad-bodied, stocky, big-headed diving duck with stiff tail, sometimes cocked. Male is pale rufous-brown, finely barred, with white head, small black crown, blacker neck, bulbous pale blue bill; young male may have blackish head. Female barred brown, with dark crown, pale stripe under eye, dark cheek stripe, pale throat, grey bill swollen at base. All-dark wings.

41

Ruddy Duck, Wood Duck & Mandarin

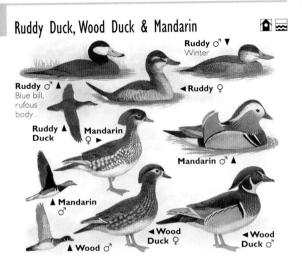

Ruddy ♂ ▼
Winter

Ruddy ♂ ▲
Blue bill,
rufous
body

◄ Ruddy ♀

**Ruddy ▲
Duck**

**Mandarin
♀ ►**

Mandarin ♂ ▲

**▲ Mandarin
♂**

**◄Wood
Duck ♀**

**◄Wood
Duck ♂**

▲ Wood ♂

Wood ♂ ▲

Ruddy is stiff-tailed diving duck: smaller, neater than White-headed, male redder with more black on crown, white undertail, slim blue bill. Female duller, less contrast on head than White-headed. Mandarin male unmistakable; female dark greyish, shaggy crest, neat white spectacle, thin pinkish bill, often in trees near water. Wood duck similar, female has yellow eye-ring.

Scaup

Long white
wing stripe ►

♂ Grey back,
white wing stripe ►

♀

Round
crown,
no tuft

Juv ►

♀ ▲ ►

♀ Pale cheek
in summer ►

Grey back ▼

▲ Tiny black
bill tip

White
face

♂ Black each end, ▲
pale middle, white flanks

♀

Big diving duck with round crown and nape, no trace of tuft. Broad, long bill sweeps into steep forehead. Male has black head and chest, grey back, white flanks, dark stern. Female dark brown with broad white facial blaze, often pale ear spot, pale grey bars on back; both have long white wingbar. Grey bill with small black tip, slightly larger on less white-faced juvenile.

Tufted Duck

♂ Black with tuft, white flanks ▼

◄ ♀ Long, narrow white wing stripe

▲ **Eclipse ♂, imm ♂**
Brownish flanks

◄▲ ♀ winter

♀ Often white ◄ undertail

♂

♀ summer
Brown overall; variable pale face, small tuft

♀ winter

Tuft on nape ►

▼ **Tufted ♀** White blaze, large dark bill tip

Tufted
Narrow bill, larger dark tip ▼

No tuft ►

▼ **Scaup ♀** Large white blaze, tiny dark bill tip

▲ ▲
Scaup Broad bill, small dark tip

Big-headed diving duck. Smaller than Scaup, with narrower body and smaller bill, much more common on inland waters. Typical bird of most lakes, reservoirs, flooded pits, along with Pochard. Male black with bold white flanks, droopy crest on back of head, yellow eyes. Female dark plain brown, variably whitish or white on face and undertail; white face sometimes sharply defined but less extensive than on Scaup. Darker than Pochard, lacking grey on body. Small tuft or bump on nape. Bill grey; broad black tip much larger than Scaup's. Male and female have long white wingbar, striking but less broad than on Ferruginous Duck. Female makes deep growling notes as it takes flight, male gives quiet whistles in courtship.

43

Red-breasted Merganser

Goosander
Thicker bill, sharp chin patch ►

♀ Blurred throat and foreneck, brownish back ▼

▲ ♂ Spiky crest, dark chest and flank

Long, slim duck with thin red bill. Male striking, with black, white, and grey body, red-brown breast, black head, spiky 'double' crest. Red bill and eye contrast with head, unlike Goosander. Female blurry brown-grey with redder head, fuzzy crest, no sharp divide on throat or foreneck. 'Stretched' shape in flight, big white wing patches. Occasional growling notes.

Goosander

Juvs like ♀ ►

◄ ♂ Clean pink-white underside and neck

◄ ♀ Sharp throat and foreneck, grey back

◄ ♂ White breast

Big, striking, long-bodied duck. Male obvious white, tinged salmon-pink, with big green-black head, dark eye, thick deep-red bill. Nape bulges but crest droops, not spiky. Female pale grey with dark red-brown head, sharp white throat patch, clearly-defined white breast. In flight looks elongated, cross-shaped, with large white inner wing patches.

Smew

♂ Boldly pied, white neck and chest ◄

Juv like ♀ ►

♀ White wing patch ►

♀ White face, dark cap, white underside

♀ Dark grey, small white cheeks ►

White crown and crest ▼

♂ ► Grey and white with black marks

Small, heavy-bodied, small-headed diving duck, sociable and active where common. Male bold white, faintly yellowish (Goldeneye starker) with grey flanks and fine black lines, black face patch. Female darker grey with white breast, deep red-brown head and small, sharp, white lower face, white wing patches. Winter male Ruddy Duck similar but browner, dark-winged.

Goldeneye

Juv ► Small white wing patch

♀ ► Large white wing patch

♂ ► Pied in flight

Big white face spot, white chest

♂ Triangular head and bill

♀ Grey, with ▲ dark, peaked head

Bulky, round-backed diving duck with high-domed head. Tail often cocked; dives constantly. Male eyecatching white with black back, black head with bold white face spot. Female dark grey with white collar (lacking on juvenile), dark brown head. Short, triangular bill, dark with variable amount of yellow. Large white wing patches show in very fast, direct, flickery flight.

Common Scoter

♀
♂
Pale wingtip
♂
Imm
♀
Imm
Tail often raised
summer
♀ ▼
Imm ♂ spring ▼
◄ ♀ **winter**
♂
♂

Typically maritime, sociable, large-bodied, slim-necked duck with pointed tail, often raised. Male black, outer wing paler below, bill black with yellow patch on top. Female dark brown (wears paler on back in summer), bill dark, cap dark, face paler greyish. Female pattern less strong than Smew or Ruddy Duck, cap darker than Red-crested Pochard.

Velvet Scoter

♂
♂
♂
♀
White wing patch ►
Imm ♂
▲ ♀ Double pale face patch
▲ **Juv**
Yellow on bill
♂ White wing patch, red legs ►

Heavy sea duck with wedge-shaped bill; usually in smaller numbers within Common Scoter flocks. Male black, with bold white rectangle on hindwing, white mark under eye, yellow sides to bill. Female dark brown with same white wing patch, variable double whitish or white face spots. Legs dark red. Watch scoter flocks, look for white on flapped wings or in flight.

46

Surf Scoter

Large North American scoter, rare in Europe, usually with other scoters. Male obvious in good view, with bold white patch on nape, smaller patch on forehead, colourful bill, no white in wing. At long range, look for nape patch among bobbing scoter flock. Female difficult, like Velvet Scoter with thick-based bill, no white in wing; may show pale nape as well as face spots.

Steller's & King Eiders

Male King Eider unmistakable with orange bill knob, pink breast, black body. Female like rufous Eider, with smaller darker-tipped bill, 'smiling' gape line, crescentic bars on flanks. Male Steller's Eider unique pale butterscotch and black with grey head, green nape spot. Female dark, square-headed, with stubby paler grey bill; double white bars on inner wing recall Mallard.

47

Eider

♀ Heavy, dark, hindwing plain

♂

Wedge-shaped head and bill, short tail often cocked

♂

▲ Eclipse ♂

Imm ♂ ▼

♀

Juv ▼

♀ ▼

♂ ►

♂ Green nape patches
◄

♀ Rufous, ▲ closely barred

Large, heavy, strictly maritime diving duck, highly social, with heavy, wedge-shaped bill. Short tail often cocked. Breeding male white above, black below, with pink breast. Head white with black cap, green nape patches. Pale bill extends as long lobe onto forehead. Immature and eclipse males piebald or very dark, with dark head and obscure pale band over eye from pale bill. Female olive-brown to reddish-brown with close, even, dark bars; bill pale greyish with whiter tip. Juvenile greyer, with strong pale line over eye. In flight female and juvenile have dark hindwing edged by two even white bars. Flight low, heavy, direct but fast. Male gives deep cooing note in courtship, female has short, repetitive, mechanical quack.

Long-tailed Duck

♀ Dark wings, white sides to rump

♂ winter
Dark wings, white neck

♂

▲ ♂ summer

♂ winter

Dives with open wings

♂ summer
White-faced type ▼

♂ summer ▶

♂ summer ▼

Long tail ▲ ▼

◀▼ Breeding ♀

▲ ♂ winter
Pale back, white on head

White flank ▲

Juv ▼

◀▼ ♀ winter

▲ Juv ♂ Red bill

Rather small, round-bodied, dark-winged and short-billed duck, maritime except when breeding. Winter male strongly pied, mostly white with dark cheek patch, dark band around foreparts, dark wings, and long, flexible, pointed tail. Bill dark with pink band. In summer has darker back and head with white patch around eye. Female dark above, pale below, whitish head with teardrop dark cheek patch. Summer female more black-brown on sides of head. Juvenile dusky, face grey-brown with dark cheek patch, pale line around and behind eye; stubby dark bill, short dark tail, dark wings, and dumpy body shape best identification clues. Flocks very vocal in late winter with yodelling *ah-ah-ahra-low* notes from courting male.

Griffon Vulture

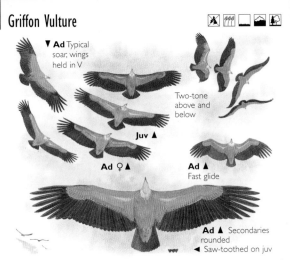

▼ **Ad** Typical soar, wings held in V

Two-tone above and below

Juv ▲

Ad ♀ ▲

Ad ▲ Fast glide

Ad ▲ Secondaries rounded
◄ Saw-toothed on juv

Massive, impressive, pale brown vulture; soars with wings raised in shallow V. Short, pale head; very short square tail. Wings long, broad, fingered, with bulging S-shaped trailing edge. Upperside pale toffee-brown with darker flight feathers, underwing two-tone with paler lines along coverts. Juvenile richer brown, flight feathers neater than worn adult.

Black Vulture

Ad ▲ Very dark overall!

Griffon ►

▼ **Griffon**

▲ **Griffon**

Black ▲ Flat-winged soar

Black ▼
◄

Plank-like shape

Griffon

Huge, plank-like, dark vulture; soars with wings flat. Wings very long, broad, straight-sided, with saw-tooth rear edge, tail wedge-shaped. Head pale with dark cheek patches, body and wing coverts all black-brown. Underwing faintly two-tone but reverse of Griffon, with coverts very dark, only faint pale streaks, flight feathers greyer. Pale feet show well.

50

Lammergeier

Ad ▲

Imm ►

◄Ad Shows white head at long range

Juv ▲

Long wedge tail

◄Ad Orange underneath

Ad ▲

Classic bow shape

Massively impressive, splendid glider, with occasional very deep wingbeat. Short head but long diamond- or wedge-shaped tail, very long wings. Adult charcoal-grey to brown above, flight feathers shine paler. Head strikingly pale at great range, with black eyestripe. Underside variably buff to orange. Juvenile grey with darker hood. Immatures variably patchy or pale below.

Egyptian Vulture

Ad ►

Ad ▲ Striking black and white

Flat-winged glide

Imm ▲

Juv ▲

Short, wedge tail; thin head and bill

Ad Yellow face, buff crest; often dirty white ▼

◄ Juv

Juv ▲

Smallish vulture with pointed head and longish, wedge-shaped tail. Soars on flat wings. Adult dirty yellowish- or greyish-white on ground with yellow face. In flight gleams white in good light, with black flight feathers, but body may look buff. Juvenile dark brown with wedge tail, thin bill. Immatures rare in Europe, staying in Africa until mature.

Red Kite

Ad Pale forewing band ►

▲ Ad

▲ Red

▲ Black

Large whitish wing patch

◄ Juv

▲ Juv

▲ Black
▲ Red

◄ Ad

Rusty tail and underside

Agile, long-winged, long-tailed bird of prey, expert in the air, wings typically angled, uses twisting tail as rudder. Looks rusty-brown and blackish with paler head. Broad pale diagonal band across inner wing above, big white patch on outer wing beneath. Tail triangular, deeply notched, rusty-brown, bright in sun. Juvenile duller, pale-tipped coverts create fine bars along wing.

Black Kite

Notched tail ▼

▲ Ad Wings dark below

Ad Pale band ▼ on upperwing

Wings angled, tail notched

Wings bowed, tail twists

◄ Juv

◄ Juv Pale wing patch

▲ Juv

▲ Ad

▲ Red

Dull, brown kite with shallow notch in longish tail. Flies with wings angled, slightly bowed, not raised as in harriers. Head pale, body grey-brown to more rufous, slightly streaked. Upperwing has broad, paler diagonal band across coverts unlike Marsh Harrier. Underwing has pale, usually diffuse patch towards wingtip. Tail dark grey-brown with faint bars.

Marsh Harrier

Soars with wings well forward, tail fanned; glides with wings raised

Juv ♀

Juv ♂ ►

◄ Sub-ad ♂

▲ Ad ♀

▲ Juv ♂
♂ narrower wings than ♀

▲ Sub-ad ♂

▲ Ad ♂

▲ Ad ♂

Ad ♀ ▲

▲ Ad ♂
Grey tail, grey wing patches, dark back

▲ Ad ♀
Pale crown, throat, wing patches

▲ Juv
Pale crown, throat

Harriers are slim, long-winged, long-tailed, long-legged birds of prey that specialize in hunting with low, quartering flight over open countryside and marshland. Marsh Harrier is biggest, heaviest, most like Black Kite; when soaring sometimes recalls Buzzard. Male smaller than female, brown with buff head and breast, grey band across wings, black wingtips and grey tail (looks more uniform at distance). Female plain dark brown, darker, less marked than Black Kite, with top of head, throat and variable forewing patch creamy-yellow. Juvenile has pale-tipped coverts above, blacker coverts below. Tail narrow, square, but spread and rounded in occasional high soar. Wings less angled than those of a kite, raised in V when gliding.

53

Hen Harrier

Glides on raised wings

Ad ♂ ►

◄ Ad ♀

Ad ♂
Black wingtip, dark trailing edge
◄

▼ Juv ♂

Juv ♂
▼

Both sexes have white rump at all ages

◄ Juv ♀
Broader wings than ♂

Ad ♀ ►
Pale brown, dark bars on cream underwing

Ad ♂ ▲

Ad ♀

A rather large harrier with striking sexual dimorphism. Juveniles look like females; all have bold white rumps. Male pale grey, whiter below, with grey 'hood', black wingtips, and dark trailing edge to underwing; white rump against often dark-centred tail. Immature male has browner back. Female dark brown above, with white rump, cream banded tail; buff below, streaked, underwing grey-buff with dark bands. Juvenile similar to female but inner underwing dark, body richer rufous-buff. Flies low, quite fast, but flight looks slow and wavering when hunting, with several deep wingbeats between glides on raised wings. Typical harrier character obvious even at very long range. Silent except for loud, rapid, nasal chatter at nest.

Montagu's Harrier

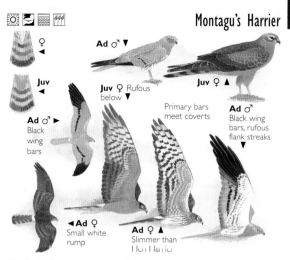

Ad ♂ ▼

♀ ◄

Juv ◄

Juv ♀ Rufous below ▼

Juv ♀ ▲

Primary bars meet coverts

Ad ♂ Black wing bars, rufous flank streaks ▼

Ad ♂ ► Black wing bars

◄ Ad ♀ Small white rump

Ad ♀ ▲ Slimmer than Hen Harrier

Small, delicate, long-winged harrier. Male grey, often darker at front than rear, with no white rump, but black bar across middle of upperwing. Underwing barred, flanks streaked. Female like Hen Harrier but white rump typically smaller, wings longer, narrower, swept back to elongated tip. Juvenile uniform rufous below, white above and below eye, dark ear coverts.

Pallid Harrier

Ad ♀ ▼

Imm ♂ ►

Primary bars away from coverts

Ad ♀ ◄

♂ ►

Juv ♀ ▲ Dark collar ▼

Ad ♀

◄ ▲ ► Juv ♀

◄ ◄ Ad ♂ Black wingtip wedge, white breast

Stocky harrier, female bigger than female Montagu's Harrier. Male very pale, gull-like, white on chest, wingtip with narrow black wedge (more on sub-adult), white underwing. Female like Montagu's with subtle underwing differences, pale ring under dark ear patch. Juvenile has stronger light collar beneath ear patch and dark neck-sides, often evident in flight.

Sparrowhawk

Ad ♀ ▲
Flap-and-glide

Carrying prey,
tail-down

Ad ♀ ►

Ad ♂ ▲
Square tail, smaller,
narrower-winged than ♀

Ad ♀ ▼ **♂ ▼**

▲ ► Ad ♂

Ad ♂ ►

♂

♀

▲ Kestrel

Juv ♂ ►

Juv ♀ ►

Ad ♂
Blue-grey above,
orange cheeks
and flanks ►

◄ Juv ♂
Short wingtips

◄ Juv
Pale nape,
rufous bars

Ad ♀ ►
Darker grey
above, whitish
below

Small, quick, agile bird-hunting hawk with rather rounded wings, long narrow tail, short squat head. Flies with distinctive fast flaps between short glides; also soars with wings spread, tail almost closed. Perches very upright, tense and alert. Male small, blue-grey above, bright rusty-orange on cheeks and breast sides. Barred orange across whole of underparts except white vent. Female grey-brown, dull white beneath with fine grey bars, thin white line over yellow eye. Juvenile brown above, with rufous-buff feather edges; uneven barring below. All have long, thin, yellow legs. Often curves wingtip back to short point in fast pursuits and glides, recalling Merlin. Quiet except near nest, where it gives loud, squealing, chattering calls.

Goshawk

Glides on flat/drooped wings

Ad ♀ ►

Ad ♂ ▲

♂ Sparrowhawk ♀
▲ Sparrowhawk ▲

Ad ♂ ►

Ad ♀ ▲

Woodpigeon ▲

S-shaped hindwing

▲ Juv ♀
Buff with dark streaks

Ad ♂ ►
Dark-barred S European bird

Long, rounded, broad tail; long head

Ad ♀ ►
White undertail

Ad ♂ ▲

Adult bluish above ►

Wears brown ▲

Ad ♀ ►
Dark bird, Italy

Juv ♀ ►

Juv ♀ ▲
Dark central European type

Juv ♀ ▲
Large, pale, northern bird

Big, heavy, broad-shouldered, thick-legged hawk, with powerful build evident in good view. Head round, protruding on longish neck in flight. Tail broad, round at tip. Male crow-sized, grey above, dull white below with dark bars; dark cap and ear coverts, white over eye. Female similar in pattern but much bigger, near buzzard-sized, long-winged. Juvenile brown above, buff below with long, drop-shaped black-brown streaks. Sits upright, sometimes on high, exposed perch but usually elusive. Direct flight strong, fast, with deep flaps between short glides. Soars high with fanned tail round at corners, wings fully spread and pushed forward, broad at base but narrower towards tip. May stoop with wings curved back to point.

Rough-legged Buzzard

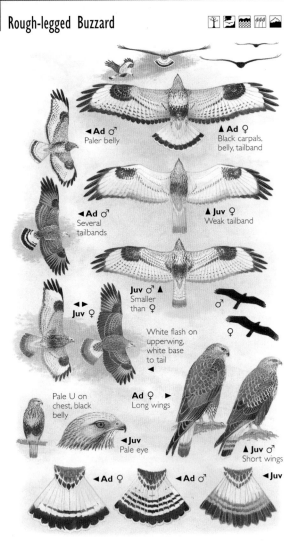

◀ **Ad** ♂
Paler belly

▲ **Ad** ♀
Black carpals,
belly, tailband

◀ **Ad** ♂
Several
tailbands

▲ **Juv** ♀
Weak tailband

Juv ♂ ▲
Smaller
than ♀

◀▶
Juv ♀

White flash on
upperwing,
white base
to tail
◀

Pale U on
chest, black
belly

Ad ♀ ▶
Long wings

◀ **Juv**
Pale eye

▲ **Juv** ♂
Short wings

◀ **Ad** ♀   ◀ **Ad** ♂   ◀ **Juv**

Big, broad-winged buzzard with small head. 'Soft' relaxed flight,
often hovers; glides with wings markedly angled at carpal joint.
Spends long periods on exposed perch, or on low post or ground.
Typically dark brown above, pale buff on head and chest, with
barred, dark belly, pale thighs and vent. Pale feather tips give
hoary look above. Tail distinctively white with dark tip, varying
from single band to several narrower ones on males. Underwing
very pale with black carpal patch, white flash on primaries above.
Variations include dark-chested birds with pale U-shape across
breast, darker underwing. Juvenile more evenly marked with
pale scaly pattern above, black belly, white uppertail with broad
black band, pale undertail with obscure band.

Honey Buzzard

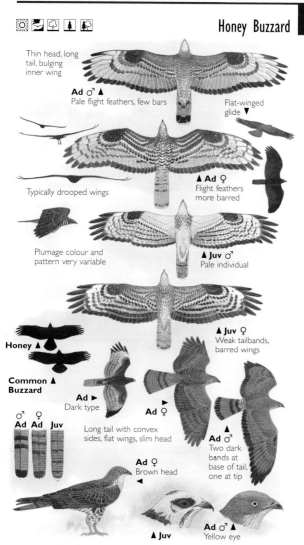

Thin head, long tail, bulging inner wing

Ad ♂ ▲
Pale flight feathers, few bars

Flat-winged glide ▼

Typically drooped wings

▲ Ad ♀
Flight feathers more barred

Plumage colour and pattern very variable

▲ Juv ♂
Pale individual

▲ Juv ♀
Weak tailbands, barred wings

Honey ▲

Common ▲ Buzzard

♂ ♀ Juv
Ad Ad Juv

Ad ►
Dark type

Long tail with convex sides, flat wings, slim head

Ad ♀
Brown head ◄

Ad ►
♀

▲ Ad ♂
Two dark bands at base of tail, one at tip

▲ Juv

Ad ♂ ▲
Yellow eye

Very variable buzzard-like bird of prey with narrow, tapered head, long tail with convex sides when closed, long wings with broad base and narrower tips giving slight S-shape to trailing edge. Soars on flat wings with tips drooped, or just very slightly raised. Active flight soft and relaxed, with elastic beats. Adult greyish above with dark trailing edge to wing, dark tail tip and two dark bands at base of tail; yellow eye. Juvenile browner, with finer bars between main bands on tail. Underside very variable, typically strongly barred, with dark carpal patches. Male has fewer bars on flight feathers and clearer pale primary patch than female. Elusive except when migrating, often in flocks, when large numbers congregate at narrow sea crossings.

Long-legged Buzzard

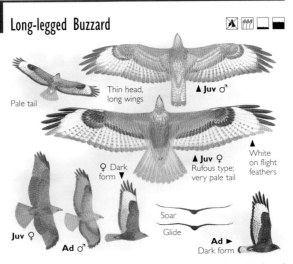

Pale tail

Thin head, long wings

▲ Juv ♂

▲ Juv ♀
Rufous type; very pale tail

▲ White on flight feathers

♀ Dark form ▼

Juv ♀

Ad ♂

Soar

Glide

Ad ►
Dark form

Large, long-winged buzzard with small, protruding head and rather long tail. Most are rusty-brown with paler head. Pale uppertail typically cinnamon, fades to whitish. Underside pale with dark belly (blacker on juvenile). Dark carpal patches and white primaries with dark trailing edge below. Tail unbarred (or fine, pale bars at close range). Rufous and dark forms frequent.

Steppe Buzzard

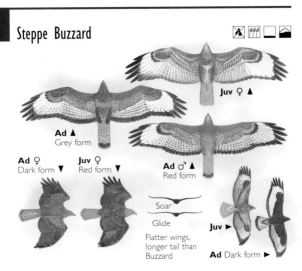

Juv ♀ ▲

Ad ▲
Grey form

Ad ♀
Dark form ▼

Juv ♀
Red form ▼

Ad ♂ ▲
Red form

Soar

Glide

Flatter wings, longer tail than Buzzard

Juv ►

Ad Dark form ►

Small buzzard, lightly-built, longish-tailed, with very variable plumage. Pale form bright foxy-red with broad pale band on flight feathers below, dark trailing edge and carpal patches. Dark form dull liver-brown, strongly contrasted underwing with largely whitish flight feathers tipped black. Small white flash on upper primaries. Large flocks migrate through eastern Europe.

Common Buzzard

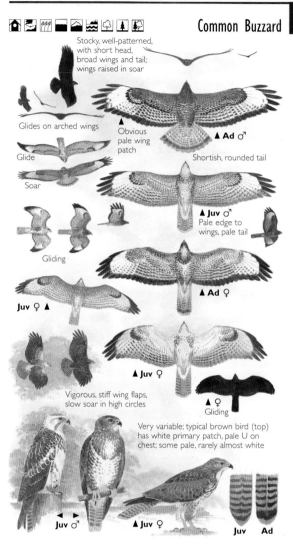

Stocky, well-patterned, with short head, broad wings and tail; wings raised in soar

Glides on arched wings

Glide

Soar

Gliding

Obvious pale wing patch

Shortish, rounded tail

▲ Ad ♂

▲ Juv ♂
Pale edge to wings, pale tail

Juv ♀ ▲

▲ Ad ♀

▲ Juv ♀

Vigorous, stiff wing flaps, slow soar in high circles

▲ ♀
Gliding

Very variable; typical brown bird (top) has white primary patch, pale U on chest; some pale, rarely almost white

◄ ► Juv ♂   ▲ Juv ♀   Juv Ad

Common and widespread, medium-large, stocky buzzard with short, broad head; shortish, broad tail; rather long wings held up in shallow V in soar. Bird by which all other buzzards are judged. Direct flight quite heavy, rather stiff, with slightly jerky action. Very variable, but great majority dark brown above, paler below, with dark flanks and belly and pale U-shape on chest. Upperwing rather uniform; underwing well-patterned with dark, mottled coverts and paler, greyish, barred flight feathers with dark tips. A few are paler with pale underwing except for primary tips and small bar on carpal area. Lightest are creamy-white on head and upperparts, but tail lacks dark band at tip. Dark forms usually have typical underwing pattern. Loud, ringing *pee-aah* call.

Booted Eagle

White 'spotlights' ▲

Glides on drooped or bowed wings

▲ Ad ♂ Pale form

Pale inner primaries

Well-marked bird

Round head

Pale inner primary patch, translucent trailing edge

▲ Ad ♀ Dark form

Stoops for prey

Medium-dark form ▼

Pale upperwing panel and white rump; pale tail

Pale rump

Ad ▲ Dark form

▲ Juv Pale form

Rufous form

Ad Rufous ► form

Ad ◄ Pale; forehead often white ▲

Dark   Intermediate   Pale

Small eagle, with markedly broad, round head, strong upperside pattern with kite-like pale covert band but also pale 'shoulders' and rump. Tips of flight feathers and tail translucent against bright sky. Pale form brownish on head and back, creamy underparts; looks black and white below with broad dark flight feather band, diffuse paler inner primary patch, pale coverts, greyish tail. Dark form all brown with paler inner primaries, dark midwing band, paler tail. All have bright white 'spotlight' at base of forewing, showing head-on. Straighter-winged than buzzards and kites, with eagle-like form; soars and glides with wings flat or slightly bowed. Plunges for prey in fast stoop. Display call is loud, shrill, whistled *kli kli kli*.

Bonelli's Eagle

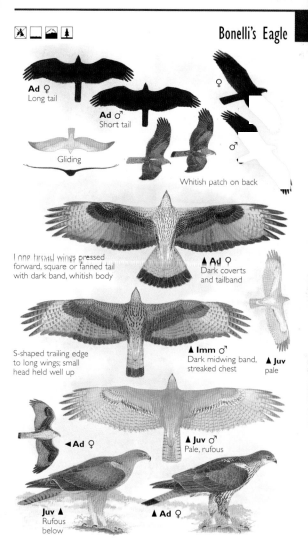

Ad ♀ Long tail

Ad ♂ Short tail

♀

♂

Gliding

Whitish patch on back

Long broad wings pressed forward, square or fanned tail with dark band, whitish body

▲ Ad ♀ Dark coverts and tailband

S-shaped trailing edge to long wings; small head held well up

▲ Imm ♂ Dark midwing band, streaked chest

▲ Juv pale

◄ Ad ♀

▲ Juv ♂ Pale, rufous

Juv ▲ Rufous below

▲ Ad ♀

Large, handsome, powerful eagle, usually elusive, not often soaring high into view. Long-winged, slightly Goshawk-like form; small, flat-topped head protrudes giving deep-chested look. Forewing typically angled, rear edge straight in glide, tail rather long, rectangular. Adult dark above with distinctive whitish patch on mid or upper back. Underbody whitish, forewing white, midwing has broad blackish diagonal band, hindwing grey with obscure fine bars. Juvenile more solidly rufous-brown, rufous below with greyer flight feathers, paler inner primaries and very narrow dark midwing band at first, broadening with age. Some juveniles much whiter below without dark band or carpal patch.

Osprey

▲ Kinked, angular wings

Juv ►
White body and coverts, grey flight feathers

Black carpal patch ◄

Variable breastband ▼

Dark above, white below, white head with black band

Very long wings; short, pale, barred tail

▲ **Ad**
Hovers well but heavily

▲ **Juv**

▲ **Ad**
Gliding

◄ **Ad**

Juv ►
Barred above

Ad ►
Not barred above

Big, long-winged, eagle-like bird of prey that uniquely plunges into water to catch fish. Small, long body, round head; rather short, broad tail with translucent bars. Long wings held at marked angle with upward kink at joint, may be held tapered to blunt point giving somewhat gull-like impression as bird circles lazily at long range. Often perches upright on exposed perch, with white head obvious. Head white with black band, underside white with more or less obvious dark breastband, upperside solid dark brown. Juvenile marked by pale, scaly feather edges above. Underside white, underwing with bold black carpal patch and usually a narrow dark central band. Noisy near nest with high, clear, whistled *pwee-pwee-pwee*.

Short-toed Eagle

Ad ♀

Gliding

♂ smaller, shorter-tailed than ♀

Ad Juv ♂
Ginger below

Soaring

Often hovers

Glides on flat or drooped wings

Pale underwing, no carpal patch

Ad
Patchy with wear

Some have dark hood

Juv
Pale edges but evenly marked

Big round head, yellow eyes

Ad

Juv

Very large eagle, often approachable, perching or soaring at close range. Flies with slow, steady beats, glides on arched wings. Frequently hovers with 'wobbling' broad wingtips, tail spread. In display stretches wings straight, with head pushed forward. Plunges onto prey from great height in dramatic stoop. Big, round, owl-like head with yellow eyes. Bare legs. Typical adult rich brown above and on head, pale below with fine dark bars. Underwing greyish- or silvery-white with no obvious dark patch, variable crisp dark bars. Dark head and chest contrast with white body. Tail has four dark, evenly spaced bars. Palest birds lack 'hood'. No dark flight feather contrast like much smaller Booted Eagle, nor carpal patches or midwing band as on smaller Osprey.

White-tailed Eagle

Huge, plank-like, with protruding head, short tail

Hindwing bulge

▲ **Juv ♂**
Narrower wing base than ♀

▲ **Juv ♀**
Juv has sawtooth trailing edge

Flat-winged glide

Wings up in soar

White tail

◀**Ad ♀**
Wide wedge tail

Ad ♂
Squarer tail ▶

Imm ▲ Dark head; pale body, wingpit

Long head in flight

Ad Very pale on head, back

▼ **Juv**

Ad ♂ ▶
Some have pale on wing

▲ **Juv**
Huge; dark bill; spotted above

◀**Juv** Tail shows white when spread, gains white streaks with age

Massive, heavy-headed eagle with long, broad wings and very short tail, typically seen near coasts or over wetlands. Flies with wings flat, wingtips broad and deeply fingered, head protruding; uses deep, floppy, flexible beats between short glides (Golden Eagle has fewer beats, longer glides). May soar at great height, swooping to water to grab food in feet. Male smaller, slimmer than female. Adult brown, with big yellow bill and striking white tail (although latter may be badly soiled). Old birds very pale-headed. Juvenile darker, streaked pale below, dark tail with white feather centres giving streaked effect. Older immatures gain browner plumage, whiter tail with narrow dark tip over several years. Shrill, yapping calls near nest.

Spotted Eagle

Very broad-winged

Pale crescent at base of primaries ▶

Juv Wing coverts darker than flight feathers ▼

Ad ♂ ▲

Juv ▶ White spots, white rump

♂ Trailing edge unbarred

Seven free tips

▲ **Juv** ♀

◀ **Ad** ♀

Juv ♀ ▲

Wide wings, longish head, short tail

▼ **Imm**

Glides on bowed wings

A big, broad-winged, wide-bodied, heavy-looking eagle with long, thin legs; flies with arched wings. Very dark in most plumages, underwing coverts darker than flight feathers. Adult brown, with pale crescent beyond carpal beneath wing, diffuse pale patch above wing, pale crescent above tail. Juvenile spotted white in rows across wings, white rump and wing trailing edge.

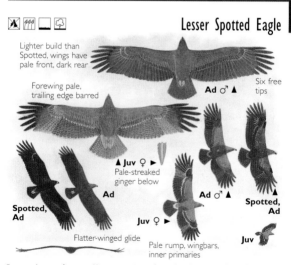

Lesser Spotted Eagle

Lighter build than Spotted, wings have pale front, dark rear

Forewing pale, trailing edge barred

Ad ♂ ▲

Six free tips

▲ **Juv** ♀ ▶
Pale-streaked ginger below

Ad

Spotted, Ad

Ad ♂ ▲

Spotted, Ad

Juv ♀ ▶

Juv

Flatter-winged glide

Pale rump, wingbars, inner primaries

Large, heavy but well-proportioned eagle. Soars and glides with broad wings slightly drooped. Adult dark brown, coverts paler than flight feathers, pale spot at base of primaries and pale patch above tail. Juvenile dark, lightly spotted across wing coverts; white rump and trailing edge. Golden Eagle raises wings in V, Spotted Eagle broader-winged with seven 'fingers', not six.

Golden Eagle

Soars on raised wings

Glides on flatter wings

Ad ♀ ▲
Big, broad-winged,
bulging trailing edge

Ad ♂ ▲
Smaller, narrower wings

Shapely wings,
long head and tail

Spectacular
dive in display

Juv ♂ ▲
Bold white
wing patches
and tail base

Ad ♀ ◄

Ad ♂ ◄

Ad ►
Pale band on
upperwing

◄ Juv
Neat, rich brown

Juv ▲

Ad Old feathers fade
pale, fresh ones dark

Very large but elegant, shapely eagle of mountains and crags, massively impressive but with almost delicate actions. Long head; long, square, broad tail; long wings with bulging S-shaped trailing edge. Soars with wings in shallow V; plunges with wings curved back in broad, bulging, tear-drop shape. Adult patchy dark brown and creamy-buff, pale on top of head and neck, often across midwing, some paler at base of tail. Flight feathers dark greyish below, darker on trailing edge of wing, faintly barred. Juvenile very dark with big splash of white across midwing below and on primaries above, and white tail with broad black tip. Becomes browner and loses white with age. Generally quiet, but some yapping notes and fluty whistle.

Imperial Eagle

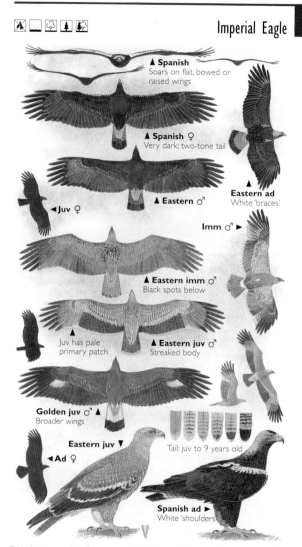

▲ **Spanish**
Soars on flat, bowed or raised wings

▲ **Spanish ♀**
Very dark; two-tone tail

▲ **Eastern ♂**

Eastern ad ▲
White 'braces'

◀ **Juv ♀**

Imm ♂ ▶

▲ **Eastern imm ♂**
Black spots below

◀ Juv has pale primary patch

▲ **Eastern juv ♂**
Streaked body

Golden juv ♂ ▲
Broader wings

Eastern juv ▼

◀ **Ad ♀**

Tail: juv to 9 years old

Spanish ad ▶
White 'shoulders'

Big, heavy eagle of forests and plains, with broad head, long tail, wings held rather flat or in shallow V. Adult dark brown with pale buff head, white marks on 'shoulders', and pale grey tail with broad blackish tip; dark coverts under wing. Juvenile sandy-brown, streaked (especially on breast), broad creamy rump; pale trailing edge, pale inner primaries, pale spots on wing coverts form double line on spread wing. Spanish adult blackish with buff head and two-tone tail; striking splash of white over forewings and 'shoulders', obvious head-on. Spanish juvenile rufous, unstreaked below, with dark flight feathers and tail, white band along wing coverts, white trailing wing edge, tail tip and rump. Pale inner primaries. Frequent multisyllabic barking calls.

Red-footed Falcon

Lightweight, agile, soars, glides, hovers

Shape between Hobby and Kestrel

Chequered primaries

1st-year ♂ ▲

Ad ♀ ▲
Orange underside, red legs

Catches insects in flight

1st-year ♂ ▲
Legs often yellowish

Ad ♂ ▲

Juv ▲

Silver-grey outer wing

▲ Juv
White nape spots

Ad ♀ ▲
Rufous cap, barred tail

Ad ♂ ▲
Blackish body

◄ 1st-year ♂

Juv ►
Barred tail

1st-summer ♂ ▲
Rufous collar, variable rusty breast/belly patch

Imm ♀ Head
▼ fades paler

Ad ♀ ▲

▲ 1st-summer ♀
Grey back appears

Ad ♂ ▲
Red legs, rusty vent

Small, agile, narrow-winged, longish-tailed falcon, between Kestrel and Hobby in shape, closer to Hobby in actions and behaviour but hovers frequently in breeding area. Flight quick or slow, relaxed, chasing insects. Adult male blackish, smoky-grey in close-up, dark face, red around eye and base of bill, greyer breast, reddish vent, red legs, outer wing silvery-grey above. Immatures frequent, grey wings with dark and whitish bars or chequered effect, some bars on tail, reddish on chest mixed with grey, orange-yellow legs. Adult female barred grey above, rich rufous on cap and underside, underwing rusty with barred grey flight feathers. Juvenile paler, less rufous, whiter face and throat with black mask, streaked below. Shrill screaming at colony.

Hobby

Elegant, agile, dashing flight with slow glides, rapid acceleration

Kestrel ▲
Soaring

▲ **Ad ♀**

▲ **Kestrel**
Broader wing, rounder tail tip

Ad ♀ ▲

▲ **Ad ♀**

Adult often looks very dark overhead, but with bold white neck

Ad ♂ ►

Juv ►
Dark, lacks red under tail

Juv ♀ ►

◄ Adult grey above, juvenile browner with pale edges

Juv ▼

Pale neck sides, throat; dense, dark streaks below

Ad ♂ ►

Juv ▲

Dynamic, smallish falcon with long, tapered, scythe-like wings, and short tail. Much narrower across body and tail base than bigger, paler-rumped Peregrine. Flight mixes elegance and speed, deep wingbeats with dashing acceleration and slow, floating glides. Adult deep grey above, buff with close black streaks below, reddish thighs, bold black moustache between white neck and throat. Immature buff on cheeks and nape, lacks red vent. All typically look dark against sky in flight, but smaller, shorter-tailed than Eleonora's Falcon. Adults shorter-tailed, sharper-winged than Red-footed Falcon; immature more similar, but tail plain, not boldly barred. Vocal near nest, with variable *keew-keew-keew* and sharper notes in flight.

Lesser Kestrel

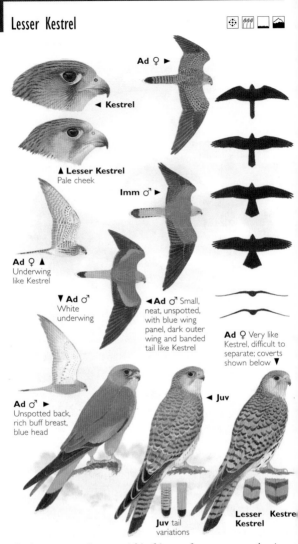

◄ **Kestrel**

Ad ♀ ►

▲ **Lesser Kestrel**
Pale cheek

Imm ♂ ►

Ad ♀ ▲
Underwing
like Kestrel

▼ Ad ♂
White
underwing

◄Ad ♂ Small,
neat, unspotted,
with blue wing
panel, dark outer
wing and banded
tail like Kestrel

Ad ♀ Very like
Kestrel, difficult to
separate; coverts
shown below ▼

Ad ♂ ►
Unspotted back,
rich buff breast,
blue head

◄ Juv

Juv tail
variations

Lesser   Kestre
Kestrel

Rather rare, southern, sociable falcon, often seen around ruins,
tall towers. Very like Kestrel, whose rather social habits around
some southern European ruins can cause confusion between
species. Hovers frequently; active flight light, wingbeats quick
and shallow. Male has slightly elongated central tail feathers,
blue-grey head and tail with black tailband, unspotted bright
rufous back and inner wing with slate-blue wing patch,
contrasted dark outer wing. Male underside rich buff, sparsely
spotted dark; underwing very white with dark tips. Female
barred like pale Kestrel, weakly marked on face but with paler
cheek patch; underwing very similar. Calls include harsh, triple
chay-chay-chay note and sharp, whining sounds.

Kestrel

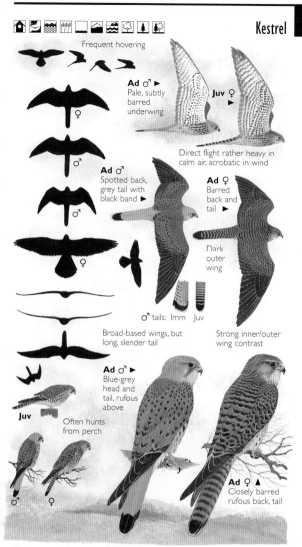

Frequent hovering

Ad ♂ ►
Pale, subtly barred underwing

Juv ♀

Direct flight rather heavy in calm air, acrobatic in wind

Ad ♂
Spotted back, grey tail with black band ►

Ad ♀
Barred back and tail ►

Dark outer wing

♂ tails: Imm   Juv

Broad-based wings, but long, slender tail

Strong inner/outer wing contrast

Ad ♂ ►
Blue-grey head and tail, rufous above

Juv

Often hunts from perch

♂

♀

Ad ♀ ▲
Closely barred rufous back, tail

Widespread, common falcon of open spaces, including farmland, often hovering as if suspended on string, or perching on poles or wires. Also capable of high soaring and quick aerobatics. Direct flight rather slow, flappy, with few glides. Slim, with long, narrow tail (often spread when hovering); short, chunky head. Male blue-grey on head and tail with black tailband. Back chestnut, spotted black; underside buff, spotted black. Underwing pale, barred grey, can shine whitish in strong light. Immature male has dark bars on sides of dull grey tail. Female rich rusty-brown with close black bars above, buff below. Both show strong contrast between pale inner wing and dark outer wing. Frequent high, whining, nasal *kee-kee-kee*.

Eleonora's Falcon

Long-winged, long-bodied

▲ Ad ♂ Pale form

▲ ♂

♂ **Hobby** ▲

Dark coverts, pale body ▼

♀

♀ **Hobby** ◄

Juv ►
Dark trailing edge

Some have pointed tail ►

▲ Ad ♀ Pale form

Dark form ►

Fast flight, changes of pace recall Hobby

◄ Ad ♀ Pale form

Ad ♀ ►
Quite brown

Juv ►
Heavy pale scaling above

Juv ♀ ►
Dark bird

Juv ►
Buff feather edges

Pale form has white throat, rufous underside ►

▲ **Ad ♂** Pale form

▲ **Ad ♀** Dark form

Medium sized falcon of Mediterranean cliffs, islands, and marshes. Rangy, long-winged, and long-tailed, with wings often sharply angled back with tapered, scythe-like tips. Flight elastic and graceful, with rapid acceleration. Two colour forms: dark and pale. Dark adult very dark, sooty brownish-grey, can look black, with two-tone underwing, blackest on coverts. Paler form has dark hood and moustache, whitish neck patch and throat, rich rusty-buff underside with black streaks; underwing strongly contrasted with very dark coverts. Juvenile greyish with buff feather edges above, dull buff with dark streaks below; underwing chequered, tail closely barred. No trace of red or orange on face, legs, or thighs. Grating, quick *kee-kee-kee*.

Merlin

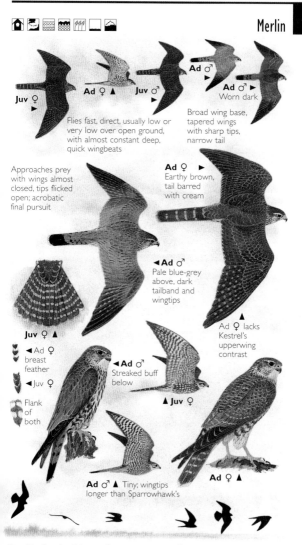

Juv ♀

Ad ♀ ▲ **Juv ♂**
▶

Flies fast, direct, usually low or
very low over open ground,
with almost constant deep,
quick wingbeats

Ad ♂ ▶
Worn dark

Broad wing base,
tapered wings
with sharp tips,
narrow tail

Approaches prey
with wings almost
closed, tips flicked
open; acrobatic
final pursuit

Ad ♀
Earthy brown,
tail barred
with cream

◀**Ad ♂**
Pale blue-grey
above, dark
tailband and
wingtips

Juv ♀ ▲

◀**Ad ♀**
breast
feather

◀**Juv ♀**

Flank
of
both

Ad ♀ lacks
Kestrel's
upperwing
contrast

◀**Ad ♂**
Streaked buff
below

▲ **Juv ♀**

Ad ♂ ▲ Tiny; wingtips
longer than Sparrowhawk's

Ad ♀ ▲

Small, chunky falcon of open country, often perching on ground
or low posts, sometimes in trees. Squat, square head. Rather
broad-based wings, tapered to sharp tip, may recall male
Sparrowhawk at times. Flies low, fast, direct, with rapid, deep
wingbeats, few glides; chases prey with fast, in-out flicks of
almost-closed wings. Male bluish-grey with dark tailband above,
rich orange-buff with dark streaks below. Sub-adult has more
marbled effect, with pale spots on rusty ground. Female earth-
brown, less rufous than Kestrel, lacking upperwing contrast; tail
barred dark brown and cream. Similar Peregrine is much bigger,
more aerial, more powerful and broader-bodied. Sharp, nasal,
rapid chittering calls, *chi-chi-chi-chi*, only near nest.

Peregrine

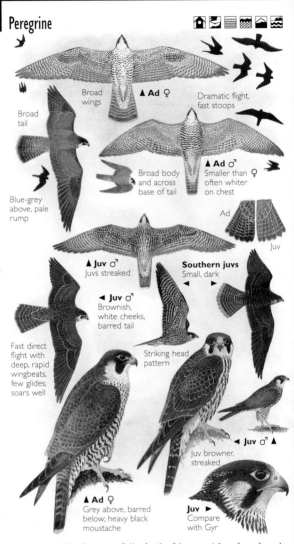

Broad wings

▲ Ad ♀

Dramatic flight, fast stoops

Broad tail

Broad body and across base of tail

▲ Ad ♂
Smaller than ♀, often whiter on chest

Blue-grey above, pale rump

Ad

Juv

▲ Juv ♂
Juvs streaked

Southern juvs
Small, dark
◄ ►

◄ Juv ♂
Brownish, white cheeks, barred tail

Fast direct flight with deep, rapid wingbeats, few glides; soars well

Striking head pattern

◄ Juv ♂ ▲

Juv browner, streaked

▲ Ad ♀
Grey above, barred below; heavy black moustache

Juv ►
Compare with Gyr

Broad-shouldered, powerfully built falcon, with a broad, pale rump and tapered, anchor-shaped wings. A dramatic and impressive bird in flight, but spends much time perched. Adults bluish-grey above, males bluer. Head dull black with broad black lobe on cheek, white neck side, white throat. Underside white with grey bars across breast, male whitest on chest, sometimes flushed pink below. In flight looks dark grey with paler rump and tail base, and striking head markings. Juvenile browner above with buff-tipped tail; buff underside with black streaks. Soars well, dives at great speed; normal flight direct, quick, with fast, deep, whippy wingbeats and few glides. Loud, raucous, harsh *haaak-haaak-haaak*, *keh-keh-keh* near nest.

Gyr Falcon

Glides on flat wings

▲ Ad ♀
Massive, broad
wings, deep,
broad belly

♂

♀

▲ Juv ♂
Dark midwing,
streaked body

◄ Blue feet

Juv can be
solidly dark

Fast, heavy,
direct flight

Juv tail variation

Juv ♀   Juv ♂

Ad ♂ ►
Often
almost
all white

Juv ♀

Juv ♂
Bluish
feet

Ad ♀
Yellow
feet

▼ Juv ♀ ►

Heavily
feathered
thighs, big
feet

▲ Juv
White
form

Lacks
elongated
moustache

Scapulars: juv
(far right) has
more black ►

Very big, heavy, broad-bodied falcon with wide wings which it
holds rather straight. Normal flight low, direct, heavy, almost
ponderous, but wingbeats quite elastic, achieving great speed in
chase. Buzzard-sized, with chunky head, broad-based wings with
blunt tips, wide tail. Very variable: adults range from white with
small black spots (Greenland) to medium grey (Iceland) or dark
grey (Scandinavia) on head and upperside. White beneath with
bars and spots of black. Immature darker overall, grey-brown
above, buff beneath with copious close, long, dark streaks. All
show darker coverts, paler flight feathers below, often with
whitish area across base of primaries. Loud, hoarse notes around
nest: cackling *rai-eh rai-eh rai-eh*.

Lanner

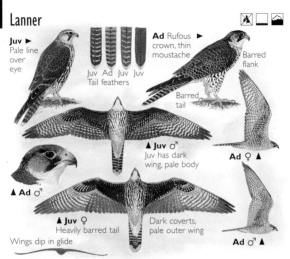

Juv ►
Pale line over eye

Juv Ad Juv Juv
Tail feathers

Ad Rufous crown, thin moustache ►

Barred flank

Barred tail

▲ **Juv ♂**
Juv has dark wing, pale body

Ad ♀ ▲

▲ **Ad ♂**

▲ **Juv ♀**
Heavily barred tail

Dark coverts, pale outer wing

Wings dip in glide

Ad ♂ ▲

Large falcon with a long tail and long, narrow, straight wings. Adult blue-grey above, whitish below with dark spots, dark bars on flanks. White cheeks and throat, buff to rufous crown with grey centre and grey nape patch, rufous hindneck. Juvenile darker: browner above, buff below with dark streaks on body, pale thighs; dark underwing coverts, pale flight feathers.

Saker

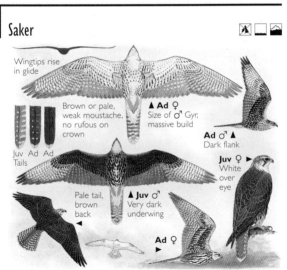

Wingtips rise in glide

Brown or pale, weak moustache, no rufous on crown

▲ **Ad ♀** Size of ♂ Gyr, massive build

Ad ♂ ▲
Dark flank

Juv ♀ ►
White over eye

Juv Ad Ad
Tails

Pale tail, brown back

▲ **Juv ♂**
Very dark underwing

Ad ♀ ►

Very large, broad-winged falcon. Adult brown above, buff below with dark spots, dark thigh feathers. Head pale buff with dark line behind eye, subtle dark moustache. Juvenile dark brown; buff-edged feathers. Streaked below, dark thighs. Underwing has strong dark coverts and pale flight feathers; upperwing has slight contrast between pale inner and dark outer half, like Kestrel.

Levant Sparrowhawk

Soars on raised wings

♂ ▲▼ Levant

▲ Sparrowhawk

Dark wingtips, pale body

Slimmer wings than Sparrowhawk

♀

Dark eye

Dumpy, thick-necked shape

◄▲ ♂

◄Juv Streaks below

♂ ◄

▲ ♀

▲ Juv ♀

▲ Sub-ad ♂

Elusive hawk on breeding grounds, but obvious in large flocks on migration. Soars with wings slightly raised. Wings broad-based but sharp-tipped. Dark eye. Male blue-grey, including cheeks; barred rufous below, whitish underwing with black tip. Female grey-brown, barred rusty below, dark throat line, dark wingtips. Juvenile has black spots below.

Black-winged Kite

Ad ▲ Striking black and white below

♂

Hovers well; soars, glides with wings in V

♂

◄► Juvs

◄Ads ►

Black on grey wings, pale head and tail

Juv Mottled above, paler feather edges ▼

◄ ♀ Wingtips exceed tail tip

▲ ♂ Wingtips equal tail tip

Medium-large, long-winged bird of prey, usually seen floating on sharply raised wings or hovering over open ground, marshes. Large, round head. Adult pale grey, head and underside whiter; striking black shoulders above, black wingtips below. Tail pale, broad, slightly notched. Juvenile marked with dull grey-brown above, with scaly whitish edges; rusty on head and chest.

Pheasant

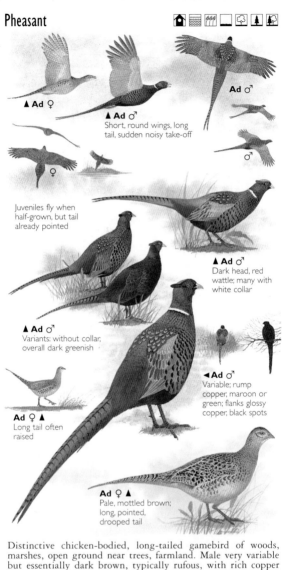

▲ **Ad ♀**

▲ **Ad ♂**
Short, round wings, long tail, sudden noisy take-off

Ad ♂

♀

♂

Juveniles fly when half-grown, but tail already pointed

▲ **Ad ♂**
Dark head, red wattle; many with white collar

▲ **Ad ♂**
Variants: without collar, overall dark greenish

◄ **Ad ♂**
Variable; rump copper, maroon or green; flanks glossy copper, black spots

Ad ♀ ▲
Long tail often raised

Ad ♀ ▲
Pale, mottled brown; long, pointed, drooped tail

Distinctive chicken-bodied, long-tailed gamebird of woods, marshes, open ground near trees, farmland. Male very variable but essentially dark brown, typically rufous, with rich copper flanks spotted black, rump rufous or pale greenish. Head green-black with or without white collar, bold red wattle around eye. Female smaller, tail less elongated but still pointed, spike-like. Pale brown to grey-brown, closely marked with lacy dark and light pattern above, dark V-shapes below, narrow bars on olive tail. Juvenile able to fly when half grown, but already has elongated, long-necked, round-headed, longish-tailed character, reducing confusion with partridges. Loud *korr-kok* crow from male, with whirr of wings; also abrupt *kutuk-kutuk-kutuk*.

Capercaillie

Ad ♀ ► Brown with orange breast, broad round tail

Ad ♂ ► Powerful, direct flight

Juv ♀ ►

Ad ♀ Greyer back than juv ►

Displays with ► raised neck feathers and fanned tail

♂
♀

Roosts in trees

◄ Orange-rufous breast

Imm ▲

Ad ♂ Huge, very dark, white on flank and white shoulder spot, round tail ►

Male is massive, dark, turkey-like woodland grouse. Female much smaller but still big, round-tailed, brown bird with rufous chest. Rare and elusive, on ground or in trees in pine forest or nearby clearings, making noisy escape if disturbed. Male dark grey, browner on back and wings, with pale, hooked bill. White spot on shoulder, white flank stripe, thin white bars on tail. White on underwing shows in fast, direct flight. Female brown above with close barring of black, grey, and buff; cream below with black and rusty bars, large clear orange patch on breast, dark grey bill. Female's tail rounded, barred, rusty against greyer rump. Male has strange, wheezy display notes building up to crackling, clicking climax with 'popping cork' sound.

81

Ptarmigan

White wings all year; fast, direct flight with flurry of flaps, long glides

Winter

Summer

Winter ♂ has thin bill, black face mark.

Juv ▼

◄ ♀ **summer**
▼ Variants ▼

▲ ♂ **winter**   ▲ ♀ **spring**

♂ **spring/ autumn** ▲

♀ **summer/ autumn**

Small, neat, handsome, white-winged grouse of high mountains, northern moors and tundra. Male greyer than female. In summer mostly dark, closely barred, wings white. In autumn and spring large patches of white on body, dark head and chest. In winter, white except for black tail and black eye patch on male. Slim bill. Low, croaking, unmusical notes.

Black Grouse

Curved tail ►

▲ White wingbar

Ad ♀ ▲
Pale wingbar; notched brown tail

♂ **summer** ►

Ad ♀ ▼

White vent

Big grouse found on edge of woodland, moorland, or heathland. Male big, striking, glossed blue on black body, curved outer tail, broad white wingbar, white vent (makes 'powder puff' under spread tail in display). Female sandy-brown, closely barred darker; tail brown, notched, wings have thin white bar. Repetitive bubbling, cooing notes and wheezy 'sneeze' in display.

Wlillow Grouse

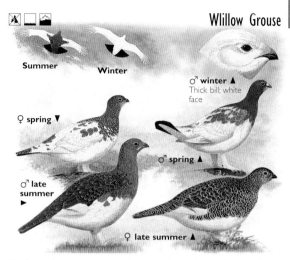

Summer **Winter**

♂ **winter** ▲
Thick bill; white face

♀ **spring** ▼

♂ **spring** ▲

♂ **late summer** ►

♀ **late summer** ▲

Stocky, rufous, white-winged grouse, becoming white in winter. Summer male rusty-brown, white belly and vent, white wings. Female paler, yellower, often patched white in spring, later closely barred overall. In winter, white except for black tail; no black face patch. Bill thicker than Ptarmigan's. Loud, staccato, rhythmic notes build into trill and *go-wa go-wa go-wa* finish.

Red Grouse

Dark wing and tail

White on underwing

Greyer Irish bird ►

Fast flight on stiff, arched wings, long glides

Arched wings ▼

♂ **spring** ▲ ♀ ▲

British and Irish race of Willow Grouse: dark-winged, dark in winter. Male red-brown, red wattle over eye, wings dark brown, tail blackish. Female paler, yellowish barring, no red wattle; dark wings and tail separate from Grey Partridge, female Black Grouse. Calls like Willow Grouse: loud, challenging, deep, fast start, slower trill in middle, staccato *go-back go-back* finish.

Rock Partridge

▲ Head pattern varies; some have black under bill (left)

Face white

Black ▲ against bill distinctive if present

Tail all ▶ rufous

Red legs

Swiss Alps bird, finely barred ▶

Stocky partridge of 'red-legged' type, found on rocky slopes and in woodland clearings in SE Europe. Rather grey, buff on belly, barred black and white on flanks. Red bill, grey crown. Black stripe curves down from above bill base through eye to surround bold white face and bib. Produces short, throaty notes and fast, irregular series of harsh, choking sounds.

Chukar & Barbary Partridge

Chukar × Red-legged Hybrid ◀

Cream face

▲ **Barbary** All-rufous tail

◀ **Chukar** Broad flank bars; neat bib border

▲ **Chukar**

Barbary Brown neck band ▶

Chukar ▲ Tail grey at base

Chukar big 'red-legged' type of extreme SE Europe; like Rock Partridge but broad white streak behind eye, small black spot at base of bill, cream face and bib. Loud *chak-era chak-era chak-era*. Barbary partridge on Canary Islands is slimmer, browner, with paler flank stripes, dark crown, wide white stripe over eye, grey bib surrounded by broad band of white-spotted red-brown.

Red-legged Partridge

Glides on flat wings

Handsome, strongly patterned, boldly barred flanks, white face

Tail all rufous

Long white stripes

Face white, border of bib breaks into spots

Red-legged ▶

Grey ▶

Red legs

Elegant, handsome partridge with red bill and legs, plain sandy-brown back, grey chest, flanks barred rusty, black, and white. Face white, surrounded by black breaking into broad band of black streaks on neck (beware Chukar × Red-legged hybrids, often lacking speckles). Call is a rhythmic, mechanical, 'chuffing' *chu-chu-chu-ka-cheka-ka-cheka-ka-cheka*.

Grey Partridge

◀ **Grey** Glides on arched wings

▲ **Red-legged** Glides on flat wings

Tail rufous at sides

Orange face, dull bill

♂

♀

Streaked back

Dull legs

Dark belly patch most marked on male ▶

♂

♀

Small, rotund, grey and brown partridge with dull legs and bill. Face orange, neck and breast grey, finely barred. Back brown with black and cream streaks. Rump barred brown, tail rusty-orange. Flanks broadly barred brown; dark belly patch, bigger on male. Barred brown wings, rufous tail unlike Red Grouse. Creaky, hoarse, mechanical *ki-errr-ik ki-errr-ik*.

Hazel Grouse

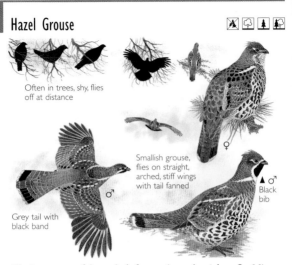

Often in trees, shy, flies off at distance

Smallish grouse, flies on straight, arched, stiff wings with tail fanned

♀

▲ ♂
Black bib

♂

Grey tail with black band

Elusive grouse of deep, dark forest, shy and quick to fly. Mixture of grey and brown, with bold white zigzag line beside throat, on side of breast and onto wing coverts; shows as white 'braces' in flight. Male has black bib. Rump and tail grey, with broad black tip to wide, rounded tail. Liquid, trilling notes and strangely thin, sharp song; loud wing noise when flushed from cover.

Little Button-quail

Pale panel on ▼ upperwing

Ad ♀

♂

♀

Tiny, elusive; orange breast, blue-grey bill

Mysterious European bird, status uncertain. Tiny, rounded, pale brown with slim, grey bill, pale legs. Back closely barred blackish; breast pale orange-brown, flanks spotted black. Male slightly duller than female. In flight shows marked pale wing coverts (like tiny Little Bittern). Calls at dusk, with deep, booming hoot: *hoooooooo, hoooooooo*; worth listening for in S Spain.

Corncrake

♂ Calls with head raised

Legs trailed in flight

Rusty wings

Juv

♂ Grey face and breast, flanks barred brown

Breeds in tall hay, difficult to see but easy to hear. Very slim but deep-bodied and stout-billed, rounded rufous wings. Head and breast grey (greyest on males), back pale brown streaked black, underside barred rusty and cream. If flushed from cover flies short way, dangles legs before settling. Distinctive repeated, harsh, rattling (close-up) or buzzy (distant) *craik craik*.

Quail

Fast, whirring flight on migration

Tiny, stocky body; rather long, pointed wings

♂ Black on throat and chin

Striped back and flanks

♀

Tiny, round, but long-winged, sharp-winged bird of dense crops, very hard to see. Brown with black spots and cream stripes above, striped cream and brown below. Striped head; male has white-sided black throat. Frequent, far-carrying, abrupt, liquid, rhythmic call, *quik, quik-ik* or *whit, whit-it*, surprisingly loud and abrupt if very close, plus quiet, nasal *mama*.

87

Water Rail

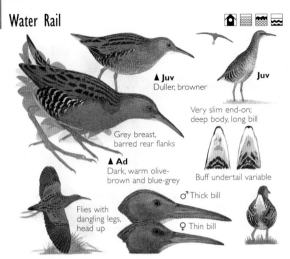

▲ Juv
Duller, browner

Juv

Very slim end-on;
deep body, long bill

Grey breast,
barred rear flanks

Buff undertail variable

▲ Ad
Dark, warm olive-
brown and blue-grey

Flies with
dangling legs,
head up

♂ Thick bill

♀ Thin bill

Slender but deep-bodied, long-billed, secretive bird of waterside
vegetation. Looks dark, with brown back and grey underside of
similar tone. Streaked back, barred flanks, variable bright buff
patch under tail. Slim, slightly curved bill, thicker on male, red
with darker tip. Pinkish legs. Flies with legs dangling. Gives
loud, repeated *kup-kup-kup*, plus pig-like squeals and grunts.

Spotted Crake

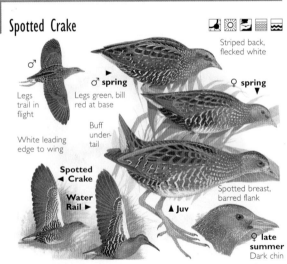

Striped back,
flecked white

♂

Legs
trail in
flight

♂ **spring**
Legs green, bill
red at base

♀ **spring**
▼

Buff
under-
tail

White leading
edge to wing

**Spotted
◄ Crake**

**Water
Rail ►**

Spotted breast,
barred flank

▲ Juv

♀ **late
summer**
Dark chin

Rounded, short-billed waterside bird, often elusive. Dark, rich
brown mottled black above, grey with brown bars and pale spots
below. Face and crown dark, chest white-spotted, big buff patch
under tail. Bill short, pale red at base with yellower tip. Green
legs. White fore-edge to wing shows in brief fluttering flight.
Loud, whiplash *hwitt hwitt hwitt* in spring.

88

Little Crake

Cream streaks on rear coverts, tertials ▼

Little

Baillon's

Ad ♂ ►
Clean blue-grey underside, green legs

Bill green-yellow, red at base on ad

Long wing point, long tail

Ad ♀ ◄

♀

♀

▲ Juv Pale bars on rear flank

Tiny waterside crake with rather long, pointed tail and wingtips. Male mid-brown above, streaked black with sparse whitish ticks, grey face and breast with only rear flanks slightly barred. Short, green bill with red base, green legs. Female brown above, buff below with greyer head. Juvenile streaked black and white on brown back, barred white on dark flanks.

Baillon's Crake

Ad ♂ White scratches above, barred rear flanks, no red on bill
◄

The tiniest crake, elusive, but not shy

Black-edged white marks on back ►

Dark tertial ▼ edges

▲ Juv

▲ Ad ♀
Short wing, barred flanks, green bill

Minute, rounded crake with no red on green bill, unlike Little Crake. Wings and tail short, wingtip projection inconspicuous. Male brown above with black streaks, white spots and rings; face and breast grey, flanks barred white. Female similar. Juvenile paler, more barred on underparts, copious white spots and lacy curls above. Elusive, but often oblivious to people nearby.

Coot

Large white facial shield ▶

◀ Ads ▲
Trailing legs; pale edges to wing

Ad ♀ ▲   Ad ♂ ▲

◀ Ist-yr
Pale chin

▲ Runs to water if disturbed

Large feet, ▲ lobed toes

White bill and shield, ▲ slaty body, blacker head

Bulging rear body

Juv ▶
Whitish face and foreneck

Dumpy, round-backed, round-tailed, grey-black waterbird.
Often dives from surface or grazes on land; sociable. Adult has
bold white facial shield and bill, red eyes, big feet with broadly-
lobed toes. Blackest on head and neck. Wings look paler when
spread, with white trailing edge. Juvenile white on face and
chest. Loud, abrupt, metallic *pit*, nasal *peu*, deep, croaky *kowk*.

Crested Coot & Purple Swamphen

▲ Tail often raised

▲ Crested, breeding ▲
Red knobs on forehead
▼

Crested, ▲
non-breeding
Wedge-shaped shield, compare with Coot

Coot ▶
Rounder head, less sloping nape

Purple Swamphen ▼

No whitish edges on wing

White undertail

Big red bill and shield

Swamphen, juv ▼
Pale, but big red bill

Ad
Huge feet

◀ Red legs

Crested Coot resembles Coot but has variable red swellings on
forehead, no pale edge to wing, rounder feather edge against bill
base, higher stern. Purple Swamphen much bigger, with huge
legs and feet, thick red bill and massive frontal shield; deep
purple-blue with large white patch under tail. Both rare and local
SW Spain, Portugal; Swamphen on W Mediterranean islands.

Moorhen

♂

Red and yellow
bill and shield,
green legs with
red garter

♀

White flank
stripe, white
undertail

▼ Juv

▲ 1st
winter

◀ Chick

▲ Ad, winter
Dark bill

▲ Ad ♂

▲ Ad ♀

▲ Juv

Ad ♂ ▲
Broad wing

Ad ♀ ▲
Narrower
wing

▲ Grey
underwing

Very dark waterside or aquatic crake, with cocked tail, short
colourful bill, white flank stripe, and white patches beside tail.
Adult glossy dark brown above, smooth slaty grey-black on head
and underbody, diagonal white flank stripe. Bill and frontal
shield scarlet with yellow tip. Legs green with reddish 'garter'
and long, narrow toes. Juvenile dull olive-brown, darkening with
age; flank stripe and undertail patches like adult, but bill dark
until maturity. Swims well with head bobbing forward and back.
Flies with quick, splashing, scuttering action across water. Moves
with half-run, half-flight over open ground. Grazes on land,
sometimes climbs (and nests in) trees. Loud, ringing *ky-orrk* or
kittuk, also *krek-krek-krek*, often in flight at night.

Great Bustard

Huge, long-winged, with eagle-like flight, much white in wing

♂ Little Bustard ►

Ad ♀

◄ More white in wing than ♀

Ad ♂

Dark patch

Ad ♀

◄ Wispy 'moustache' in spring

Ad ♂ ►

Imm ♂

Ad ♂ ▲
Broad tail, big white wing patch

Ad ♀ ▲
Smaller, neater head, less white

Very large bird of open spaces. Strides slowly across ground, flies with deep wingbeats on broad vulturine wings, with head outstretched. Male immense, thick-necked, with short, stout bill. Extensive white in wing and underbody, head grey, back and tail rich rusty-brown. Female smaller, browner, with less white in wing, but still large and strikingly patterned.

Little Bustard

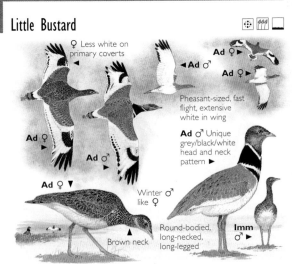

♀ Less white on primary coverts

Ad ♀

Ad ♂ ►

Pheasant-sized, fast flight, extensive white in wing

Ad ♀

Ad ♂ ♂ Unique grey/black/white head and neck pattern ►

Ad ♀ ▼

Winter ♂ like ♀

▲ Brown neck

Round-bodied, long-necked, long-legged

Imm ♂ ►

Pheasant-sized, pale bustard with largely white wings. Elusive on ground but flies fast with rapid wingbeats and short glides, revealing startling pattern. Male sandy-brown, white below, with black and white bands on neck and upper chest. Female browner, with brown head and neck. Male makes a short, dry note in display, and wings whistle in flight.

Stone-curlew

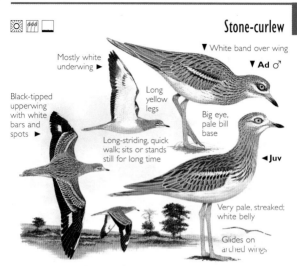

Mostly white underwing ▶

Black-tipped upperwing with white bars and spots ▶

Long-striding, quick walk; sits or stands still for long time

Long yellow legs

Big eye, pale bill base

▼ White band over wing

▼ Ad ♂

◀ Juv

Very pale, streaked; white belly

Glides on arched wings

Secretive, shy, pale sandy-brown ground bird with pale-striped head, pale band across closed wing, long pale legs. Pale bands above and more obvious yellow bill base and whitish face. Large yellow eye and more obvious yellow bill base and whitish face. In flight looks long-bodied, long-tailed; wings have pale midwing panel and white patches on black tips. Loud, screeched *kierr-lew, kip-ip-ip* notes.

Pratincoles

No white on rear wing; uniform above ▶

Collared, juv
Scaly above; plain throat ▶

Collared, summer ▼

◀ Black edged throat

Black-winged
Black underwing

Two-tone above

Collared ◀ ▼

Collared, winter ▲

Oriental ▶

No white, short tail

White ▶ trailing edge

Red underwing, white trailing edge

Collared \ Bl-winged Oriental

Red underwing

Rotund birds with short legs on ground, yet elegant, slender, long-winged with forked tails in flight. Collared is earth-brown, upperwing darker on outer half, dark secondaries tipped white. Underwing coverts chestnut, often look blackish, trailing edge white; bold white rump. Black-winged black beneath wing with no white trailing edge. Oriental chestnut, no white, shorter tail.

93

Black-winged Stilt

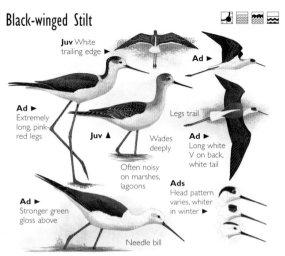

Juv White trailing edge ▶

Ad ▶
Extremely long, pink-red legs

Juv ▲
Wades deeply
Often noisy on marshes, lagoons

Ad ▶
Legs trail

Ad ▶
Long white V on back, white tail

Ad ▶
Stronger green gloss above

Ads
Head pattern varies, whiter in winter ▶

Needle bill

Remarkable black-and-white bird with improbably long legs, in or around shallow water. Fine, straight bill, long wings, and glossy black head. Most of head and body gleaming white with variable dark head markings. Legs amazingly long, deep red-pink. Juvenile browner above with white trailing edge to wings. All show striking white V on back in flight. Loud scolding calls.

Avocet

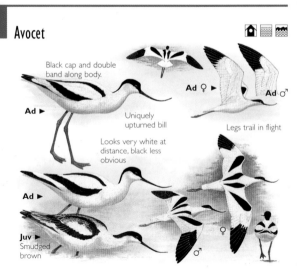

Black cap and double band along body.

Ad ▶

Ad ♀ ▶

Ad ♂

Uniquely upturned bill

Looks very white at distance, black less obvious

Legs trail in flight

Ad ▶

Juv ▶
Smudged brown

♀

♂

Bright white wader with long legs and unique upturned bill, used to sweep sideways through shallow water. Black cap and hindneck, black-outlined oval shape each side of back. In flight black wingtips obvious on rather straight, slightly blunted wings. Legs very long, pale greyish. Immature washed browner on back, black areas dull. Frequent loud, liquid, abrupt *klute*.

Oystercatcher

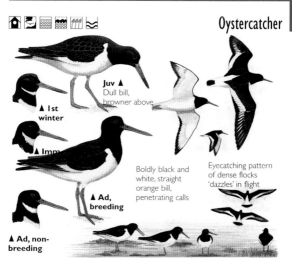

Juv ▲
Dull bill, browner above

▲ 1st winter

▲ Imm

Boldly black and white, straight orange bill, penetrating calls

Eyecatching pattern of dense flocks 'dazzles' in flight

▲ Ad, breeding

▲ Ad, non-breeding

Noisy, sociable, stocky wader with eyecatching pied plumage, vivid orange bill, and thick pink legs. Adult in summer glossy black on head, chest, and back. Broad white band along wing, white rump, and underside. In winter has whitish frontal collar, back fades duller. Immature has dark bill tip, browner back. Piercing *kleep kleep, p'keep*, strident piping notes and trills.

Dotterel

Dark cap; pale stripes over eyes meet in V on nape

Pale eyestripe ▶

Plain in flight

Breeding ♂ ◀

▲ Non-breeding ♀

White breast-band

Juv ▲

▲ Juv ♂

◀ Breeding ♀
Brighter than ♂

Winter ad and juv have ghost of summer pattern

Neat, rounded, elegant, short-billed but quite long-legged plover. Breeds on mountains in summer, migrants on lowlands and coasts. Adult has dark cap and broad white stripes above eyes, meeting in V on nape. Grey breast with white band, rusty underside with black belly. Male dullest. Juvenile paler, buffy, no black below, but pale breastband and buff stripes on head.

Ringed Plover

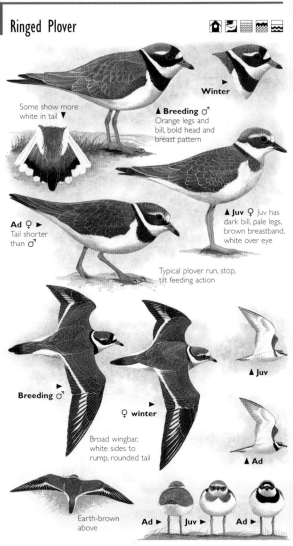

Some show more white in tail ▼

▲ **Breeding** ♂
Orange legs and bill, bold head and breast pattern

Winter ►

▲ **Juv** ♀ Juv has dark bill, pale legs, brown breastband, white over eye

Ad ♀ ►
Tail shorter than ♂

Typical plover run, stop, tilt feeding action

Breeding ♂ ►

▲ **Juv**

♀ **winter** ►

Broad wingbar, white sides to rump, rounded tail

▲ **Ad**

Earth-brown above

Ad ► **Juv** ► **Ad** ►

Small, rotund, pale plover with striking head and breast pattern, fluty calls, distinctive run, stop, tilt-forward feeding action. Typical of sandy beaches in summer, but on almost any coasts and inland waters with sandy margins. Summer adult brown above, white below, long white wingbar. Black band above white forehead, black stripe though eye, black band around upper body. Orange bill with black tip, orange legs. Duller in winter, black areas reduced, breastband narrower in centre. Juvenile has brown cap, white forehead and white stripe over eye, dark band through eye and brownish breastband, widest at sides. Sweet, liquid, fluting call note: a soft, rising *poo-eep*. Song is a rhythmic, quick *tee-loo-ee, tee-loo-ee, tee-loo-ee* in stiff-winged, rolling song flight.

Kentish Plover

Breeding ♂
Rusty nape, black chest mark ▼

♀ White ►
tail sides and wingbar

Juv

Small, pale, black-billed, dark-legged plover

▲ **Juv**

▲ **Ad ♀**
Pale sandy; face and chest marks brown

Small, pale, rather thick-billed plover with dark legs and an incomplete breastband. Male has rusty nape, white forehead and white over eye, black eyestripe and narrow patch at side of breast. Female has brown where male is black. Juvenile even paler. Legs grey-black, bill black. White bar on wing. Sharp *kip* or *kit*; short, bright, whistled *brrip*.

Little Ringed Plover

Yellow eye-ring, widest in ads, dark bill, dull legs

Bill all-dark or small pale base

Breeding ♂ ▲

No wingbar or just narrowest hint

▲ **Breeding ♀**

Narrow breastband

Juv Brown hood, ▲ no white over eye; broken breastband

Dark band across tail sides

Small freshwater plover. Pattern recalls Ringed, but no white wingbar (at best a fine pale line). Breastband narrower, more even in width. White band across front of crown behind black. Bright yellow ring around eye. Black bill with small pale base, legs dull pinkish. Juvenile has brown cap, no white over eye. Call distinct, abrupt, short *piw*; song a harsh *cree-a cree-a cree-a*.

Sanderling

Spring ▼
Greyish,
wears off

◄ Winter
Dark wing with
wide white stripe

Late spring ►
Wear gives rusty
back, mottled breast

White tips
wear off in
summer

Winter ►

Juv ►
Blackish
chequers
above

Small, usually seaside wader of sandy beaches, with black legs, straight black bill, and white belly. In winter pale grey above, white below, wings blacker with broad white stripe. Juvenile chequered darker above. In spring and autumn head, breast, and back variably rufous, marbled dark and silver-buff; underside always white. Short, hard *kit* in flight.

Broad-billed Sandpiper

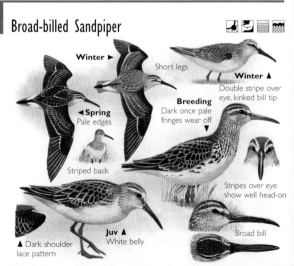

Winter ►

Short legs

Winter ▲
Double stripe over
eye, kinked bill tip

◄ Spring
Pale edges

Breeding
Dark once pale
fringes wear off
▼

Striped back

Stripes over eye
show well head-on

**▲ Dark shoulder
lace pattern**

Juv ▲
White belly

Broad bill

Mostly scarce, inconspicuous, short-legged wader with longish bill slightly downtilted at tip. Two pale stripes over eye each side of head, most obvious in summer. Spring birds mottled greyish and dull brown above, darker in summer with long creamy back stripes, rufous edges. In winter grey above, dull whitish below, dark cap, double stripes less clear.

Temminck's Stint

◀ **Winter**
Dull, plain, dusky
breast above white
belly, plain back

Pale legs, no V
on back, grey
breastband

◀ **Summer**
Blotched back

♂ ▲
Short tail

♀ ▲
Long tail

Elongated shape and
pattern like Common
Sandpiper

White-sided tail

▲ **Juv**
Lacy back
pattern

Tiny freshwater wader, quiet and slow unless flushed, when rises
fast, high, with trilling call. Short, pale legs, pale outer tail, no
V on back. Early spring birds dull, later variably spotted blackish
on back with a few rufous spots. Autumn juvenile pale brown,
upperside feathers neatly edged with thin dark line and pale
fringe, breast streaked, paler in centre, white 'hook' on side.

Little Stint

Juv ▶
Rufous,
black and
cream
above

Streaked
chest patch

Pale stripes form
V on back

Thin
black
bill

▲ **Juv**

Summer ▲
Rusty; pale V above

White belly at all
times, black legs

Grey tail sides,
dark centre

Winter ▲
Dull grey

**Ad, early
spring** ▼

Miniature wader with short, straight, black bill, black legs, clean
white underside. Summer adult rusty above with pale V-shape.
Autumn bird more boldly spotted dark in bands along scapulars
and coverts, with creamy feather tips, striking cream V on back;
breast washed buff, faintly streaked only at sides. Thin white
wingbar, grey outer tail. Short, quick *stit* or *tit-it*.

99

Dunlin

Winter

Autumn ►
Moulting, grey appears above

White sides to rump, thin wingbar

Juv ►
Rufous back, pale V, bright buff breast

Winter

Grey replaces rufous above in autumn ▼

▲ Juv

Breeding

◄ Juv
Rufous back, streaked flank

Juv ►
Moulting into winter plumage

Tail length varies between individuals and populations

Little Stint

▲ Winter
Brown-grey above and on chest

A common, small, rather round-shouldered wader, with a slim, slightly downcurved bill, slim dark legs, a thin white wingbar, and a white-sided, dark rump. The 'benchmark' standard by which rarer waders are judged. Found singly, in small groups or large, dense flocks. Winter adults (shown above) grey-brown, closely streaked grey-buff chest, white below. Summer adults (shown opposite) variably chestnut above with black and buff streaks, greyer on head and closely-streaked chest, with bold black belly patch. Juveniles buff on head and chest, pale brown with rufous and black above, cream stripes on back, white on underside with smudgy dark streaks on flanks. Call a thin, hoarse, reedy whistle, *trreee*; song a vibrant, purring whistle.

Dunlin

Greenland, ▲ breeding Short bill, yellowish fringes

N Europe, breeding Broad pale edges wear off to show brighter colour ►

Britain, breeding ◄

Breeding adults rusty above, grey on breast, square black belly patch

N Europe, breeding ◄
Worn plumage

Summer adult Dunlins vary according to breeding range. British breeders have big black feather centres on upperparts creating boldly mottled pattern. Northern breeders have smaller black spots in more extensive chestnut, revealed when broad, pale grey feather edges of spring plumage wear away. Black rectangle underneath separates from any other small, slim-billed wader.

Curlew Sandpiper

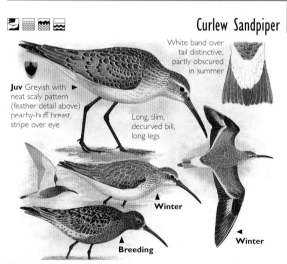

White band over tail distinctive, partly obscured in summer

Juv Greyish with ► neat scaly pattern (feather detail above) peachy-buff breast, stripe over eye

Long, slim, decurved bill, long legs

Winter ◄

Winter ◄

Breeding ◄

Slightly larger, more elegant bird than Dunlin: longer black legs; slightly longer, more evenly downcurved bill. Autumn juvenile (commonest in W Europe) scaly greyish above, clean, unmarked apricot-buff on breast; white band above tail without dark centre. Spring adult dark reddish with white around eye, greyer back. Autumn adult patchy red and grey. Trilled, soft *chirrup*.

Turnstone

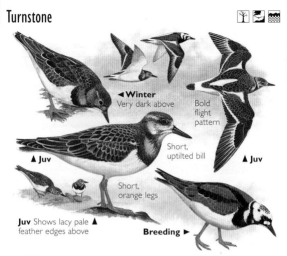

◄ Winter Very dark above

Bold flight pattern

▲ Juv

Short, uptilted bill

▲ Juv

Short, orange legs

Juv Shows lacy pale ▲ feather edges above

Breeding ►

Smallish, stocky, elongated wader of stony and rocky shores, with short, wedge-shaped bill and short, vivid orange legs. In winter very dark: brown and blackish above, black on chest, clean white below, giving piebald effect in flight. Spring and summer birds whiter on head, with much pale, bright, orange-chestnut plumage above. Loud, abrupt *kitikikik*, *tuk-a-tuk* and *tit-tit* notes.

Purple Sandpiper

◄ Summer Rufous feather edges, black mottling

Broad dark rump

1st-winter ▲ Pale edged coverts, greyish head and chest

▲ Winter

Winter ▼

Specialist of coastal rocks in splash of waves

▲ Juv

Slightly curved, yellow-based bill, slim yellowish to dull orange legs

Small, stocky wader of rocky seashores, with downcurved bill, yellow at base, and dull orange-yellow legs. Winter birds grey-brown, marked with scaly white feather edges on upperside. Breast mostly dark, merging into blurry streaks of grey-brown and white below, with white belly and white chin. Broad blackish rump, narrow white wingbar. Sharp *tit*, *quit-it*.

Knot

◄ Winter
Rump looks
plain pale grey

▼ Winter

**◄ Thin white
wingbar**

Medium size, medium bill,
medium legs: smaller than
Redshank, bigger than Dunlin

**▲ Breeding
▼**

Winter ►
Dull, pale grey,
darker at long
range on estuary

Juv ►
Lacy grey-white
feather edges
above

**◄ Pale
apricot
wash, fine
streaks**

**▲
Winter**

Ads, autumn
Transition from
breeding to winter
▼

▲ Breeding
Soft orange-red

Medium-small wader: smaller than Redshank, bigger than
Dunlin, with stocky shape, shortish bill, rather short greenish
legs. Typically sociable, often in huge, dense flocks, yet
surprisingly quiet. Bill faintly decurved, about same length as
head (more like Sanderling than longer-billed Dunlin). Winter
birds grey, paler below, with thin whitish wingbar and paler grey
rump; can look dark against gleaming wet estuary mud. Spring
and summer adults marbled black, buff, and rufous above; light,
rich, orange-red beneath, legs blacker. Autumn juveniles greyish
above with lacy dark lines and pale crescents on feather edges,
pale below with buff-pink wash, faint grey mottles. Occasional
liquid, short whistle and dull, nasal *whet* or *nut nut*.

Terek Sandpiper

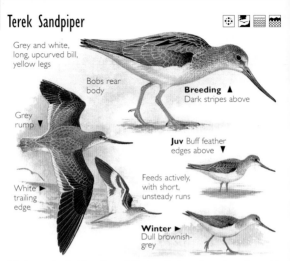

Grey and white, long, upcurved bill, yellow legs

Bobs rear body

Breeding ▲
Dark stripes above

Grey rump ▼

Juv Buff feather edges above ▼

White ► trailing edge

Feeds actively, with short, unsteady runs

Winter ►
Dull brownish-grey

Medium-sized, slim, long-billed and short-legged wader with quick, lurching walk. Tapered, slightly upcurved bill, strong orange-yellow legs. Grey above, with blackish curved band along shoulder area. Juvenile has hint of this band. Pale grey rump, whitish hindwing (not so strong as on Redshank). Quick, soft, rapid whistles in flight.

Common Sandpiper

White patch in front of wing

Breeding ►
Dark spots above

White ► wingbar

Flicked wingbeats

Streaked chest, pale in centre

Patterning on upperside subtle, looks plain at longer ranges

Winter ►

Long, straight wings held stiffly bowed

Legs dull greyish, sometimes yellower

◄ **Juv**
Pale feather fringes, barred coverts

Small, slim, long-tailed wader, mostly on freshwater edges, also rocky coast. Bobs head, constantly swings rear end up and down in loose, springy action. Pale olive-brown above, breast pale brownish with whiter centre, white underside and strong 'hook' of white in front of closed wing. Long white wingbar. Flies with stiff, arched, flicked wings. Loud, ringing *tswee-wee-wee*.

Wood Sandpiper

Non-breeding ▼
Clear white rump, barred tail, dark upperwing

Breeding
Pale spangling above ▼

▲ Juv
Buff spotting above, pale stripe over eye

Tall, slim wader with long yellowish legs, short dark bill; bobs head and tail

Long stripe over eye from bill, dark cap ▼

Pale underwing ▶

Finely barred tail ▶

Taller, longer-legged, longer-billed than Common Sandpiper, with broad white rump, barred tail, dark upperwing, grey-buff underwing. Strong pale stripe over eye. Breast finely mottled grey-buff. Back brown with variable whitish spots, more mottled blackish and buff on summer adult. Long, pale yellow legs. Loud, sharp, nasal, peevish *chiff-if-if* in flight.

Green Sandpiper

▼ Short stripe from bill to eye

▼ Underwing dark

Few broad bars on tail

Black and white in flight

◀ **Breeding**
Pale spots above

Bold ▲ white rump

Very dark wing ▶

Bobs head and tail; looks very dark with bright white belly

Greenish legs

Dusky breast pale in centre

◀ Juv

Darker, stockier than Wood Sandpiper, bobs like Common Sandpiper. Dark greyish head and chest, white stripe from bill to (but not behind) eye. Back dark olive-brown (may look blackish) with fine white specks. Broad, obvious white rump, few dark bars at tail tip, upperwing all-dark, underwing blackish. Legs greyish-green, never yellow. Loud, rich, fluty *tluwee-wee-wee*.

Redshank

◀▼ **Breeding**
Heavily marked

Bold white
back and
hindwing

◀**Winter**
Rather plain

Vivid red legs ▲

Big splashes of
white in flight

Juv Buff edges above;
legs yellowish-orange ▶

Middle-sized wader, neither bill nor legs very long, on all kinds
of waterside. Brown back and head, dark mottled chest, whiter
belly. White V on rump; big, broad, white hindwing triangle.
Bill red at base, legs rich bright red. In summer has blacker spots
above, streaked below. Juvenile paler with buff feather edges
above, yellower legs. Loud, ringing *teu-hu-hu, tyip tyip tyip.*

Greenshank

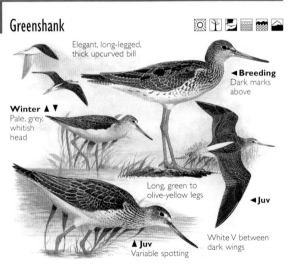

Elegant, long-legged,
thick upcurved bill

◀**Breeding**
Dark marks
above

Winter ▲▼
Pale, grey,
whitish
head

Long, green to
olive-yellow legs

◀**Juv**

▲ **Juv**
Variable spotting

White V between
dark wings

Taller, greyer than Redshank with longer, yellowish-green to
greyish-green legs, slightly upcurved bill with grey base.
Summer adult marked blackish above. Paler in winter, with
whiter head, white underside, breast streaked pale grey. In flight
wings look dark, contrasting with long white V on back. Loud,
clear, *tew tew tew*, more even-spaced than Redshank.

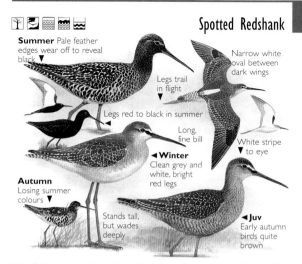

Spotted Redshank

Summer Pale feather edges wear off to reveal black

Narrow white oval between dark wings

Legs trail in flight

Legs red to black in summer

Long, fine bill

White stripe to eye

◀**Winter** Clean grey and white, bright red legs

Autumn Losing summer colours

Stands tall, but wades deeply

◀**Juv** Early autumn birds quite brown

Slim-billed, stout, long-legged wader, often swims and up-ends. Dark wings, white oval on back. Winter adult pale grey above, white below, white stripe over and dark line through eye. Long bill, faintly downtilted, red at base; bright red legs. Summer adult blackish, legs dark red to black. Juvenile barred brown over whole body. Loud, clearly-enunciated *chew-it*.

Marsh Sandpiper

Summer ▶

◀**Juv** Buffish above

Very delicate bird; needle-fine bill

Winter ▶

Flight pattern recalls Greenshank, tail whiter

Breeding ▲ Brownish, spotted black above; some are whiter on chest

Long, slim, greenish legs

▲ **Winter** Grey and white, looks very pale

Small, very slim, elegant, needle-billed wader with long legs, on freshwater edges. Like Greenshank but smaller, with longer, thinner legs and straight bill. Slimmer than Wood Sandpiper, greener legs, stands higher. Summer adult has blackish spots above and fine dots on flanks. Paler, plainer in winter. Juvenile browner above. Sharp, high *kyew* or *kyew-kyew-kyew* in flight.

Grey Phalarope

Aquatic wader, at sea outside breeding season. Swims, with head up, tail uptilted, stocky. Cap and eye-mask black, nape dark, back pearly-grey, underside white. In summer cap and face black, cheeks white, body orange-red, back striped buff. Juvenile striped buff and black, gains grey patches in autumn. Bill quite broad, yellow at base. Long white wingbar. Sharp, metallic *pit*.

Red-necked Phalarope

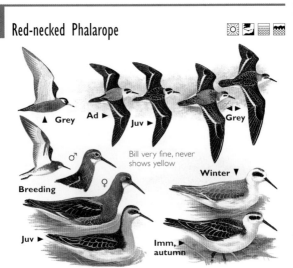

Small, elegant swimming wader with needle-fine all-black bill. In winter grey with white stripes above, white below, black through eye. Summer adult darker, greyer, striped buff, with white throat, dark cap, red neck or side of neck (brightest on female). Juvenile dark, long lines of buff above; in autumn darker and more streaked above than Grey Phalarope. Short, deep *chep*.

108

Ruff

Juv ♂ ▶
Bright pale
feather edges,
white sides
to rump

Juv ♀ ▶
Like male
except for
small size

Long wings,
pale beneath

Fine white
wingbar ▼

Juvs buff
below

Juv ♀ ▶

Neat, small head;
thickish, slightly
curved bill

▲ White rump
sides may meet
in U-shape

Juvs have ▶
neat V-shaped
scales above

Ad ♀
Heavily
blotched
in spring ▼

Juv ♂ ▲ ▶

Juv's legs
ochre to
greenish

♂ bigger
than ♀

♂

spring

♂ summer ▼ ▶
Great variation

♀ winter ▲
Winter birds
plain; males
often white-
headed with
red legs

♀ ▲

Variable wader, male much bigger than female. Short, rather
thick, slightly downcurved bill. Long olive, yellow-ochre, or
orange-red legs. Small, neat head on longish neck, elongated
body. Flies with soft, slowish action of long wings. Summer male
strikingly patterned, with crest and wide, erectile ruff: black,
white, barred, or chequered. Winter male greyish with white on
head. Female boldly spotted in summer, plainer in winter, more
buff-brown. Autumn juvenile (commonest migrant Ruff on
freshwater edges in many areas) neat, evenly patterned with
black-brown feather centres and scaly, bright buff edges above,
plain olive-buff on head and breast, ochre legs. White wingbar,
large white sides to rump may form U-shape. Almost silent.

Bar-tailed Godwit

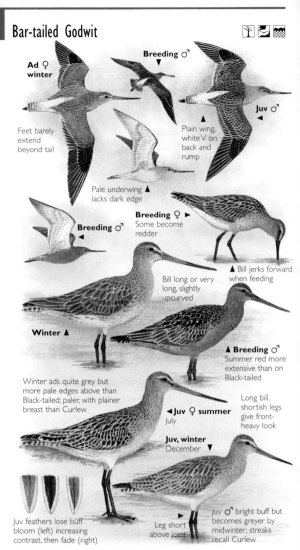

Breeding ♂

Ad ♀ winter

Feet barely extend beyond tail

Juv ♂

Plain wing, white V on back and rump

Pale underwing lacks dark edge

Breeding ♀ ►
Some become redder

Breeding ♂

Bill long or very long, slightly upcurved

▲ Bill jerks forward when feeding

Winter ▲

▲ Breeding ♂
Summer red more extensive than on Black-tailed

Winter ads quite grey but more pale edges above than Black-tailed; paler; with plainer breast than Curlew

Long bill, shortish legs give front-heavy look

◄ Juv ♀ summer
July

Juv, winter
December ▼

Juv feathers lose buff bloom (left) increasing contrast, then fade (right)

Leg short above joint

Juv ♂ bright buff but becomes greyer by midwinter; streaks recall Curlew

Large wader, but much smaller than Curlew, with long or very long, tapered, fractionally upcurved bill. Rather short legs. Less compact than Black-tailed Godwit, stands lower. Scatters over estuarine mud to feed, gathers in lines and tight groups at high tide. Winter birds paler than Curlew, adults subtly streaked greyish and buff-brown above, grey-buff on chest, white below. Immatures buffer, breast clean buff. Streaked dark cap above pale line over eye. In flight shows pale inner wing, darker outer wing but no wingbar, white V on back, barred tail. Bill pink at base. Summer males striking rich coppery-red with dark back, females paler orange-buff. Flies in long lines and V-shapes. Loud, low, nasal *wicka-wicka-wicka* or *k'wee k'wee*.

Black-tailed Godwit

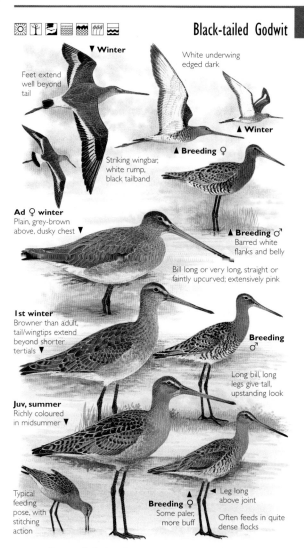

▼ Winter

Feet extend well beyond tail

White underwing edged dark

▼ Winter

▲ Breeding ♀

Striking wingbar, white rump, black tailband

Ad ♀ winter
Plain, grey-brown above, dusky chest ▼

▲ Breeding ♂
Barred white flanks and belly

Bill long or very long, straight or faintly upcurved; extensively pink

1st winter
Browner than adult, tail/wingtips extend beyond shorter tertials ▼

Breeding ♂

Long bill, long legs give tall, upstanding look

Juv, summer
Richly coloured in midsummer ▼

Typical feeding pose, with stitching action

Breeding ♀
Some paler, more buff

Leg long above joint

Often feeds in quite dense flocks

Large, tall, long-billed wader, in winter more uniform on ground than Bar-tailed Godwit, but strikingly patterned in flight. Thick-based, straight or fractionally upswept bill (less than Bar-tailed). Longer legs, especially above joint. In winter dull greyish above, head and chest plain, pale grey, only short pale line to eye. Immatures rusty at first, upperparts spotted black with rufous feather tips, greyer in winter with spotted back. Summer adults copper-red on head and breast, white belly, flanks barred black unlike Bar-tailed; females paler, more orange-buff. In flight reveals dark wings with long, broad white bar (white underwing edged dark), white rump and tail base, black tailband. Quick, nasal, *vee-vee-vee* or *ke-ke-ke* and Lapwing-like notes.

Golden Plover

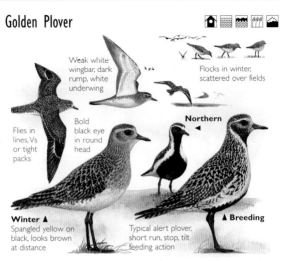

Weak white wingbar, dark rump, white underwing

Flocks in winter, scattered over fields

Flies in lines, Vs or tight packs

Bold black eye in round head

Northern ◄

Typical alert plover, short run, stop, tilt feeding action

Winter ▲
Spangled yellow on black, looks brown at distance

▲ Breeding

Stocky, short-billed bird of moorland and pasture, in dense flocks in winter. Flies fast in packs, long lines. In winter yellow-brown, chequered black and yellow above, mottled below, whitish over eye. In summer has black belly, mottled black face and foreneck (southern birds) or solidly black edged with white (northern). Pale wingbar, dark rump. High, fluty *pieu* call; *pu-peeooo* song.

Grey Plover

♀ Moulting

Strong white wingbar, white rump

▲ Ad, winter
Dull greyish; large bill and eye

Breeding ►
Spectacular silver, white, black

Unique black wingpit

▲ ►
Winter

▲
Breeding

▲ Juv & 1st winter
Buffish; big bill

A seashore bird, larger than Golden Plover with a bigger bill. Winter adult dull grey, closely chequered blackish above, buffish on chest. In summer striking silver-grey above, black below, black face and foreneck broadly edged white. Immatures strongly tinged yellowish-brown. Flight reveals white wingbar, white rump, unique black 'wingpit' axillary patch. Whistled *pee-u-eee*.

Lapwing

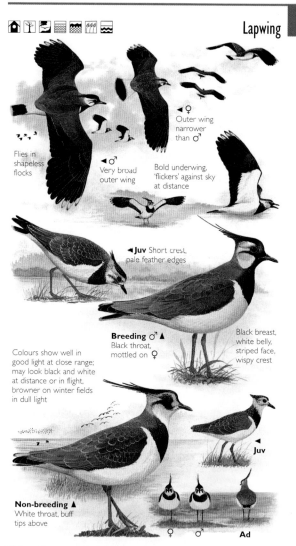

Flies in shapeless flocks

♂ Very broad outer wing

Bold underwing, 'flickers' against sky at distance

♀ Outer wing narrower than ♂

◄ Juv Short crest, pale feather edges

Breeding ♂ ▲ Black throat, mottled on ♀

Black breast, white belly, striped face, wispy crest

Colours show well in good light at close range; may look black and white at distance or in flight, browner on winter fields in dull light

► Juv

Non-breeding ▲ White throat, buff tips above

♀   ♂   **Ad**

Unique European bird, black and white at distance (especially in flight) with broad, rounded wings, black chest, white belly. Black and white underwing gives flickering effect in flight at long range. Forms dense flocks from late summer to late winter, flying in irregular masses. Pairs or small groups in summer. Black cap, buff-white over eye, buff nape, thin crest. Face buff and black, whiter in spring. Broad black chest band and throat (narrows in winter, throat pale), dark green upperparts glossed purple and blue, white underside with rufous patch under tail. Short black bill, thin dark pink legs. Shows broad white band over base of tail in flight. Nasal, sharp *peet*; variations on *pe-wit*, longer, raspy *pway-eet*; ecstatic song with throbbing wingbeats.

Spur-winged Plover

Spurs on wings

Pied underwing shows more white than Lapwing, contrasts with black body

♀ Longer tail ▼ than ♂ (below)

♂

♂

◀ Juv is barred

Unmistakable black, white and grey-brown with bold white cheek and neck patch, black belly, white wing panel

Striking waterside bird of extreme SE Europe. Lapwing-like form, stands more upright, head sunk into shoulders unless alert. Feeds with typical plover forward tilt. Black cap, throat, breast contrast with vivid white cheeks and neck. Upperparts dull sandy-grey or grey-buff. Wings have white central panel, black tips; half black, half white below. Repeated, harsh, loud *pik pik*.

Whimbrel

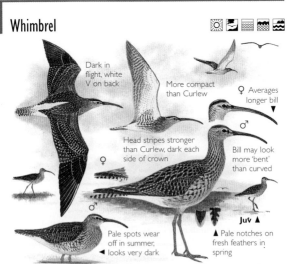

Dark in flight, white V on back

More compact than Curlew

♀ Averages longer bill ▼

♂

Head stripes stronger than Curlew, dark each side of crown

♀

Bill may look more 'bent' than curved

♂

Juv ▲

Pale spots wear off in summer, looks very dark ◀

▲ Pale notches on fresh feathers in spring

Large, dark, Curlew-like, mostly spring and autumn migrant. Buffish, closely streaked dark. Very dark cap with pale central line (stronger than hint on some Curlews), dark eyestripe. Dark outer wing, white V on back in flight. Downcurved bill slightly shorter, more 'bent', less smoothly curved than typical Curlew. Flight quicker. Fast, staccato, even whistle *ti-ti-ti-ti-ti-ti-ti*.

Curlew

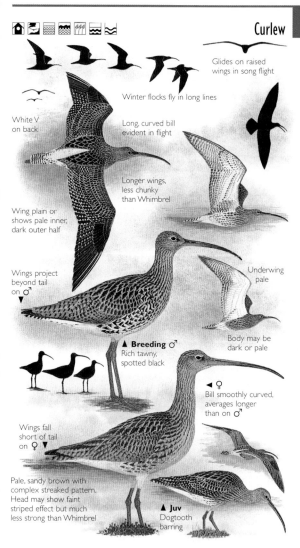

Glides on raised wings in song flight

Winter flocks fly in long lines

White V on back

Long, curved bill evident in flight

Longer wings, less chunky than Whimbrel

Wing plain or shows pale inner, dark outer half

Wings project beyond tail on ♂ ▼

Underwing pale

Body may be dark or pale

▲ **Breeding** ♂
Rich tawny, spotted black

◄ ♀
Bill smoothly curved, averages longer than on ♂

Wings fall short of tail on ♀ ▼

Pale, sandy brown with complex streaked pattern. Head may show faint striped effect but much less strong than Whimbrel

▲ **Juv**
Dogtooth barring

Very large brown wader of moors, heaths, pastures, estuaries, all kinds of watersides and shores. Bill long, smoothly downcurved (longest on females, shortest on juveniles). Buffy-brown, closely streaked dark; looks pale against moorland vegetation, but generally dark on shiny estuarine mud or sand. Head plain, with only slight trace of Whimbrel-like pattern on some. In flight outer wing darker than inner; rump and lower back white. Large size, long dark-tipped wings, rather slow, steady flight, but wingbeats more even and continuous. Flocks roost in groups or lines, markedly larger than other waders on the shore. Loud, pure *cur-lee*, hoarse throaty variations, long-drawn *whaup*, hard *hi-hi-hu*. Brilliant, fast, bubbling song.

Woodcock

Heavy in flight, deep belly, broad-based wings swept back to blunt point

Rufous rump

Bill angled down

Black-barred nape ▼

Complex 'dead leaf' pattern ▼

Long, straight bill

◄ Barred below

May feed by day in cold weather

A woodland bird, usually seen when flushed from cover (fast, noisy, low getaway, rufous rump) or over woods at dusk, when rotund form, broad-based wings, long straight bill obvious. Patterned with rufous, brown, black, cream. Pale forehead, broad dark cross-bars on nape, fine bars on underparts. Whistled, sharp *tsiwik* and repeated, deep, throaty *gwork gwork* in display flight.

Great Snipe

Short, heavy flight before dropping into cover

Barred grey underwing

Bold white tips to wing coverts ▼

◄ **Juv** Less barred below than adult

Bill held more level than Snipe's

Dark midwing panel edged white ◄

▲ **Ad** Heavy bars below

Thick bill

Ad   Juv

Snipe-like form and pattern, with bulk approaching Woodcock. Straight, thickish bill, shorter than Snipe's. Flight low, straight. Bold cream stripes on back, striped head. Heavy bars over underside. Broad white wing covert tips aligned as bars across midwing in flight, with dark central panel. Adult has large white tail corners, shown best when about to settle. Gruff croak.

Common Snipe

Flies up at close range, towers to a height

Quick, high flight with back-flick of angled wings

◄ Juv

Bold cream stripes on back

▲ Ad

Striped crown ▼

◄ Juv

Rufous patch across tail

Short legs; usually stands in half-crouch

Very long straight bill

Long-billed wader of wet mud and floods. Sedate on ground, but rises with fast, high, zigzag flight. Rich brown, striped cream. Head striped cream and black. Mottled breast, unbarred white belly. In flight wings dark with white trailing edge, tail rufous; long bill points down. Harsh *scarp!*, bright *chip-per* often from high perch. Dives in display with tail fanned to make bleating hum.

Jack Snipe

Small, weak flier, with shorter bill than Snipe

Strong cream stripes along upperside

Flies up at very close range, quickly settles again

Centre of crown black (cream on Snipe) ▼

Bold stripes above ▼

Grey underwing, white belly

Springy vertical bob as it feeds

Wedge-shaped tail

Small, elusive snipe of dense vegetation; flies up under feet and usually drops again quickly. Dark, striped cream above, pattern more even and contrasted than Snipe's. Head stripes include dark centre to crown (pale centre on Snipe). Bill shorter. Bouncy, springy action on ground. Flight weaker; pale trailing edge less obvious than Snipe's. Call infrequent, quiet *gat* note.

Great Skua

Blackish bill

Big, heavy, dark skua with bold white wing flashes

Wings long, pointed, but look broad, flight ponderous

Juv Rufous to blackish except for wing patch ▼

Short, wedge-shaped tail, dark rump, unlike young gulls

Ad ▶

Fades to bleached buff around neck and chest, darker cap

Juvs: Arctic ▲ Pomarine ▲ Great ▲

Big, heavy bird of open sea and northern isles. Dark brown with variable dark cap, paler head and neck, pale buff streaks overall. Short, dark, wedge-shaped tail (unlike any gull's) and long, broad wings, tapered to point, with large white patch towards tip. Juvenile duller, darker, some blackish, some rufous with dark hood, smaller wing flash. Bill thick, blackish.

Pomarine Skua

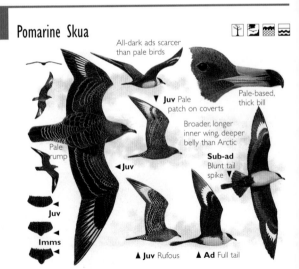

All-dark ads scarcer than pale birds

▼ **Juv** Pale patch on coverts

Pale-based, thick bill

Broader, longer inner wing, deeper belly than Arctic

Pale rump

◀ **Juv**

Sub-ad Blunt tail spike ▼

Juv

Imms

▲ **Juv** Rufous   ▲ **Ad** Full tail

A big skua, almost as bulky as Great Skua but with Arctic Skua pattern. Flight steadier than Arctic. Pale adult has black cap, dark upperside, white underside with brown breastband and flank bars. Dark adult brown. White flash on outer wing. Tail spike broad, spoon-like. Juvenile dark, square tail, 'double' pale crescent under wing, heavy pale-based bill, pale barred rump.

Arctic Skua

Fast-flying, supremely elegant bird, chases terns and gulls

Slim bill

Ad has straight tail spike

▲ Ads Pale form

Ad Intermediate form **▼**

Ad Dark form **▲**

Juv ►

Juv ► Slim, rufous, dark-rumped

◄ Juv

Juv ▼

Ad ▼

Imm ►

Slender, elegant, agile skua, with long wings and fluent flight, acrobatically chases terns. Adult has pointed tail spike, juvenile has very short pointed spike. Pale adult dark above, dark cap, white below with dusky chest sides. Dark birds brown overall. Small white wing flash. Juveniles barred rufous, unbarred dark brown, or sandy with pale bars, head paler. Slim bill looks dark.

Long-tailed Skua

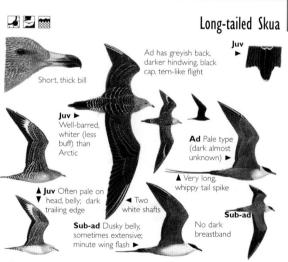

Short, thick bill

Ad has greyish back, darker hindwing, black cap, tern-like flight

Juv ►

Juv ► Well-barred, whiter (less buff) than Arctic

Ad Pale type (dark almost unknown) **►**

▲ Very long, whippy tail spike

▲ Juv Often pale on **▼** head, belly; dark trailing edge

◄ Two white shafts

No dark breastband

Sub-ad

Sub-ad Dusky belly, sometimes extensive; minute wing flash **►**

Chesty skua, but looks small, slender in flight, like a tern. Adults greyish above, with black cap, yellowish cheeks, white breast, dusky belly, only tiny pale wing flash on very dark wingtip. Very long, whippy tail spike. Juveniles pale greyish to very dark, typically greyish with pale belly, pale bars on rump and vent, barred underwing; tail projection short and blunt.

119

Black-headed Gull

Long white flash on outer wing

Thin, sharp bill

Small, agile, sharp-winged; very pale

♀ **winter** ▲
Cheek spot; red bill and legs

♂

Summer ►
Brown hood, red bill similar tone; white nape
♀

Juv ▲

♂ **1st winter** ▲

Dark cheek spot, dark-tipped orange bill, orange legs

Ad ►
Underwing has dark outer patch, white leading edge

♀ **1st summer** ►
(Longer tail of ♂ outlined)

♂ **1st winter** ►
White flash on wing obscured by dark feather edges, which gradually wear off

♀ ►

Ad, winter
Black trailing edge to wingtip ►

White flash on leading edge

Small, noisy, pale, often abundant gull with white forewing flash, dusky underwing. Silvery-grey above, white neck, body, and tail. Outer wing has narrow black trailing edge and broad triangle of white on front. Underwing dark grey with narrow white stripe along outer primaries. In summer has dark brown hood from bill to lower throat and nape, dark red bill, dark plum-red legs. In winter has white head, greyish nape, black ear spot, bright red bill with dark tip, scarlet legs. Incomplete hood in spring and autumn. Immature has dark tailband, dark brown on coverts, less clear-cut white flash on upperwing, paler grey underwing, paler, more orange legs and bill base, brown hood in summer. Loud, squabbling calls, *kreee-arr, kek, kekeke*.

Mediterranean Gull

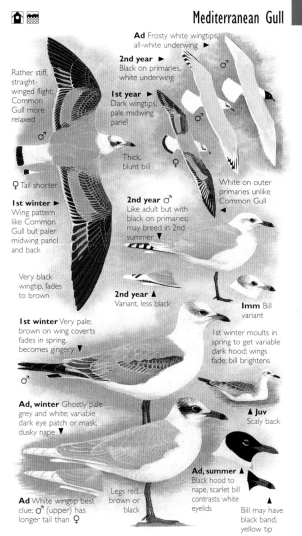

Ad Frosty white wingtips, all-white underwing ▶

2nd year ▶
Black on primaries, white underwing

1st year ▶
Dark wingtips, pale midwing panel

Rather stiff, straight-winged flight; Common Gull more relaxed

Thick, blunt bill

♀ Tail shorter

White on outer primaries unlike Common Gull

1st winter ▶
Wing pattern like Common Gull but paler midwing panel and back

2nd year ♂
Like adult but with black on primaries; may breed in 2nd summer ▼

Very black wingtip, fades to brown

2nd year ▲
Variant, less black

Imm Bill variant

1st winter Very pale; brown on wing coverts fades in spring, becomes gingery ▼

1st winter moults in spring to get variable dark hood; wings fade; bill brightens

Ad, winter Ghostly pale grey and white; variable dark eye patch or mask, dusky nape ▼

▲ **Juv**
Scaly back

Ad, summer ▲
Black hood to nape, scarlet bill contrasts; white eyelids

Ad White wingtip best clue; ♂ (upper) has longer tail than ♀

Legs red, brown or black

Bill may have black band, yellow tip

Stocky, handsome gull, rare breeder, small numbers on coasts. Palest grey above, with white body and tail. Wingtip frosty white (tiny black leading edge), underwing strikingly white. Head jet black to hindneck in summer, with big white 'eyelids'. Bill contrasting scarlet with black and yellow tip, legs deep red. In winter head white, nape greyish, dark smudge behind eye more a mask, less a spot, than on Black-headed. Thicker bill, more angular head. Immature like adult but with variable black wingtip spots. First year pale grey on back, pale midwing panel, dark trailing edge, black-brown wingtips (primaries show white streaks when spread), dark tailband, dark mask, thick orange bill, buff or red at base. Distinctive nasal *miaoow* at colony.

121

Slender-billed Gull

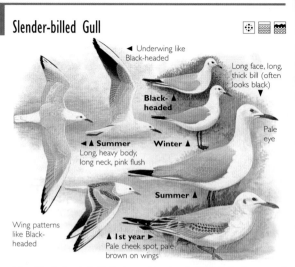

◄ Underwing like Black-headed

Long face, long, thick bill (often looks black) ▼

Black-headed ▲

Pale eye

◄▲ **Summer**
Long, heavy body, long neck, pink flush

Winter ▲

Summer ▲

Wing patterns like Black-headed

▲ **1st year** ►
Pale cheek spot, pale brown on wings

Like Black-headed Gull, but white-headed, slightly larger and longer on water and in flight, with big, long, bulbous head and longer bill; wing pattern almost identical. Summer adult flushed pink. Bill deep red in summer, often looks black; pale reddish in winter. Red legs. Pale eye hard to see. Immature pale, with washed-out wing pattern, grey ear spot, dull orange bill and legs.

Fulmar

▼ Pale patch near wingtip

Grey rump and tail

Big white head

Stiff-winged in wind, banking onto wingtip ►

Dark form brownish-grey ▼

Thickset, flies low over flat sea in calm air ►

Underwing grey and white, no black ►

Swims with head and tail raised

▲ **Ad**
Grey upperwing fades browner with patchy effect

Bold black eye and eye-patch, thick, blunt bill

A petrel, unrelated to gulls, but with gull-like plumage, on cliff ledges in summer. Grey upperwing uneven, pale patch inside dark grey tip. Rump and tail grey, unlike any gull's. Head large, bulbous, striking white over sea at long range. Eye and patch in front blackish. Flies with stiff, straight wings, with shallow beats in calm weather, masterful glides in wind. Loud, cackling calls.

Little Gull

◄ 1st summer
Retains juv wings (faded) but gains hood

2nd summer
Most 2nd-years as adult, some with black on wing

1st winter ►
Black zigzag above; dark cap; tiny bill

Ad, winter ►
White rim to grey wing

Ad, summer
Underwing blackish with white rim ►

1st autumn ►
Moult from juv to 1st winter may give collar effect, also dark rump

Ad, winter
Dark cap, ear patch; thin black bill ▼

▲ 2nd summer
Underwing greyer

White wingtips (black under far wing)

Ad, summer
Large black hood, no white eyelids ▼

Bill red or blackish

Red legs

2nd summer
Variable hood

Juv ▼

Juv Moulting to ▲ 1st winter: quickly loses brown on back and neck

Smallest gull, rather tern-like action and proportions. Small, fine bill, shorter than terns', short legs, wings slightly broader than terns', blunter at tip on adult. Pale grey above, white body and tail. Upperwing grey, underwing blackish, both with white rim. Summer adult has black hood and bill, no white eyelids, red legs. In winter has white head, small dark cap, dark ear patch, pale legs. Immature has variable black on wingtip. Juvenile dark on head and neck, dark back barred black-brown. Loses dark on back in autumn, at first retaining dark nape (broader than Kittiwake's) and dark rump (never on Kittiwake); crisp black zigzag on upperwing. One-year-old has patchy hood; dark zigzag on wings fades, inner wing diagonal breaks up. Short, nasal, hard *kek*.

Kittiwake

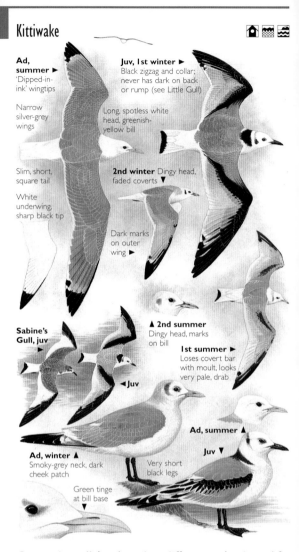

Ad, summer ►
'Dipped-in-ink' wingtips

Narrow silver-grey wings

Slim, short, square tail

White underwing, sharp black tip

Juv, 1st winter ►
Black zigzag and collar; never has dark on back or rump (see Little Gull)

Long, spotless white head, greenish-yellow bill

2nd winter Dingy head, faded coverts ▼

Dark marks on outer wing ►

Sabine's Gull, juv

◄ **Juv**

▲ **2nd summer**
Dingy head, marks on bill

1st summer ►
Loses covert bar with moult, looks very pale, drab

Ad, summer ▲

Juv ▼

Ad, winter ▲
Smoky-grey neck, dark cheek patch

Very short black legs

Green tinge at bill base ▼

Ocean-going gull, breeds on sheer cliffs, rests on beaches and flat rocks; rare inland. Adult grey above, outer wing paler, fades to whitish, 'dipped-in-ink' black tip. Underwing white with black tip. White head, body, short tail. In flight shows striking white head, narrow grey back. Bill greenish-yellow, eye and legs black. Immatures duller, tinged buff on wings, greyish nape, bill blackish at base, legs browner. Winter adult has blackish ear patch, grey nape. Juvenile has sharp, narrow black half-collar, black diagonal on inner wing, whiter hindwing, black triangle on outer wing, forming W broken by pale back (never dark, as on Little Gull), black bill. One-year-old wing diagonal browner, thinner, then breaks up. Loud, nasal *kitti-ar-wake* at colony.

Glaucous Gull

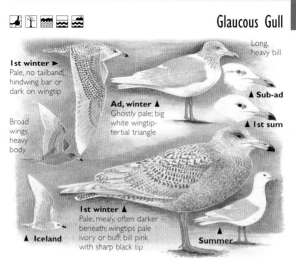

1st winter ▶
Pale, no tailband, hindwing bar or dark on wingtip

Long, heavy bill

▲ **Sub-ad**

▲ **1st sum**

Broad wings, heavy body

Ad, winter ▲
Ghostly pale; big white wingtip-tertial triangle

▲ **Iceland**

1st winter ▲
Pale, mealy, often darker beneath; wingtips pale ivory or buff; bill pink with sharp black tip

▲ **Summer**

Large to very large long-billed gull, with no black on wings or tail. Adult pale grey with big white wingtip. In winter has white head and streaked grey-buff chest. Bill yellow with red spot, legs pale pink. First year pale buff, closely barred, often darker below than above, buff wingtips, pink bill with black tip (reduces with age); patchy white in summer, gains grey with age.

Iceland Gull

1st winter ▶

▲ Iceland (top) lighter than Glaucous (lower)

Short bill, round head

▲ **1st winter**
Black bill tip wedge extends back

Pale tail, hindwing, wingtips striking in mixed flock

Long wingtip

Short legs

2nd winter ◀

Ad, winter ▼

Short bill

Long wingtip at all ages

▲ **Glaucous**

▲ **Ad, summer**

1st summer ▲
Becomes very white

1st/2nd yrs hard to age

Size of Herring Gull, but with rounder head and slimmer, shorter bill, longer wingtips. Plumage pattern matches Glaucous Gull, but has rounder head, stubbier bill, longer wingtips at rest. Adults often look dark-eyed at distance. Legs dark pink. First year birds have darker bill, dark tip extending towards base as wedge. Older immatures have bill pattern like young Glaucous.

Common Gull

Juv Pale midwing band, brown-black outer wing; sharp black band on white tail ▶

Ad Two large white spots on black wingtip ▶

1st year Brown spots on underwing, dark tip ▼

1st summer has white head, grey back, creamy-brown wings

Medium size, greyer than UK Herring Gull, no red on bill, green legs, dark eye

Ad Underwing has more black than Herring Gull

Underwing

◀ **2nd winter**

2nd year ▶

Large white tertial tips

◀ **Ad, winter** Dark eye; slim bill with thin dark ring

▲ **Ad, summer**

▲ **Juv**

◀ **1st winter** November

Pattern like Herring Gull but darker grey back than UK birds, bolder white patch between back and wingtip, and bolder white wingtip spots on more extensive black. Head and neck streaked dark grey in winter. Eye dark, unlike Herring Gull. Legs green, yellower in summer. Bill small, tapered, greenish-yellow, no red spot, often with small dark band in winter. In first year has sharp black band on white tail, solid brown-black wingtips (not streaked white as on Mediterranean), neatly chequered coverts with greyer midwing panel (darker than on Mediterranean). Fades pale buff in summer with grey saddle, brown wingtips and tailband. Second year like adult but more black, less white in wingtip. Distinctive high, strangled, squealing calls.

Ring-billed Gull

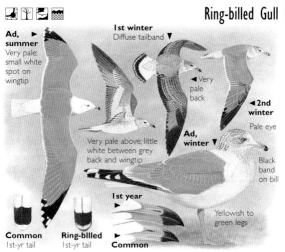

**Ad, ►
summer**
Very pale;
small white
spot on
wingtip

1st winter
Diffuse tailband ▼

◄ Very
pale
back

◄**2nd
winter**

Pale eye

Very pale above; little
white between grey
back and wingtip

**Ad,
winter** ▼

Black
band
on bill

1st year
►

Yellowish to
green legs

Common
1st-yr tail

Ring-billed
1st-yr tail

►
Common

Like stockier, often slightly larger version of Common Gull, but
paler. Smaller than Herring Gull, but can be similar in pattern.
Adult very pale above, with white between back and wingtips
inconspicuous. Thick, stubby, yellow bill with black band near
tip, pale eye unlike Common Gull. First year has less clear cut
tailband, more barred body, paler back, blacker wing markings.

Audouin's Gull

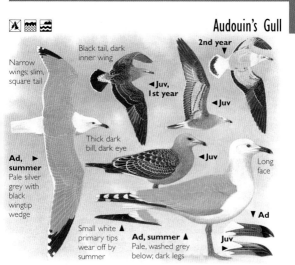

Narrow
wings; slim,
square tail

Black tail, dark
inner wing

2nd year

◄**Juv,
1st year**

◄ **Juv**

Thick dark
bill, dark eye

◄ **Juv**

Long
face

**Ad, ►
summer**
Pale silver
grey with
black
wingtip
wedge

Small white ▲
primary tips
wear off by
summer

Ad, summer ▲
Pale, washed grey
below; dark legs

▼ **Ad**

Juv

Large, elegant, thin-winged gull. Adult silver-grey with white
head, wingtips with black wedge, tiny white spot. Body washed
palest grey. Underwing white with Gannet-like black tip. Bill
thick, square-tipped, dark red (looks black at distance) with
black band and yellow tip. Black eyes, grey legs. Juvenile dark,
mostly black tail, U-shaped white rump, plain brown breast.

127

Yellow-legged Gull

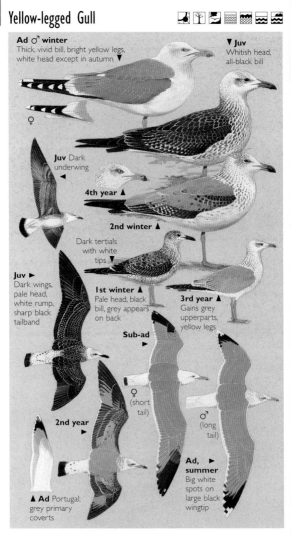

Ad ♂ winter
Thick, vivid bill, bright yellow legs, white head except in autumn ▼

▼ Juv
Whitish head, all-black bill

♀

Juv Dark underwing ◄

4th year ▲

2nd winter ▲

Dark tertials with white tips ▼

Juv ►
Dark wings, pale head, white rump, sharp black tailband

1st winter ▲
Pale head, black bill, grey appears on back

3rd year ▲
Gains grey upperparts, yellow legs

Sub-ad

♀ (short tail)

♂ (long tail)

2nd year ►

**Ad, ►
summer**
Big white spots on large black wingtip

▲ Ad Portugal; grey primary coverts

A large, white-headed, grey-backed gull with black and white wingtips, mostly marine. Thick bill, long wings held rather flat. Adult immaculate grey above, paler than Lesser Black-backed but darker than UK Herring Gull. Head white except in late summer and autumn, when streaked pale grey. Wingtips have extensive black. Bill vivid yellow, large red spot, legs bright yellow. First year dark brown above, tinged rusty, head whiter with dark mask, thick black bill, dark primaries (less obvious pale inner patch than Herring Gull), neat blackish tailband; gradually develops grey above. Eastern race *cachinnans* a rare visitor: adult paler above, longer, slim bill often with dark band, dark eyes, much paler underwing.

Herring Gull

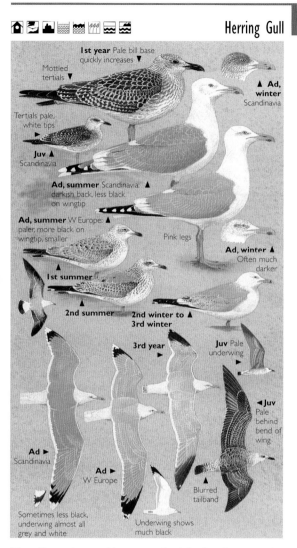

1st year Pale bill base quickly increases ▼

Mottled tertials ▼

▲ **Ad, winter** Scandinavia

Tertials pale, white tips ►

Juv ▲ Scandinavia

Ad, summer Scandinavia: darkish back, less black on wingtip ▲

Ad, summer W Europe: paler, more black on wingtip, smaller

Pink legs

Ad, winter ▲ Often much darker

1st summer ◄

2nd summer ▲

2nd winter to ▲ **3rd winter**

3rd year ►

Juv Pale underwing ►

◄ **Juv** Pale behind bend of wing

Ad ► Scandinavia

Ad ► W Europe

Blurred tailband

Sometimes less black, underwing almost all grey and white

Underwing shows much black

Big gull, mostly coastal in summer, but inland at tips, reservoirs in winter. Adult white-headed with grey back, black and white wingtips, yellow bill with red spot, pink legs. In winter head and breast extensively clouded and streaked brownish. Paler than Yellow-legged, much more contrast on wings than Lesser Black-backed and flight feathers much paler grey beneath. Bigger than Common Gull, distinguished by pink legs, pale eye. Immature starts dark brown with dark bill, soon develops paler back (grey increasing with age), pale-based bill; upperwing shows obvious paler patch on inner primaries behind angle, unlike Lesser Black-backed, tailband blends into barred tail base, mottled rump at first. Loud, yelping calls, *kyow*, long, strident laugh.

Great Black-backed Gull

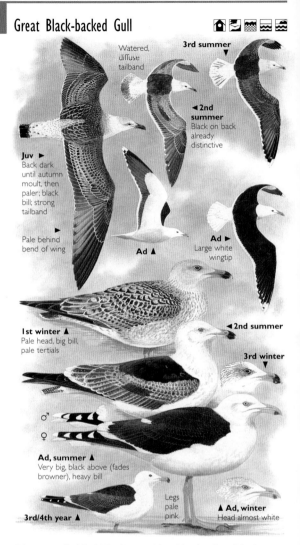

3rd summer

Watered, diffuse tailband

◄2nd summer
Black on back already distinctive

Juv ►
Back dark until autumn moult; then paler; black bill; strong tailband

Pale behind bend of wing

Ad ▲

Ad ►
Large white wingtip

1st winter ▲
Pale head, big bill, pale tertials

◄2nd summer

3rd winter

♂
♀

Ad, summer ▲
Very big, black above (fades browner), heavy bill

Legs pale pink

▲ Ad, winter
Head almost white

3rd/4th year ▲

Biggest gull, blackish above with white head and body, more white on wingtip than Lesser Black-backed. Very heavy yellow bill with red spot, legs whitish or pale pink. Head almost white in winter, keeping very strong contrast with back and wings, which fade slightly browner. Immature starts pale, boldly chequered blackish on back, very big black bill against white face; upperwing pale, strong dark brown bar on secondaries, dark outer primaries, obvious pale patch behind angle; tailband narrow, broken against white tail base. Gradually develops black back over three or four years. Bill becomes pale olive-brown with black band, then yellow with black and red near tip. Loud, deep *owk-owk-owk*; 'laughing' call shorter, deeper than Herring Gull's.

Lesser Black-backed Gull

1st summer Baltic Gull, Scandinavian ▼

Ad Baltic Gull, Scandinavian, long-winged, white head all year ▼

White primary tips wear off ▲

Ad, summer Netherlands: very dark, slender, long-winged ▶
Paler end of range ▼

Yellow legs

♂

Sub-ad ▼

Winter ▲

Juv Baltic: very dark on wing and tail ▶

Ad, summer UK: ▲ palest, heaviest; dark head outside breeding season

◀ Darker under flight feathers than Herring Gull

♀

Juv

1st W Dark greater coverts, all-dark primaries

Ad UK: ▶ most contrast between grey of wing and tip

Ad Baltic: longest, thinnest wing ▶

1st year ▲ Underwing

Ad Netherlands

A white-headed gull with dark back, long wings, bright yellow legs. Race *graellsii* (W Europe) has slate-grey back, darker than Yellow-legged or Herring Gull, black wingtips, dark grey beneath flight feathers; dark head and chest in winter. Race *intermedius* (NW Europe) is darker, almost black above; *fuscus* (Baltic Gull, probably separate species) longest-winged, blackest above, white-headed all year. Immature dark brown, mottled darker, dark smudge around eye on grey-buff face, black bill; upperwing shows dark band across midwing, darker band across hindwing, primaries all dark without pale patch behind angle; tail blackish, rump white. Develops dark grey 'saddle' and progressively gains adult plumage with age.

Common Tern

Juv Dark forewing, dark trailing edge, paler midwing, greyish rump, pale bill

Long head, long inner wing, medium tail

Ad ► Broad dark trailing edge squared off

Underwing ► translucent only behind angle

Ad ► Inner primaries pale, outer wing marked darker

1st summer ▲ Rare in Europe

1st winter Loses buff tinge, bill black ▼

Ad, winter ▲

Flattish head; wide white line between bill and cap ►

Long bill with black tip

Ad, summer ▲ Long primaries dark, shorter innermost primaries pale

Medium-short legs

Juv ► Buffish tinge above; pale bill base; longer legs than Arctic

A typical tern, common on coasts from spring to late autumn, frequent inland. Black cap, pale grey back, white body and forked, white tail. Bill dagger-shaped, bright red with black tip. Short red legs. Spring adult shows slight contrast between darker-streaked outer and plain grey inner primaries, with dark 'wedge' near middle. By autumn outer primaries streaked blacker (no such contrast on Arctic Tern). Autumn adult has white forehead, darker forewing (Arctic retains black cap longer). Juvenile has pale forehead tinged ginger, grey back washed buff, pale midwing panel with grey hindwing bar, pale-based bill. All show broad dark tips to outer primaries below, only innermost ones translucent. Sharp *kik*, nasal, rasping *kieri kieri kieri*.

Arctic Tern

Ad Very pale, narrow, tapered outer wing, all pale grey ►

Very long tail

Juv Dark forewing, white trailing edge, white rump, dark bill ►

Neckless, spike-billed

Short head, short inner wing, long tail give different profile from Common

▼ **Ad**

Very white, translucent underwing, narrow, sharp dark trailing edge tapers inwards

1st-summer Upperwings ▼

Arctic

Common

1st summer ▲ Rare in Europe

Ad Pale individual ▲

Round head; thin white line between bill and cap

Ad ▲ Primaries all pale

Grey below, cheeks white

Short, all blood-red bill

Tiny legs

Juv White forehead, fine black bill, barred grey back ▼

◄ **Juv** Buff wash, pale bill when very young

Much like Common Tern, but bill shorter, more spike-like, deeper red with no black tip; cap rounder, less flat. More stocky, neck and head project less in flight while longer tail projects more; inner wing shorter, less 'arm', while outer wing narrower, tapers into longer point. Primaries all pale above, no wedge or dark outer feathers. Underbody darker grey, but underwing white except for crisper, dark trailing edge to all-translucent primaries. Wing longer, more tapered, less broad than on Common Tern. Red legs noticeably shorter. Flight lighter, airy and elastic. Juvenile has whiter forehead, dark-barred grey back, whiter rump, underwing like adult; upperwing dark at front, with white trailing edge; all-dark bill. Rising *krree-eh*, sharp *kik*.

133

Roseate Tern

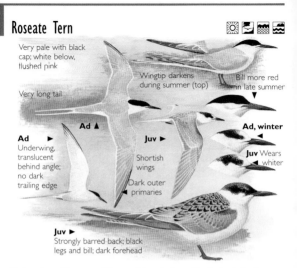

Very pale with black cap; white below, flushed pink

Very long tail

Wingtip darkens during summer (top)

Bill more red in late summer

Ad ▲

Ad ►
Underwing, translucent behind angle; no dark trailing edge

Juv ►

Ad, winter ►

Shortish wings

Dark outer primaries

Juv Wears whiter

Juv ►
Strongly barred back; black legs and bill; dark forehead

Paler than Common Tern, whiter below, flushed pink. Longer, blacker bill, with red base that increases during summer. Long red legs. Upperwing very pale grey, outer primaries streaked blackish. Underwing shades to grey tip with white rim, no black trailing edge. Very long tail. Juvenile barred dark above, dark forehead, blackish bill and legs. Harsh *kraak*, bright *chi-vik*.

Gull-billed Tern

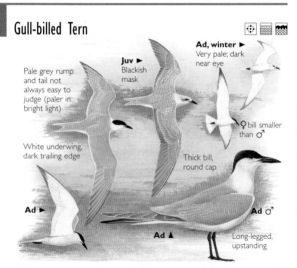

Ad, winter ►
Very pale; dark near eye

Juv ►
Blackish mask

Pale grey rump and tail not always easy to judge (paler in bright light)

♀ bill smaller than ♂

White underwing, dark trailing edge

Thick bill, round cap

Ad ►

Ad ▲

Ad ♂

Long-legged, upstanding

Medium-large, pale tern of freshwater and brackish marshes. Thick all-black bill, black legs. Looks grey in summer, whiter in winter, with black eye-patch. Upperwing grey with blackish tips to outer primaries; underwing has obvious black trailing edge towards tip. Rump very pale grey, not always obvious. Tail short, forked, pale grey. Deep, nasal *ger-wik*.

Sandwich Tern

Proportionately longer inner wing than Common Tern

▲ **Sandwich**

▲ **Common**

Outer primaries wear blackish in contrast with inner ones

◄ **Ad, spring**

Very pale overall, white below unlike grey-bodied Common Tern

Shaggy crest; long black bill with pale yellow tip

Juv ►

Ad, summer ▲

◄**Ad, spring**
Loses black forehead by June or July

Longish black legs

Juv has dark V-shaped marks across back and wing coverts, shorter all-dark bill at first

▲ **Juv** Moulting to 1st winter

▲ **Juv, Aug–Sept**

Ad, late ▼ **summer**

▲ **Gull-billed Tern, juv**

Large, strikingly pale, rangy tern of sea coast. Long bill, black with pale yellow tip. Long, very pale wings, outer primaries contrasted like Common Tern, becoming blacker near wingtip. Rump and rather short forked tail white, underparts very white, unlike grey of Common and Arctic Terns. Black legs. Black cap early in summer, soon gets white forehead. Juvenile scaly above with black-brown marks; upperwing has darker primaries and tailtips, darker wingtip; bill shorter, all-dark at first. Flight strong, often quite high, with deeper wingbeats than Common, more powerful than Arctic and smaller (but equally pale) Roseate. Dives with obvious splash and 'smack' into water. Distinctive loud, grating, rhythmic calls, *kier-rik*; juvenile has high, shrill whistle.

Black Tern

Ad, winter
Three-lobed cap; dark bill and legs ▼

Ad, summer ▲
Dark grey and smoky black, white undertail

Juv, autumn Three-lobed cap, dark patch beside breast, barred back ▼

Ad, winter
Shoulder patch

Juv Grey, browner on dark forewing; grey rump ►

White-winged Black Tern
Stubby bill, no shoulder patch

Buoyant, erratic, airy flight, dipping to water

Ads, summer ◄ ▲

White-winged Black, ad ►

usually grey

Black, imm ►

Ad, winter
Shoulder patch ▲

Whiskered, ▲ **imm**

Small, elegant 'marsh' tern of freshwater, migrates over sea. Dips to surface rather than dives, often beating slowly into wind, low over water, head down. Summer adult black on head and body, white undertail, with pale underwing. Grey back, wings and tail. Bill fine, sharp, blackish. Black legs. In autumn black body becomes patched with white, and upperwing often has darker outer primaries. Winter plumage white below with dusky patch at side of chest, three-lobed black cap against white face. Immature like winter adult, but brownish-grey above, back feathers tipped paler; back browner than slightly paler grey wings; distinctive dark chest patch and cap. Has nasal, squeaky, short flight call, but usually a quiet bird.

White-winged Black Tern

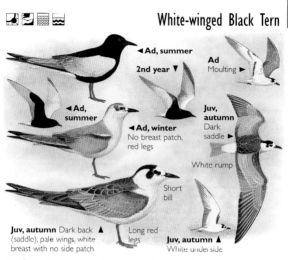

◄ **Ad, summer**

2nd year ▼

Ad
Moulting ►

◄ **Ad, summer**

◄ **Ad, winter**
No breast patch,
red legs

Juv, autumn
Dark saddle ►

White rump

Short
bill

Juv, autumn Dark back ▲
(saddle), pale wings, white
breast with no side patch

Long red
legs

Juv, autumn ▲
White underside

Stockier than Black, shorter-billed, longer-legged, with stiffer, less elegant, more direct flight. Summer adult glossy black, wings grey above with white forewing patch, black on coverts below. White rump and tail, red legs. Winter adult pale, rump whitish, dark ear patch. Autumn juvenile has dark 'saddle', pale wings, white rump, no dark chest patch, grey tail edged white.

Whiskered Tern

Ad, summer
▼

Ad, winter
▼

Ad, winter
Very pale, recalls
Common Tern ►

Red bill

White
face

Grey
rump

Ad, summer ▲
Black cap, blackish belly

Buff forehead
fades white;
cap streaked
white

Juv, autumn ▲
Gingery brown soon
replaced by grey; clean
white breast, long red legs

Black on nape of juv touches
back, no white collar

Larger than Black Tern, dagger-billed, with more direct, less airy flight. In summer has black cap, white face and throat, dark grey underbody, white underwing, very pale upperwing fading almost to whitish towards tip. Dark red bill. In winter, cap streaked, back and rump pale grey. Juvenile also has coarse ginger-brown bars on back, soon lost whiter wings without dark leading edge.

Little Tern

Adult tiny, fast-moving, nervous and noisy

◀ **Juv** Dark bill, dark upperwing, barred back

Juv ▶

▲ Tail fork longest on breeding ♂

◀ **Ad** Black wing fore-edge

Winter ▲

May lose dark bill tip ▼

White forehead at all seasons, yellow bill with tiny black tip

Summer ▲ Orange-yellow legs

Tiny, fast, pale tern of seashore, always with white forehead. Black cap, silvery back, white body. Short, notched white tail. Upperwing has black wedge at tip. Quite stout dagger bill, yellow with tiny dark tip. Orange-yellow legs. Juvenile barred dark above, with dark forewing bar, blackish bill. Quick, irritated *kittiri kittirit*, rasping *kreet*.

Caspian Tern

◀ **Ad** Big black patch under wingtip

Juv ▶

Ad ▶ Pale grey; short tail, heavy head and bill

◀ **1st year**

1st year has ▲ thin tailband

Sub-ad ▼

◀ **Ad, winter**

◀ **Ad, breeding** Big, shaggy black cap, massive bill, black legs

Massive tern, bigger than Common Gull, with shaggy black cap, very large (but not disproportionate) red bill, black legs. Underwing has Gannet-like blackish area at tip. In flight shows long, angular wings, short tail, heavy head. Juvenile barred darker above, cap closely streaked but no clear white; bill orange-red, dark tip. Dives with big splash. Deep, heron-like *kree-ahk*.

Little Auk

Dark underwing, white belly

Dark above, lacy white scapular edges

◄ Winter

Breeding ►
Frog-like profile; black chest

Winter ▲ ▼

◄ Winter ▼

◄ Winter ▼

Tiny, dumpy, maritime bird with round, frog-like head and short, deep bill. In summer has black head and breast. In winter, black cap to below eye, rest of underside white. Black above with fine white streaks on scapulars. Flies with rather wavering, wader-like action, showing white trailing edge to narrow wing. Adults dive with slightly opened wings like tiny Eider.

Puffin

◄ Breeding
Age 5+ years

◄ Breeding
Age 4–5 years

◄ Breeding
Age 2–3 years

◄ Ad, winter

◄ Ad, winter

◄ Juv/1st winter

▲ All black above; stocky, big-headed

▲ Ad, winter

◄ Ad, breeding

Black and white auk with orange legs. Summer adult has grey-black cap and breastband surrounding greyish facial 'disc', outrageous red, yellow, and blue-grey bill. In winter, bill smaller, duller, face much darker grey. Juvenile has even smaller bill: triangular, mostly dark grey. No white trailing edge to wing. Flight quick, low, direct, with whirring wings set well back.

Guillemot

Ad, winter Dark above, white trailing edge; pointed bill

Brown above in S; square tail

Winter Northern: barred underwing, black necklace

Ad, winter ▲

▲ Bridled variant, commoner in N

▲ **Ad** August ▲ **Ad** September

◄ **Breeding**

Ad, winter ►

Long-bodied, short-legged seabird with dagger bill. Dives from surface, nests on sheer cliffs. Dark brown (southern birds) or black (northern) above, white below. In summer dark breast, in winter dark cap and stripe behind eye on white cheek. Tail short, square. Underwing pale (mottled dark on northern birds). Rolling *whooaarrrr* at colony; chick gives loud whistles at sea.

Brünnich's Guillemot

Winter ►

Summer ►

Winter ▲

Thick bill with white gape streak in summer

Breeding
♀
♂

Winter Cap below eye, thick bill, unstreaked flank, long tail ▼

Winter

Guillemot

Like blackish Guillemot, with thicker bill and pale streak along gape line. White of breast more pointed in centre in summer, flanks clear white, lacking dark streaks. In winter bill streak smaller, but thick, stubby bill useful clue; cap down to below eye, no dark stripe on paler cheek, only lower face white. Broader white sides to rump, whiter underwing coverts.

Razorbill

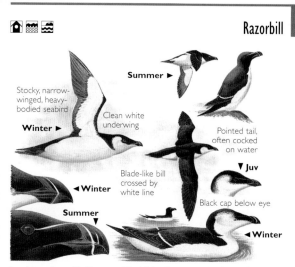

Stocky, narrow-winged, heavy-bodied seabird

Summer ►

Clean white underwing

Winter ►

Pointed tail, often cocked on water

Blade-like bill crossed by white line

▼ Juv

Black cap below eye

◄ Winter

◄ Winter

Summer ▼

Stockier than Guillemot, blackish above, with deep, flattened blade-like bill crossed by white line. White line in front of eye, pointed tail. In winter has dark cap to below eye, whitish area behind eye but no thin dark stripe, broader white sides to rump and sharper white underwing coverts. Thick bill obvious at close range. Deep, whirring *urrrr* at cliff colonies.

Black Guillemot

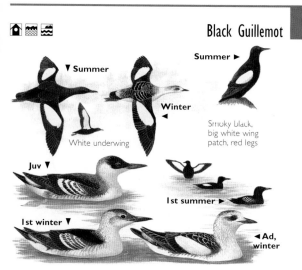

▼ Summer

Summer ►

Winter ◄

Smoky black, big white wing patch, red legs

White underwing

Juv ▼

1st summer ►

1st winter ▼

◄ Ad, winter

Small seabird, solitary or in pairs around rocky islets, at base of cliffs (not on high ledges or in huge rafts below). Smoky black in summer, with big oval white patch on wing, white underwing, red legs and red inside mouth. In winter barred above, head mostly whitish, wing patch still clear white. Juvenile browner, becomes like winter adult but with barred wing patch.

141

Black-bellied Sandgrouse

Underwing black and white, bold black belly, short tail

Strong contrast on upperwing

♂ ♀ ♂ ♀ ♂

Stockier, larger than Pin-tailed, with short tail, no central spike. Male has grey head and breast with orange throat, black belly, and brown back spotted with orange-buff. Female buffer, finely barred and spotted, also has black belly. Underwing like Pin-tailed in flight, but black belly obviously different even if tail cannot be seen well. Rolling, slowing *churrr-re-ka* in flight.

Pin-tailed Sandgrouse

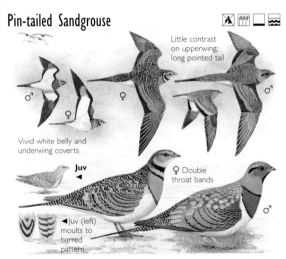

Little contrast on upperwing; long pointed tail

Vivid white belly and underwing coverts

Juv

♀ Double throat bands

◄ Juv (left) moults to barred pattern

♂ ♀ ♂ ♂

Small-headed, round-bodied, long-tailed, rather pigeon-like bird with long, angled, pointed wings. Male has coppery-orange face and breastband, green neck, and yellow-spotted greenish back. Female browner, with three narrow black bands on orange-brown chest, barred above. White belly and underwing coverts, black wingtips below, pointed tail spike. Nasal, harsh *kata kata*.

Laughing Dove

▼ **Ads** ►

Dark, compact, with bluish wing patch, white corners to tail

Turtle Dove

Dark underwing contrasts with white belly

▼ **Juv**

◄ **Ad** Dark rufous back, black speckles on pink breast

Long dark tail

Small dove of extreme SE Europe only. Dark with rusty-brown upperparts, dark slaty-bluish wing patch, blacker wingtips, pinkish head and black-speckled rusty breastband. Tail dark with pale tip. Wings shorter, tail longer than Turtle Dove. Often tame in cities, around hotels, street cafes. Fast, five-syllable cooing call, *do-do du du do*.

Rock Dove

Long, tapered wing, narrow head

Rock Dove ►
Thin bill, tiny white patch (cere) above

White rump, two wingbars

Town/feral pigeon ▲
Thick bill, large white cere

White underwing

◄ **Ad** Pale blue-grey, ▲ black bars on wing

Wild bird has slim bill with tiny white fleshy patch (cere) at base; domestic variants have thick bill, big pale cere. True wild pattern a handsome blue-grey with green and purple gloss on neck, dark nape, two broad black bands across wing, white rump and white underwing. Domestic and feral town pigeons vary greatly, often parti-coloured. Deep, rumbling coo.

Stock Dove

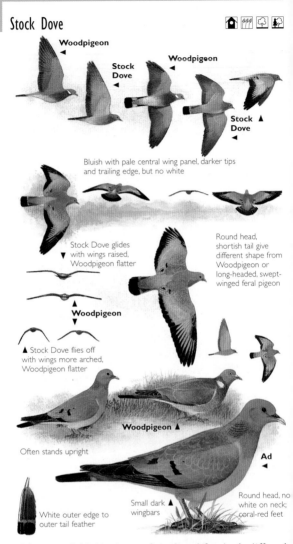

Woodpigeon

Stock Dove

Woodpigeon

Stock Dove

Bluish with pale central wing panel, darker tips and trailing edge, but no white

Stock Dove glides with wings raised, Woodpigeon flatter

Round head, shortish tail give different shape from Woodpigeon or long-headed, swept-winged feral pigeon

Woodpigeon

▲ Stock Dove flies off with wings more arched, Woodpigeon flatter

Often stands upright

Woodpigeon ▲

White outer edge to outer tail feather

Small dark ▲ wingbars

Round head, no white on neck; coral-red feet

Ad

Medium-sized, bluish pigeon of woods and farmland, cliffs and quarries. On ground looks more blue-grey than very similar Woodpigeon. Head small and round, tail quite short. Pink chest and glossy green neck patch. Two short dark bars on wing. Legs deep, bright rose-pink. In flight, underwing smooth mid-grey, upperwing with contrasted pale midwing panel, dull black trailing edge and tip. Pale rump and tail with dark band. More protruding, rounder head but shorter wings and tail than Woodpigeon; usually has broader head, less back-swept wings than feral/town pigeon. Glides on raised wings in display; flies with arched wings. Calls with slow, deep, rhythmic notes, increasing in volume with repetition, *oorr-oow*, *orr-oow*.

Woodpigeon

Woodpigeons

Broad pale rump, dark tailband

Large, long-winged, long-tailed

Stock Dove ▶

Bold white band across wing, white neck patches, pale central band under tail unique combination

Steep climb, curving stall and wing-clap in display

Flies up with clatter; gets away in long, fast, direct flight

Winter sun reveals bright pink against dark tree or hedge

◀ **Juv** White on wings but not on neck; looks untidy

Ad ◀

Big, handsome, long-winged and long-tailed pigeon, with heavy, broad body and small round head. Head blue-grey, back duller grey, rump pale, tail with pale central band and dark tip. Breast deep dusky pink, appears bright in good light. Neck has broad white patch, closed wing shows white along edge. In flight, wings reveal dark tips and bold white patch cutting across wing, half way to tip. Pale pink legs. Bright red and yellow bill, striking at close quarters. Juvenile dull, uneven in colour, lacks white on neck. Often flies and feeds in big flocks in winter. Wild and wary on farmland, tame in town parks, it often enters large gardens. Loud wing claps on take-off but no alarm calls; song a pleasing, soothing coo: *coo-cooo, coocoo, cook*.

145

Collared Dove

Angled wing with blunt point; grey underwing, grey panel across upperwing, but little contrast overall

Blackish base, broad white tip beneath long tail

Flies with wings raised, arched; display includes steep climb then long, circling glide back to perch

Pale, with dark eye, thin dark half-collar on back of neck

♀ has longer wingtip, less bluish head than ♂

♀

♂

A common, widespread, pale, long-tailed dove of warm, southern conifer woodland, towns, villages, parks and gardens, and the vicinity of farms and stables. Small, pinkish head, with thin black half-collar on adult (absent on juvenile). Body pale sandy-grey-brown, wing dark at tip and pale blue-grey across centre. Tail has white tip above, dark base with broad white tip below. Eyes very dark (reddish at close range), bill fine and dark, legs dark pink. Flies with wings arched and long tail obvious. Soars with tail spread in display. Loud flight note, a nasal *kwer*. Song an oft-repeated triple coo, with some variation: *coo-cooo-coo* or *cu-cooo-cuk*, usually with emphasis on middle note but some strained versions have a more even emphasis throughout.

Turtle Dove

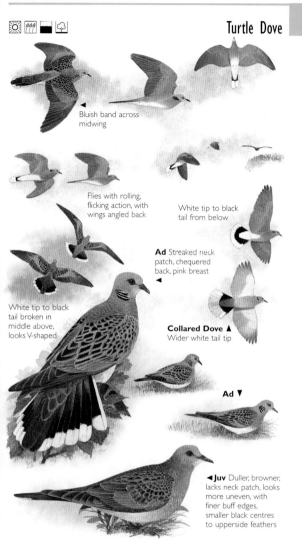

Bluish band across midwing

Flies with rolling, flicking action, with wings angled back

White tip to black tail from below

Ad Streaked neck patch, chequered back, pink breast

White tip to black tail broken in middle above, looks V-shaped

Collared Dove ▲ Wider white tail tip

Ad ▼

◄**Juv** Duller, browner, lacks neck patch, looks more uneven, with finer buff edges, smaller black centres to upperside feathers

Small, neat countryside dove of woodland edge and tall hedgerows in farmland. Neat, pale, with strong tail pattern. Flies with flicked beats of angled, arched wings and slight side-to-side rolling. Head grey, underside pale pink and buff. Back rufous-brown, neatly chequered brown-black. Blue-grey midwing patch. Brown rump, dark tail with sharp, wedge-shaped white tip above, blackish with white tip below (narrower but purer white than Collared). White vent shows against darker body and underwing. Adult has bluish and black striped neck patch, absent on duller juvenile. Display flight includes flat, circling soar at moderate height. Call a rolling, purring, shapeless but pleasing crooning note, *turr-turrrrr* or *rorrrr-rorrrrr*.

147

Cuckoo

Often sits with tail raised, wings drooped ▼

Slim head, long tail, sharp wings obvious at a glance ►

◄ ♂ Blue-grey chest

Often swings tail sideways

♀ Brownish on chest

May perch very upright on top of post, tail held down

▲ Juv Barred below, pale spots on tail

Juv ▲ Pale nape spot

◄ ♀ 1st summer Showing juvenile secondaries

Broad pale band across underwing

Ad Grey with ▲ darker tail (white spots show when spread)

Juv ►

Ad ►

Flies with deep beats below body level, head raised

Ad ♀► Rufous form

A familiar disembodied voice, the cuckoo has long wings and tail, both rather broad-looking, a slim, narrow, tapered head, and short, downcurved bill. Perches on branches, wires, low posts, wings slightly drooped, tail swayed from side to side or raised and fanned. Flies fast, direct, head up, wings beating down below body level. Adult grey, paler below with fine bars, whiter undertail. Underwing has broad, pale central band. Juvenile grey-brown or rufous, heavily barred, with pale nape spot. Some females (regular in E Europe, rare UK) are rich red-brown. Loud, far-carrying, clear *cuck-coo*, sometimes *cuk-uk-coo* or followed by chuckling *wuck-uk-uk*; various hoarse, hissing, and guttural calls. Female has rich, bubbling note.

Great Spotted Cuckoo

Ad

Juv ▶

Big white spots under long tail

Long, quite broad wings, curved edges

Ad Grey cap ▶

Juv Black cap, rufous wings

1st year ▶

◀ Ad

Cuckoo-like character but wings longer, slender, curved back in flight; long slim tail. Adult has grey, crested cap, yellow-buff throat and breast, grey upperside with large white spots, white underside. Juvenile has black cap, darker back with smaller spots, blacker tail with large white tips and bright rufous outer wings. Quick, cackling *churr-churr-che-che-che-che*.

Hawk Owl

White braces

Hawk-like effect in flight, but big head

Fierce, black-framed white facial disc, yellow eyes

Sometimes very upright

Long tail obvious

♂

Northern forest owl, upright, with large, square head and long tail; rather short, slim wings. Bold face pattern and close yellow eyes; white cheeks edged black and pale V on forehead give striking expression. Much white above, barred below. Juvenile very dark with white forehead V, staring yellow eyes. Shrill, falcon-like chatter; song is long, bubbling trill for 8–9 seconds.

Tawny Owl

Black eyes

◄ Watches from
perch, drops onto prey

Greyer and rufous
forms both
common

White spots ►
on shoulders

Big, rounded,
short-tailed

Large, brown owl of woods and parks, nocturnal. At roost looks big-headed, rufous-brown or grey-brown with row of pale spots each side of back. Wide, round facial disc, thinly edged black; black eyes. Sleepy and rotund, or alert and upright. Identified at dusk by silhouette and call: loud, nasal *ke-wick*, and hooting song, a clear, breathy *hoo; hu-hu - hoo-oooooooooou u u*.

Barn Owl

White underwing

Quite quick, jerky beats
of shortish wings

Heart-shaped
white face,
black eyes

Dark-breasted ►

Pale-breasted ►

Wingtip
varies
◄

Striking pale owl: white-faced, with white (W Europe) or deep buff breast (E Europe). Variably peppered grey and white above. Heart-shaped face, with black eyes and bill creating V in centre. Thin legs with knock-kneed stance. Flies low, erratically, with quite quick wingbeats, pausing, twisting, or hovering to detect prey; looks bright buff and white. Hoarse squeal, strident shriek.

Short-eared Owl

Flies high in display; hunts low, in gliding, quartering flight

White trailing edge ►

Dark carpal patch ◄

Yellow eyes set in black; white around bill

Dark bars on tail ▼

Mottled above, streaked below

White belly

Bright buff near black wingtips ►

Large, pale, yellow-brown owl, with black-rimmed yellow eyes set in pale facial disc. Mottled above, streaked on breast, white belly. In flight reveals long wings, short, barred tail. Wings have bold dark carpal patch, bright golden-buff outer wing and dark tips, white trailing edge. Often flies by day, in low, frequent harrier-like glides. Deep, abrupt *hu-hu-hu-hu*, wheezy *shay-ay*.

Long-eared Owl

Tufts raised in alarm, often relaxed into wider V

Dark carpal patch ◄

Grey hindwing ►

Orange eyes

Fine, weak bars on tail

Dark underbody

Deep orange near ▲ barred wingtip

Large, upright, nocturnal owl, round when relaxed but taut, slim, upright when alarmed. Ear tufts raised when alert, creating V that continues black and white face pattern above deep orange eyes. Strongly mottled and streaked, darker below than Short-eared Owl. Wings have similar carpal patch, richer orange-buff on primaries, no white trailing edge. Deep, moaning, short hoot.

Scops Owl

Tiny, 'eared' owl with yellow eyes

Tufts often lowered, forming bumps at corners of head

◄ Tufts raised

Flies to next perch with quite quick action, often downward swoop

◄ Greyer and rufous forms both frequent

Barred underwing

Small, large-headed owl of parks, woodland edge, rooftops and wires. Top of head square, or with short tufts at corners. Eyes yellow, face rather plain. Body grey-brown to rufous with dark rusty areas on upperparts. Pale spots in line along shoulders, streaks below. Looks pale in torch beam or street lights. Frequent, simple, musical *peuw* repeated every 2–3 seconds.

Pygmy Owl

Tiny but catches prey almost its own size

Yellow eyes, white eyebrows

Round head

Fluffed feathers change silhouette

Pygmy Scops Little

Barred tail

Barred flight feathers below ►

Tiny, dark, round-headed northern owl. Rotund body, obvious stumpy tail, often raised. Dark rusty-brown, whiter underside, streaked on breast and barred on flanks. Short white 'eyebrow' above each small, yellow eye. Woodpecker-like bounding flight. Autumn song up to 10 thin whistles rising in pitch; full song a piping whistle, longer than Scops Owl's, repeated 6–7 times.

Little Owl

Thickset, solidly-built, small owl with flattish head; low, pale brows and yellow eyes

Quick, undulating flight

Closely spotted above, mottled and streaked below

Often seen in daytime, open countryside

Small, stocky, chunky owl with 'solid' look. Spotted forehead above long, flattish white 'eyebrows'; black-rimmed yellow eyes. Earthy-brown with whiter underside, white spots on back, streaked below. Sits upright on branches, poles, barn roofs, boulders, often by day. Flight low, fast, bounding. Loud, high, emphatic *kee-ew* or *eee-ow*; song thin, long, questioning hoot.

Tengmalm's Owl

Underside pale, spotted or barred ▶

High brows, questioning look

Nocturnal, elusive, in forest

Juv ◀

◀ Rusty-brown, pale spots on shoulders, yellow eyes

Nocturnal forest owl, hard to see, with constant 'surprised' look on high-browed, round face. Pale facial disc edged black, bold yellow eyes. Back bright rufous brown, spotted white; underside whitish with broad brown spots. Juvenile plain dark brown with paler face. Low, husky *chak*, song rapid series of short, whistling hoots, *pu pu-po-po-po-po-po-po*.

153

Ural Owl

Very large owl of ancient forest. Like big, upright, pale, rather elongated Tawny Owl, but with longer tail, plainer face, smaller black eyes, pale yellow bill. Longer tail and wings obvious in flight; action buzzard-like. Upperwing lacks obvious pale patch on primaries shown by Great Grey and 'eared' owls. Call coarse, heron-like; song a deep, cooing hoot, with two, then five notes.

Great Grey Owl

Giant, magnificent owl. Huge dish-like head bulging at sides, flattened at front in deep disc, with small yellow eyes separated by back-to-back white C-shapes. Black patch around small yellow bill tip. Body mostly grey. In flight shows barred buff patch near wingtip. High *chiep chiep chiep*, growling notes and prolonged, deep growl; song a series of deep, booming hoots.

Eagle Owl

Massive, heavy in flight, wings closely-barred

Piercing orange eyes, wide-set ear tufts

Huge, dark, 'eared' owl of forests and cliffs

ears erect

Massive, broad-bodied, big-headed owl with broad, powerful wings. Wide ear tufts, dark face with fierce orange eyes, pale patch around bill tip. Blackish or dark brown above, barred and spotted. Buff below with black streaks. Bright patch on outer wing in flight. Call a harsh bark or very loud series of barks in alarm; song deep, booming, quiet but far-carrying *oo-hu, oo-hu*.

Snowy Owl

Huge, white owl of far north; ad ♂ whitest, ♀ barred

Yellow eyes look dark at distance

♂ ▼

Slightly jerky wingbeat

♀ ▶

◀ **Juv** Grey, white-faced

▼ Barn Owl

◀ ♀

Unique, massive, big-headed, big-footed owl of far north. Male white, sparse dark bars on wings and tail. Female closely barred dark on underside, broader bars above. Juvenile dull grey-brown, white on face and wings, develops adult plumage over several years. Black-rimmed yellow eyes often look dark at all but closest ranges. Strong flight, with quick, deep downstroke.

155

Alpine Swift

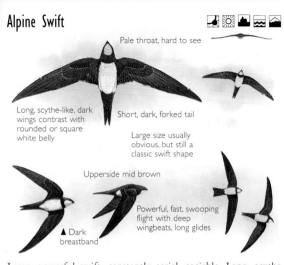

Pale throat, hard to see

Long, scythe-like, dark wings contrast with rounded or square white belly

Short, dark, forked tail

Large size usually obvious, but still a classic swift shape

Upperside mid brown

Powerful, fast, swooping flight with deep wingbeats, long glides

▲ Dark breastband

Large, powerful swift, constantly aerial, sociable. Long, scythe wings, broader than Swift's but with obvious swift form. Short, blunt head, notched tail. Mid brown above, inconspicuous white chin, brown breastband, white belly. Often flies at great height, belly patch flashing in the sun. Chattering chorus of rapid, rising and falling *ti ti ti tititit ti ti ti titititit ti ti.*

White-rumped & Little Swifts

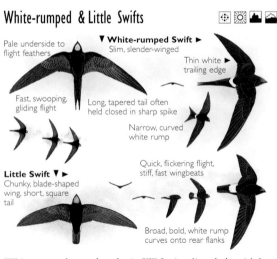

Pale underside to flight feathers

▼ **White-rumped Swift** ►
Slim, slender-winged

Thin white ► trailing edge

Fast, swooping, gliding flight

Long, tapered tail often held closed in sharp spike

Narrow, curved white rump

Quick, flickering flight, stiff, fast wingbeats

Little Swift ▼ ►
Chunky, blade-shaped wing, short, square tail

Broad, bold, white rump curves onto rear flanks

White-rumped a rare breeder in SW Spain: slim, dark, with long pointed tail, sometimes spread in deep fork, scythe wings, small curved white patch on rump. Thin pale trailing edge to inner wing, quite large white throat patch. Little a rare vagrant: stocky, with short square tail and broader, straighter wings, big white rump patch wrapped around rear flanks, white throat.

Swift

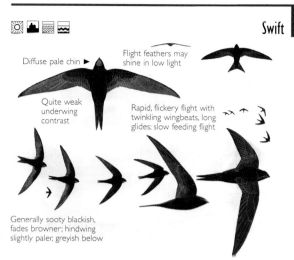

Flight feathers may shine in low light

◄ Diffuse pale chin

Quite weak underwing contrast

Rapid, flickery flight with twinkling wingbeats, long glides; slow feeding flight

Generally sooty blackish, fades browner; hindwing slightly paler, greyish below

Only swift in most of Europe. Blackish, with blunt head, narrow body, forked tail and long, stiff, swept-back, scythe-like wings lacking flexibility of swallows and martins. Flies very low in bad weather, otherwise high. Inconspicuous pale throat. Flight feathers may shine paler in bright light. Loud, sharp, screaming chorus over breeding areas, often from dashing groups.

Pallid Swift

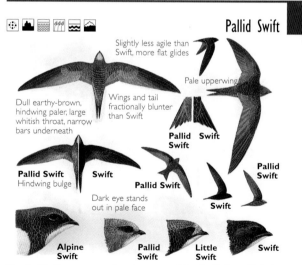

Slightly less agile than Swift, more flat glides

Pale upperwing

Dull earthy-brown, hindwing paler, large whitish throat, narrow bars underneath

Wings and tail fractionally blunter than Swift

Pallid Swift

Pallid Swift Swift
Hindwing bulge

Pallid Swift

Pallid Swift

Swift

Dark eye stands out in pale face

Alpine Swift   **Pallid Swift**   **Little Swift**   **Swift**

Mostly Mediterranean, often in towns. Like Swift but slightly blunter in head, wingtip and tail. In good light perceptibly paler, earthy brown overall, with larger pale face and throat, paler area on inner wing and hindwing above and below. Close views reveal fine, pale scaly effect on body. Calls very similar, sometimes slightly lower and falling in pitch.

157

Nightjar

♀ has all-brown tail (juv)

◄ ♂ Big white spots on wingtips and tail sides

♀

♂

♀ ► No white spots

Camouflaged at rest

Nocturnal summer bird of heaths, woodland edge. Flat-headed, tiny-billed, long-bodied form, with long, broad, square tail and long, bluntly-pointed wings, often widest near middle. Flies erratically, weaving and twisting acrobatically, tail often broadly fanned. Male has white wing and tail spots, otherwise dark. Call nasal *goo-eek*; song remarkable prolonged wooden churr or rattle.

Red-necked Nightjar

Slightly larger, longer-tailed than Nightjar

♂

◄ ♀ spots buff

White throat patch, white wing spots biggest on ♂

▲ White outer tail (on ♂)

Rufous collar hard to see: song best clue

◄ ♀ Tail (juv)

Rusty collar ▼

In Europe only in Iberia, on sandy heaths with aromatic herbs and clumps of trees. Very like Nightjar but a little more orange-buff below, grey (less dark) on forewing, inconspicuous rusty collar. Usually seen as silhouette at dusk, located by hearing song: mechanically-repeated, nasal *kut-uk kut-uk kut-uk kut-uk* with a slightly squeaky quality.

Kingfisher

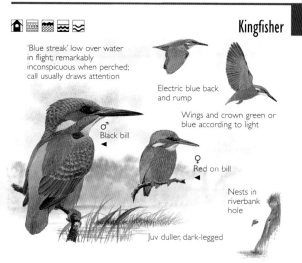

'Blue streak' low over water in flight; remarkably inconspicuous when perched; call usually draws attention

Electric blue back and rump

Wings and crown green or blue according to light

♂ Black bill ◄

♀ Red on bill ◄

Nests in riverbank hole

Juv duller, dark-legged

Unique waterside bird, often detected by voice or seen briefly flying over water, but may give close-up views at times. Dagger bill, big head, short-tailed form. Perches upright or leans forward, often hunches when resting. Striking green-blue above, electric blue on rump. White face patches and throat, rufous below. Female has orange bill base. Sharp, high *ch'keeee*.

Bee-eater

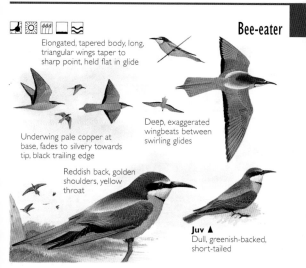

Elongated, tapered body, long, triangular wings taper to sharp point, held flat in glide

Underwing pale copper at base, fades to silvery towards tip, black trailing edge

Deep, exaggerated wingbeats between swirling glides

Reddish back, golden shoulders, yellow throat

Juv ▲ Dull, greenish-backed, short-tailed

Sharp-billed, long-bodied, long-tailed bird of open spaces, earth cliffs. Long, triangular wings like elongated Starling, held flat in glides, with back or downward flicks giving sudden acceleration. Red-brown with golden shoulders, bright yellow throat edged with black, green-blue below. Underwing silvery to pale copper with black trailing edge. Frequent deep, ringing *prrup prrup*.

159

Roller

◀ **Juv** Dull, greenish, back pale yellow-brown

Ad ▶

Underwing deep violet and pale turquoise

Ads, summer Vivid blue, turquoise and bright brown; duller, paler in winter

Slim, Jackdaw-sized, often on wires or low in trees. Thick dark bill, short square tail, rather long wings with blunt point. Pale turquoise-blue, greener below, bright in early summer. Back pale rufous. In flight angled wings reveal vivid blue, purple, and black. Juvenile and winter birds much duller. Repeats harsh, raspy *hack hack* in short side-to-side rolling display flight.

Hoopoe

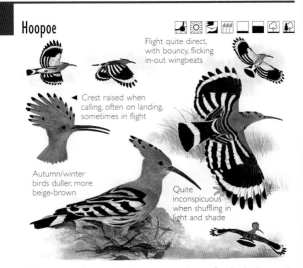

Flight quite direct, with bouncy, flicking in-out wingbeats

◀ Crest raised when calling, often on landing, sometimes in flight

Autumn/winter birds duller, more beige-brown

Quite inconspicuous when shuffling in light and shade

Often inconspicuous, despite pattern. Long, flat-bodied, erectile fan-like crest (or backward pointing tuft), long slightly curved bill, long triangular tail, short legs. Waddles on ground, flies up in sudden flurry and off in long, smooth, springy flight. Pinkish to pale buff, crest more orange with black tips. Back and wings boldly barred black and white. Soft, deep, hooting *poo-poo-poo*.

Wryneck

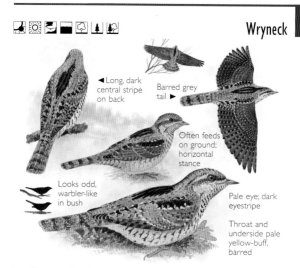

◄ Long, dark central stripe on back

Barred grey tail ►

Often feeds on ground; horizontal stance

Looks odd, warbler-like in bush

Pale eye; dark eyestripe

Throat and underside pale yellow-buff, barred

Peculiar woodpecker-like bird with short sharp bill, rounded head, rather long tail. Hops on ground, creeps around branches in trees. Closely patterned grey, brown, and buff, with long dark central stripe on back. Finely barred below with golden-buff throat. Wide, closely barred tail. Call a fast, soft, nasal, whining *kee-kee-kee-kee-kee-kee*.

Black Woodpecker

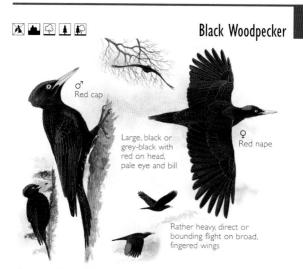

♂ Red cap

Large, black or grey-black with red on head, pale eye and bill

♀ Red nape

Rather heavy, direct or bounding flight on broad, fingered wings

Like large Green Woodpecker in form, with slim neck and large head. All black except for red crown (male) or nape (female), pale eye and pale bill. Likes large pines, beeches, poplars, riverside willows; roams widely in winter. Calls frequently in spring, with loud, high, fading *p'eeee*, startling *kvi-vi-vi-vi-vi-vi*, and rougher, deep, rattling *krruk krruk krruk krruk*. Quieter in summer.

161

Green Woodpecker

♀ Spanish

♂ Spanish

◀ **Juv** ♂
Greyish head,
bold bars below

♀ Spanish

♂ Red cap, red
moustache ▶

Apple green,
with bright
yellow rump

♀ Black
moustache

Large, solid, long-bodied woodpecker, often on ground. Apple-green above with yellow rump. Red crown, black face, dark moustache (male's with red centre). Juvenile closely streaked and barred. Flight low, fast, undulating, yellow rump conspicuous. Loud, shrill *kyu-kyu-kyu-kyu*; song more laughing, musical, a longer series of evenly-pitched, slightly accelerating notes.

Grey-headed Woodpecker

◀ **Green**

Like Green
in flight
but stocky,
greyer

◀ **Juv**

▲ **Grey-
headed**

♂ Red cap ▼

♂

♀

Grey head,
thin black
moustache

Slim bill, neckless
shape, slender
body, greyer
than Green
Woodpecker

Like smaller, more 'neckless' Green Woodpecker, without big red crown. Small round head, short bill. Head grey with thin dark moustache (no red), male has red forehead. Eye darker than Green's. Flight swooping, quick, looping between trees. Song has character of Green but slower, lower, less 'laughing' and both descending and decelerating; 'fades away' unlike Green.

Three-toed Woodpecker

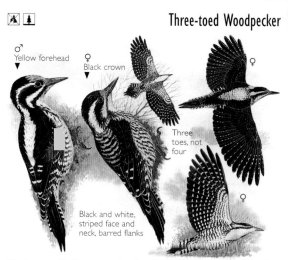

♂
Yellow forehead ▼

♀
Black crown ▼

♀

Three toes, not four

♀

Black and white, striped face and neck, barred flanks

Elusive, small forest woodpecker in N Europe and mountains, shy but sometimes gives close views. Quite large, slim-billed, very dark, with dull yellow cap (black streaked on female with no yellow) but no trace of red. White stripes on black face and neck, barred or unmarked white back. Underside white, closely barred dark. Soft *kik*; short, fast, powerful drumming.

Lesser Spotted Woodpecker

♂ Red cap ▼

♀

♂

a
b
c

a Chaffinch
b Lesser Spotted
c Great Spotted

♀ Black cap ▼

Very small, stocky, small-billed. White bars above may merge into square patch; barred wings; buff below

♀

Smallest woodpecker, often in treetop twigs. Round-headed, short-billed, slim-looking. Barred black and white above, white or buff below. Broad white patch on side of neck, black beneath buff cheek. Male has red cap, female black, but no red on body. Flight weak, fluttering, undulating. Call a short, sharp, weak *kik*; song a high, peevish quick *pee-pee-pee-pee-pee-pee*.

Great Spotted Woodpecker

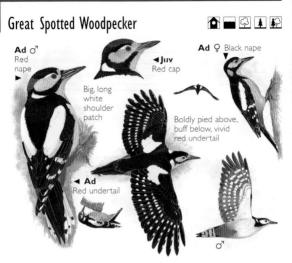

Ad ♂
Red nape ▶

◀ **Juv**
Red cap

Ad ♀ Black nape ▼

Big, long white shoulder patch

Boldly pied above, buff below, vivid red undertail

◀ **Ad**
Red undertail

♂

Striking woodpecker, black and white above, buff below, with bold white shoulder patch, vivid deep red under rear body. Buff forehead, black crown. Adult male has red nape, juvenile has red crown. Black stripes from bill to nape and shoulder meet black of hindneck and wing. Call sharp, metallic *tchik*; fast rattle of alarm. Short, abrupt, echoing drum.

Syrian Woodpecker

White neck separates black of back and cheek

◀ **Juv** Red cap

Big white shoulder spot, pink-red undertail

◀ **Ad ♀** ▶
Black nape

◀ **Ad ♂**
Red nape

Great Spotted ▲　　▲ **Syrian**

♂

Large, spotted woodpecker of far E Europe. Looks like Great Spotted but has weaker, pinker red area beneath tail. Often on roadside poles. Male has large red nape patch, juvenile small red crown. Black on cheek does not join black of hindneck, giving slightly whiter face. Call softer *kik*; fractionally longer drum with less abrupt finish.

Middle Spotted Woodpecker

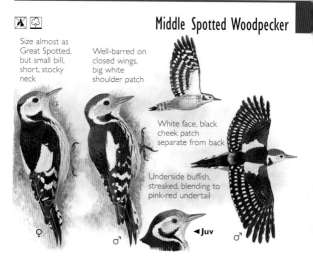

Size almost as Great Spotted, but small bill, short, stocky neck

Well-barred on closed wings, big white shoulder patch

White face, black cheek patch separate from back

Underside buffish, streaked, blending to pink-red undertail

♀ ♂ ◀ Juv ♂

Boldly pied like Great Spotted, but smaller head and bill. Red crown. Pale pink-red undertail blends into streaked warm buff underside. Reduced black on face does not meet neck or wing, so whiter-faced than Syrian. Wings more closely barred white. Male's crown flame-red when raised in display. Occasional weak *kik*; quick *kuk kuk kuk kuk kuk kuk*; does not drum.

White-backed Woodpecker

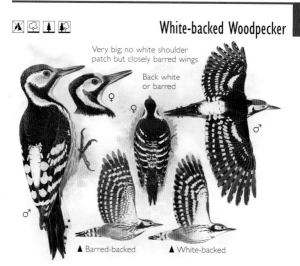

Very big; no white shoulder patch but closely barred wings

Back white or barred

♀ ♂

▲ Barred-backed   ▲ White-backed

Largest 'spotted' woodpecker. Long spike bill, long body and tail. Male's crown red, female's black. Very white face; black moustache and cheek patch do not meet hindneck or shoulder. Weak pink-red undertail. No clear white shoulder patch: wing coverts barred overall. Back white (N and E Europe), or closely barred (Pyrenees, SE Europe). Weak *kik*; accelerating drum.

165

Skylark

◄ Angular shape, wings square-ended, straight-edged

Grey underwings contrast with pale body

Dark upperside, white tail sides and pale trailing edge to wing

1st winter Bright, buffy ▼

♀ Short tail

Short, blunt crest flattened or raised

Gorget of streaks across chest, belly pale and unmarked

♂ Long tail

▲ **Ad** Worn, dark

Very long hind claw

Juv ▲ Dark, greyer, scaly above

White tail sides

Farmland and moorland lark, with short, blunt crest, closely-streaked chest and white underside. Wings triangular in flight, with obvious pale trailing edge. Streaked buff-brown above, with typical lark pattern of drooped streaks along scapulars. Finely streaked cap, pale stripe over eye. Bill quite thick, pointed (but much slimmer than, for example, Corn Bunting's). Tail pale in centre, black each side with broad white edges. Pale pink legs, long hind claw. Flies with hindwing fairly straight, forewing angled back to blunt point. Calls with short rippled *prrip*, high thin *seee*. Sings from perch or high, hovering songflight: prolonged stream of high, varied warbling, richer at close range, silvery at distance. Baseline for judging rarer larks and pipits.

Woodlark

Small, dumpy, broad-winged lark with short, round-tipped tail.

Inconspicuous on ground; sings from tree or in high circling flight

Undulating flight with open-closed wing action

Crest can be raised; pale stripes over eyes meet on nape; rufous cheeks

Black and white patch on edge of wing

Pale-centred tail white at ▶ corners

Short-tailed, broad-winged lark, with undulating flight. Streaked crown, long pale stripes over eye to nape, dark-edged rufous cheek. Boldly streaked, black-white-black patch at edge of wing. No white wing trailing edge, tail white only at corners. Soft *t'looo it*; sings in high, circling flight with discrete rich, fluty, falling phrases: *lyu lyu lyu, oodl oodl oodl, loee loee loee loee*.

Shore Lark

◀ Plain wing, longish tail white on sides

♂ **Balkans** ▼ grey above

♂ has longest 'horns', brightest yellow on face

♀ **spring** ▼

♀ **Balkans** ▲

Black obscured by brown tips in winter, yellow paler

♂ **non-breeding** ▼

♀ ▶ No 'horns'

Thin white outer edge to tail ▶

Sleek, long lark with bold head pattern, especially in summer. Dull brown above, white below (back grey on SE European breeders). Dark crown and eyestripe, black patch through eye, variable black band under throat (and brown band beneath that in winter), face pale yellow. Dark wings, white-sided tail. Call short, pipit-like *seee*; song a repetition of short phrases.

167

Lesser Short-toed Lark

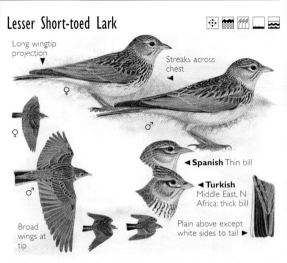

Long wingtip projection

Streaks across chest

♀

♂

♂

◀ **Spanish** Thin bill

◀ **Turkish** Middle East, N Africa: thick bill

Broad wings at tip

Plain above except white sides to tail ▶

Small, streaky lark of sand dunes and dried mud, with streaked chest and long wingtips. Short, blunt, erectile crest; pale eye-ring and stripe behind eye. Wings rather evenly coloured with little contrast between rows of coverts. Breast closely streaked, like Skylark. No white trailing edge to wings. Primary projection usually clear in good view. Dry, purring, buzzy *drrrt*.

Short-toed Lark

Narrow wings

♂

♀

♀

E Europe: pale; stocky bill ▼

Two pale wingbars

Pale, dark-capped; white breast with dark side patch

♀

Short wingtip

Dark band across coverts

Worn tertials ▲ reveal more of primaries

♂

SW Europe: Longer bill, streaky chest

Small, pale lark of dry, cultivated areas and grassland. Streaked above with dark median and paler greater coverts. Long tertials cloak all but extreme tip of primaries. Breast usually unstreaked, but variable dark patch or streaks at side of chest. Rufous or streaked cap, white stripe over eye. Two pale wingbars obvious in flight. Stuttering, sparrowy or Linnet-like *drit, drit-it-it*.

Crested Lark

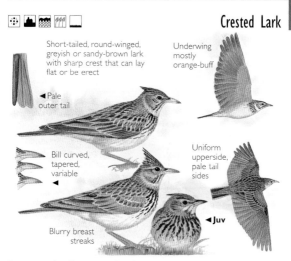

Short-tailed, round-winged, greyish or sandy-brown lark with sharp crest that can lay flat or be erect

◄ Pale outer tail

Underwing mostly orange-buff

◄ Pale outer tail

Bill curved, tapered, variable ◄

Uniform upperside, pale tail sides

Blurry breast streaks

◄ Juv

Large, stocky, big-winged lark with upstanding sharp, pointed crest (may lay flat). Long, rather thick bill with curved upper edge. Rather soft dark streaks on breast. Upperwing plain, no white trailing edge; underwing rusty. Pale greyish rump and centre of tail, outer tail blackish with pale sides. Floppy, undulating flight. Loud, fluty, whistled *tree-lee-pioo*.

Thekla Lark

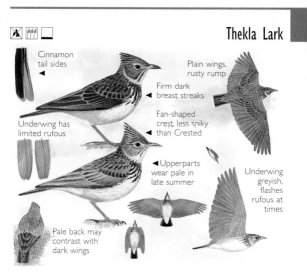

Cinnamon tail sides ◄

Plain wings, rusty rump

Firm dark breast streaks ◄

Fan-shaped crest, less spiky than Crested ◄

Underwing has limited rufous

◄ Upperparts wear pale in late summer

Underwing greyish, flashes rufous at times

Pale back may contrast with dark wings

Very like Crested Lark, difficult to separate, in bushier places or on rocky slopes. More fan-shaped crest, sharper streaks on chest, straighter bill. Underwing greyish, some rusty on flight feathers in some lights. Rump brown, uppertail coverts and central tail rusty, more contrast than Crested. Call piping, similar to Crested but more often several syllables: *tu-tewi-tew-tilli-tee*.

Calandra Lark

Blackish underwing edged white

Big, heavy lark; flight low, powerful, on angled wings, deep wingbeats

White trailing edge

Thick, pale bill

◄ Dark neck patch shows when head raised

◄ ♂ sings with tail cocked

Big lark with thick bill, broad white stripes over eye and under cheek, blackish patch on side of neck and chest. Spread wings dark, blackish below, broad white trailing edge. Looks long- and broad-winged, short-tailed, flies with quick downbeats of angled wings. Call a dry, buzzy *schreeep*; song in high flight with outstretched wings, slightly slower, less flowing than Skylark.

Dupont's Lark

White tail sides

Pale stripe over eye

Streaked gorget ►

Elusive, secretive lark, often runs rather than flies

Plain wings

Slim, curved bill

Worn, grey plumage

Fresh, scaly plumage

Elusive lark of short vegetation on steppe, salty depressions. Often stands upright, neck stretched up, with slim, slightly downcurved bill distinctive; runs rather than flies off. Spanish birds dark brown above, streaked dark on chest; dark, plain wings. African populations more rufous. Sings from great height, with slow, brief, repetitive series of whistles and nasal note.

Crag Martin

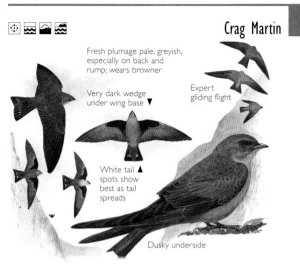

Fresh plumage pale, greyish, especially on back and rump; wears browner

Expert gliding flight

Very dark wedge under wing base ▼

White tail ▲ spots show best as tail spreads

Dusky underside

Thickset martin with broad-based wings, seen flying over high river valleys or around cliffs and gorges, often pendulum-style across rock faces. Looks greyish (wears browner) above, paler on rump. Pale grey-buff below with no clear white, dusky under tail, dark wedge on underwing coverts. White spots near tip of tail visible as bird turns and fans tail. Short, dry, clicking notes.

Sand Martin

Broad-based, swept-back wings

Bright brown above, white below

Weak, flicking, fluttery flight

Thin brown ▶ breastband

▼ Juv

Plain tail with shallow notch

Tiny brown and white martin of waterside areas, reservoirs, sand and gravel quarries. White underside with brown breastband; plain brown above. Flight rather weak, fluttering, with backward, in-out flick of angled, triangular wings. Breeds in colonies, in tunnels in sand or earth cliffs. Call dry, unmusical: a rasping *chrrt chrrt, chirrr*.

Swallow

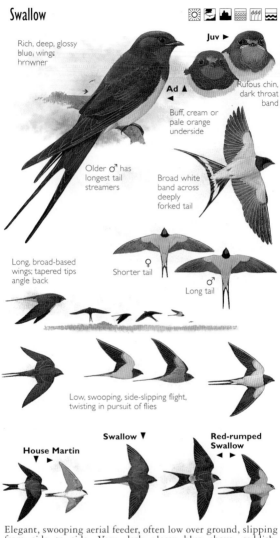

Rich, deep, glossy blue, wings browner

Juv ▶

Rufous chin, dark throat band

Ad ▲
◀

Buff, cream or pale orange underside

Older ♂ has longest tail streamers

Broad white band across deeply forked tail

Long, broad-based wings; tapered tips angle back

♀ Shorter tail

♂ Long tail

Low, swooping, side-slipping flight, twisting in pursuit of flies

House Martin
▼ ▶

Swallow ▼

Red-rumped Swallow ◀ ▶

Elegant, swooping aerial feeder, often low over ground, slipping from side to side. Very dark glossy blue above, reddish-chestnut on forehead and throat above dark blue breastband. Underside pale to orange-buff. Tail deeply forked, with elongated outer streamers (longest on old male) and row of broad white patches across middle. Lacks white rump of House Martin and pale rump of Red-rumped Swallow; much more fluent and flexible-winged than Swift, pale beneath. Juvenile duller, with paler face and throat, shorter tail, no long streamers. Breeds in open buildings, outhouses, carports; often perches on wires, aerials. Roosts in flocks in reeds in autumn. Call a repeated, short *fit fit*, or *slif-it*; soft, twittering song with characteristic trill.

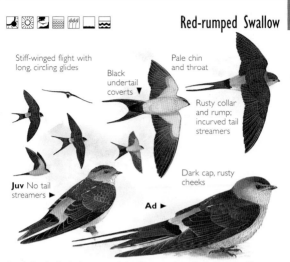

Red-rumped Swallow

Stiff-winged flight with long, circling glides

Black undertail coverts ▼

Pale chin and throat

Rusty collar and rump; incurved tail streamers

Juv No tail streamers ►

Dark cap, rusty cheeks

Ad ►

Dark-backed, dark-winged swallow with pale rufous-buff rump. Dark blue cap above rusty face and collar; buff underside, no dark throat, black vent and all-black tail with 'stuck-on' effect and thick, incurved streamers. Flight stiffer than Swallow, with long, flat-winged, circling, falcon-like glides. Call nasal, abrupt or longer, rasping *chit, chreet*.

House Martin

Ad Bold white rump ▼

All-white underbody

Stiff-winged, flickery flight

Juv Duller rump ►

Tends to feed high up

Ad Blue-black above, wings browner ▼

White legs and toes

Small, stocky martin of towns and suburbs, with obvious bold white band across rump. Dark blue above, brown-black wings, all-white underside. Juveniles duller, washed buff on rump but never like slimmer Red-rumped Swallow. Short, forked tail without streamers. Nests in mud cups under eaves, on cliffs. Call a short, dry, scratchy *prrit, prri-tit*.

173

Rock, Scandinavian Rock, & Water Pipits

Rock, breeding
Wears dark above, whiter below, blurry streaks ▶

Rock, ad ▶

Rock, autumn ▶
Greyish above, yellow-buff below, dark legs, dusky outer tail

Dark legs

Rock, juv ▶
Darker, greener, shorter tail than ad

Rock, ad ▶
Wing width = tail

Rock ▶
W Scotland

Rock
♂ ♀
▶

SRP, Water ♂
SRP, Water ♀

◀ SRP
Wing wider than length of tail

◀ SRP, juv

♂ ▶

◀ ♂ SRP

◀ ♂ SRP
Dark malar streak

Water
Breeding, Pyrenees

Dark legs, pale wingbars

◀ Water
No streak

Water Greyish on head, pale stripe over eye

◀ ▲ Water, winter

Rock   SRP   Water

▲ Water, juv
Brown until Nov

Rock Pipit dull, greyish-olive above with soft, dark, grey streaks, yellower-buff below with blurry streaks. Smoky-grey outer tail feathers, dark brown to blackish legs. Coastal all year. Scandinavian Rock Pipit (SRP) similar in winter. In summer may have white stripe over eye on greyer head, flushed pinkish below with streaked chest sides. Fuller call than Meadow, *fist* or *feesp*. Water Pipit a summer bird on high pastures. Grey-headed with white stripe over eye, plain back, pale unstreaked underside, washed pink on breast. In winter like brown-backed Rock, with bolder pale stripe over eye, white throat and bib surrounded by dark. Underside cold whitish; dark streaks on chest and flanks. Two white wingbars, white outer tail, dark brown legs.

Richard's Pipit

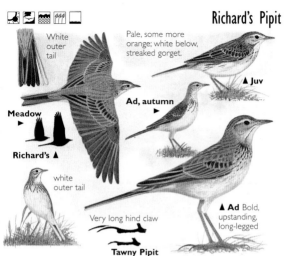

White outer tail

Pale, some more orange; white below, streaked gorget.

▲ Juv

Meadow ►

Ad, autumn ►

Richard's ▲

white outer tail

Very long hind claw

▲ **Ad** Bold, upstanding, long-legged

Tawny Pipit ▲

Big, long-legged, long-tailed pipit, with bold upright stance. Strong, thrush-like bill. Long legs have very long hind claw. Pale to orange-brown, washed buff on chest and flanks but whitish below. Closely streaked above; a few small, fine streaks on chest. Long tail, very dark with broad white sides. Hovers briefly before landing. Loud, rasping, dry *schrree* or quieter *schrew*.

Tawny Pipit

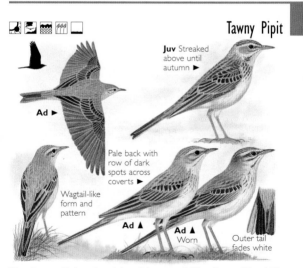

Juv Streaked above until autumn ►

Ad ►

Pale back with row of dark spots across coverts ►

Wagtail-like form and pattern

Ad ▲

Ad ▲ Worn

Outer tail fades white

Big, long-tailed, pale pipit with wagtail-like form. Slim bill. Adult pale sandy-buff above, hardly streaked, underside buff. Row of dark-centred median coverts across closed wing. Long, pale yellowish-orange legs, with shortish hind claw. Juveniles streaked above and below for a few weeks in late summer. Call a rasping or grating *tzeeeip*, shorter *chup*.

Tree Pipit

Small, streaked pipit, often perches on bushes, walks about on large branches of trees

Ad, summer ▶
Darker, worn plumage

'Parachuting' song flight ends on tree, bush or post

Ad, spring
Fresh plumage ▶

Dark band across coverts

Rather strong bill

Pale beneath, flank largely unmarked buff

Short hind claw ▶

▲ Juv

Small, streaked pipit: more elegant, forceful, longer-looking than Meadow Pipit, with brighter, yellower or buffer appearance. Firmer stripe over eye, stouter bill, flanks pale with much finer streaking, much shorter hind claw. Call buzzy *teees*. Sings in parachute flight from and returning to tree top or bush (not ground): rich, sweet, with long *sweea-sweea* finish.

Red-throated Pipit

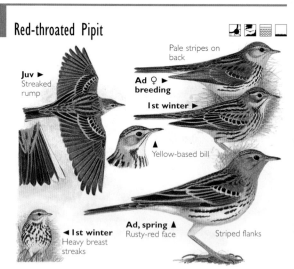

Pale stripes on back

Juv ▶
Streaked rump

Ad ♀ ▶
breeding

1st winter ▶

Yellow-based bill

◀ 1st winter
Heavy breast streaks

Ad, spring ▲
Rusty-red face

Striped flanks

Thick-bodied, short-tailed pipit of damp places, tundra. Adult has two-tone bill, plain sandy-orange to red face and throat; some darker, some pale and washed-out. Bold stripes on back, striped black underside, streaked rump. Autumn juvenile lacks red: often greyish, with strongly streaked buff breast, pale lines on back. Call high, thin, penetrating, explosive *pseeeeee*, fading away.

Meadow Pipit

Flight rather weak, flitting

Nervous, twitchy winter flocks fly up and bound weakly away, then split up

◄ **Tree Pipit**

Tree Pipit Bolder, longer, with shorter hind claw ▼

◄ **Meadow Pipit**

Long hind claw compared with short claw of Tree Pipit ►

▲ White tail sides

◄ **Meadow Pipit** Bill weaker, flanks more streaked than Tree Pipit

'Parachuting' song flight ends on ground

◄ **Juv** Greenish type

Very variable: grey, olive, yellowish types frequent

◄ **Ads**

◄ **Juv** Yellowish type

Small, nervy, hesitant pipit, very like Tree Pipit and autumn juvenile Red-throated Pipit. Often more olive or greyish in spring; typically with weaker pale line over eye than Tree, less streaked rump/uppertail coverts than Red-throated. Buff breast, whiter belly, long dark streaks (more than Tree, less than Red-throated). Autumn birds buffer beneath, with warm buff throat. Legs bright orange-brown, hind claw much longer than on Tree. Flight weak, fluttery, but rises with erratic, bouncy effect, with peevish, sharp calls, *tseep tseep*, *tsip* or *pseet pseet pseet*. Call much less explosive than Red-throated; weaker, thinner than dark-legged Rock and Water Pipits. Song prolonged, thin, with varied trills in parachute flight from ground.

177

Grey Wagtail

Long white bar above and below wing

Juv ▶

▲ **Juv** yellow undertail, greeny-yellow rump

Breeding ♂ ▼

Very long, white-edged tail

♂ **winter** ◀

Pale pink legs

1st winter ▲

♀ **summer**

Longest-tailed, shortest-legged wagtail, with yellow-green rump, yellow undertail combined with grey back (unlike any Yellow or Pied Wagtail). Summer male has black throat, flush of vivid yellow on breast. Long white-sided tail. Broad white wing bar, obvious from below. Call explosive, much sharper than Pied/White, often single note, *tchi* or *tisik*.

Citrine Wagtail

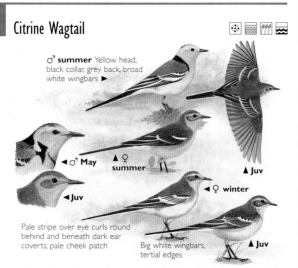

♂ **summer** Yellow head, black collar, grey back, broad white wingbars ▶

◀♂ **May**

▲♀ **summer**

▲ **Juv**

◀ **Juv**

◀♀ **winter**

Pale stripe over eye curls round behind and beneath dark ear coverts; pale cheek patch

Big white wingbars, tertial edges

▲ **Juv**

Rather like mix of Yellow and Pied Wagtails. Summer male has grey back, yellow underside and head, broad black collar. Female and winter male paler; pale yellow line over eye curls around pale-centred ear coverts. Juvenile greyish, washed yellower on chest sides, pale underside, white beneath tail, bold white wing bars, pale around pale-centred cheeks. Harsh, buzzy *slee* or *bseep*.

Yellow Wagtail

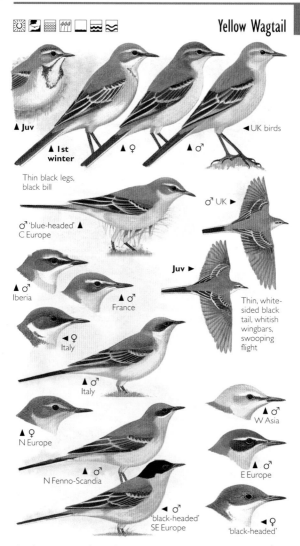

Juv

1st winter

♀

♂

◄ UK birds

Thin black legs, black bill

♂ 'blue-headed' ▲
C Europe

♂ UK ►

Juv ►

▲ ♂
Iberia

▲ ♂
France

◄ ♀
Italy

Thin, white-sided black tail, whitish wingbars, swooping flight

▲ ♂
Italy

▲ ♀
N Europe

▲ ♂
N Fenno-Scandia

▲ ♂
W Asia

▲ ♂
E Europe

◄ ♂
'black-headed'
SE Europe

◄ ♀
'black-headed'

Slender wagtail of meadows and waterside, very variable across Europe. Males bright yellow below, greenish above; dark wings with pale bars. Females duller, greenish above (some very grey), creamy beneath, yellower beneath tail. Juveniles browner still, buff beneath with dark gorget, eyestripe and moustache, pale stripe over eye. All have long, slim tail, black with white sides, and spindly black legs. Male in UK has yellow head with green crown and cheeks. W European 'blue-headed' form has blue-grey head, white stripe over eye. Spanish form has grey head with dark cheeks, white over eye. Scandinavian grey with darker cheeks, no white. Black-headed Wagtail of SE Europe has glossy black cap. Loud, full, rising *tsweep* in undulating flight.

Pied & White Wagtails

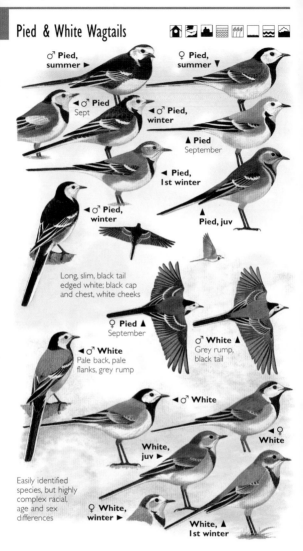

♂ **Pied, summer** ▶

♀ **Pied, summer** ▼

◀ ♂ **Pied** Sept

◀ ♂ **Pied, winter**

▲ **Pied** September

◀ **Pied, 1st winter**

◀ ♂ **Pied, winter**

▲ **Pied, juv**

Long, slim, black tail edged white; black cap and chest, white cheeks

♀ **Pied** ▲ September

♂ **White** Grey rump, black tail

◀ ♂ **White** Pale back, pale flanks, grey rump

◀ ♂ **White**

♀ **White**

White, juv ▶

Easily identified species, but highly complex racial, age and sex differences

♀ **White, winter** ▶

White, ▲ **1st winter**

Distinctive, common, widespread black, white, and grey wagtails with long, white-edged tails. In UK Pied has black or sooty back, dark flanks, blackish wings with white bars and feather edges; summer males blackest. Continental White has pale grey back, browner wings, paler flanks. Male handsomely pale, silvery grey above, female duller. Immatures complex: juvenile has grey-brown cap, drab face, dark moustache and incomplete black bib, underside washed yellow-buff, grey back (autumn Pied hard to tell from White); older immatures gain adult plumage through various patchy transitions. Winter adults lose much black; throat white above dark breastband. Calls with hard *chissick* and sweet *chrew-eee*; song twittering variation of these with warbling notes.

Waxwing

Foxy-red face, black throat, bushy crest

Rusty-red undertail

◄♂

◄♀ Short crest

♂ imm ►

◄♂ imm

◄♀

◄Ad

Grey rump, black tail with pale tip

Stocky, upright, acrobatic bird with unique pointed crest, dumpy body, short legs, short tail. Starling-like triangular wings in flight, but longer body. Body mostly pale dusky grey-pink, rump blue-grey, undertail darker dull rufous. Black tail, yellow tip. Black wings have white bar, striped white and yellow on primaries. Shrill, vibrant *shrrreee*.

Dipper

N Europe, NW France: black belly

◄Ad Big white breast patch

▲ Black bellied

UK, Ireland, C Europe: rufous belly

▲ Rufous bellied

◄Juv Paler below, barred

Short tail, strong legs and feet; springy, bouncing action; swims, wades, dives under water

Round-bodied, short-tailed, dark bird of running water. Bold white breast against dark body. UK race has browner head, chestnut breastband. 'Black-bellied' populations darker on head, black below. Juveniles greyer, with duller, more diffuse white bib. Bobs and flicks tail, walks into water, swims, dives from surface. Flight low, fast along watercourse. Hard, metallic *zik*.

181

Dunnock

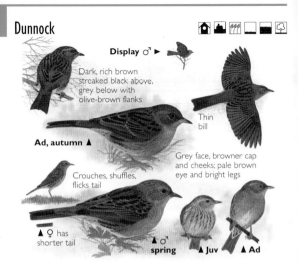

Display ♂ ►

Dark, rich brown
streaked black above,
grey below with
olive-brown flanks

Thin
bill

Ad, autumn ▲

Grey face, browner cap
and cheeks; pale brown
eye and bright legs

Crouches, shuffles,
flicks tail

▲ ♀ has
shorter tail

▲ ♂
spring

▲ Juv

▲ Ad

Small, dark, shuffling bird of gardens, woods, thickets. Thin bill,
mid-grey face and breast, brown cheeks, pale eye. Back striped
brown and black, flanks buffish, streaked dull brown. Orange-
brown legs. Robin-like form, but much more crouched when
feeding; upright when singing from exposed perch. Call sharp,
strong *teee*; song fast, flat, rather even warble.

Alpine Accentor

◄ **Ad, spring**
Grey back

◄▼ **Ads, autumn**
October; darker,
browner above

♂ Bright colours obscured
at long range; bold black
wingbar best clue

▲ ♀ tail

▲ White tips
beneath tail

Juv ►

Like large Dunnock of mountain areas: more thickset, longer
wings and tail. Looks rather dark and grey with blackish band
across wing, edged white. Grey head, streaked brown back, rusty
streaks on flanks all inconspicuous except at close range. Dark-
spotted pale throat and yellow base to bill, often hard to see.
Lark-like, rippling call, *tschirrr*; irregular, short, trilling song.

Wren

Loud song with vibrant trill, given with short tail cocked

Thin, faintly downcurved bill

Flies low and fast on whirring wings

Warm brown above, pale below, long stripe over eye, barred wings and flanks

Juv ▶

Tiny, dumpy, irascible bird of woods, thickets, gardens, ditches. Bright rusty brown, long pale stripe over eye; barred wings. Some larger island races darker, more heavily barred. Tail short, broad, often raised. Rather long, stout legs and spike-like bill. Calls dry, hard *zurrr* and repeated scolding notes; song very loud, bright, fast warble with distinctive low, quick trill.

Robin

Ads Olive-brown above, face and breast reddish-orange, fades paler, duller; blue-grey on side of neck

Bold dark eye in plain face

Whitish breast spot palest point on underparts

Juv Warm buffy-brown with paler spots on back, dark mottles on breast ▶

Dips head, flicks tail and wings

Round-bodied, slim-tailed bird of woods, gardens. Olive-brown above, buff below, face and gorget reddish-orange; fades paler. Variable blue-grey sides to gorget. Bold dark eye. Juvenile lacks red at first; mottled buff and dark brown. Cocky, alert, quick actions with frequent upward tail flick. Call metallic, short *tik*; sharp, thin *seee*; song rich, varied, slightly melancholy warble.

183

Nightingale

Juv ►
Mottled above

A few are more
mottled or washed
brown across chest

Rufous tail

Greyish head,
pale eye-ring,
typically plain
underside

Tiny 1st primary ►
(shown dark)
reaches tips of
primary coverts

Tail has rusty
underside ►

Secretive bird of deep thickets. Plain brown above except for
rustier rump and tail, grey on neck, bold dark eye in plain face,
pale eye-ring. Underside pale grey-buff. Rather long wings often
drooped beside thick rear body. Calls loud *hweet*, croaking *kerrrr*.
Song loud, fast, very varied, with long pauses, sudden changes in
quality and pitch, frequent long *pew piew piew* crescendo.

Thrush Nightingale

Tiny 1st primary
(shown dark) falls
short of primary
coverts ►

Relatively dull
tail and rump

Dull rufous
tail

Variably grey or
buffish below,
mottled on
chest; slight dark
moustache

Western birds
greyish, eastern
ones brighter

Very like Nightingale but typically greyer (less so in E Europe).
Tail less rufous, breast dull grey-brown, more or less mottled,
hint of darker moustache. Like Nightingale, has tiny first
primary, but shorter than primary coverts (Nightingale's just
visible beyond coverts). Song a loud, shouted warbling of
Nightingale character, with more clicks; lacks crescendo.

Bluethroat

Red panels at base of tail

◀♂ Spain

Robin-like form

White stripe over eye

◀♂ Blue form, Netherlands

♂ ▲ White-spotted, C Europe

◀♀ spring

◀♀ Blue type

♀ winter ▲

▲ ♂ 1st winter

Variable blue, black, buff on face and chest

▲ ♂ Red-spotted, N Europe

Robin-like form but contrasted pattern, with distinctive rufous panels at sides of broad tail. Long pale stripe over eye. Summer male has vivid blue breast, with white or red (or no) central spot, black and rufous lower border. Female has little or no blue, pale throat outlined black. Juvenile has bold pale stripe over eye and under cheek, black moustache; tail as adult. Hard *tlak* call.

Rufous Bush-robin

Long tail cocked, flirted, swayed sideways in exaggerated actions

Face pattern varies

Eastern birds ▶ dull on back

Western birds more white, less black on tail ▼

▲ Western birds rufous

White spots under tail

Short, quick dash to cover

Juv Eastern ▲

Western   Eastern

Large, fan-tailed warbler with exaggerated tail-cocking, leaping hops; often around cactus in orchards, or gullies on dry, sandy slopes. Pale orange-buff with bright rufous tail in W Europe, brown-backed with rufous rump, brown tail in SE Europe. Bold pale stripe over eye. Tail tipped with black and white spots, striking in flight. Clicking and whistling calls, thrush-like song.

Redstart

Breeding ♂
Bold black face,
rufous underside

♀ Plain head, rich
buff underside

Juv More
mottled ▶

Rufous rump and
constantly-flicked tail

♂ **Juv**

◀ **Breeding ♂**
SE Europe: pale
wing panel

♀

♂

◀ ♂
**autumn,
winter** Pale
tips obscure
colours

Slim, Robin-like woodland bird with flickered, bright, pale
rufous tail and rufous rump. Male grey above with white
forehead, black face. Female plainer, buffy-brown. Autumn male
has black obscured by white feather tips. Juvenile has pale wing
feather edges, pale orange-buff chest. Pale eye-ring. Call a sweet
whee-tik; song a short warble, starts with rolled *srree sree sree*.

Black Redstart

◀ ♂ Iberia: steely-black,
paler cap, white wing panel

♂

♂ Black and slaty,
dark reddish tail,
pale wing
panel ▶

♀

Small rusty rump,
dull red tail

1st winter ▼

♀ Sooty,
brownish
grey ▶

Underside of ♀
and 1st winter
grey, tinged buff
or brownish,
always darker,
greyer than
Redstart

♂

♀

Dark redstart of urban areas and cliffs. Male sooty grey with
black face, white wing flash, rufous rump and tail sides. Female
and many breeding immature males greyer with browner wings,
weaker pale flash. Young females brownish-grey overall, a little
darker but less buff than Redstart, less rufous on tail and rump.
Song includes grating, stone-rubbing sounds and dry rattles.

Whinchat

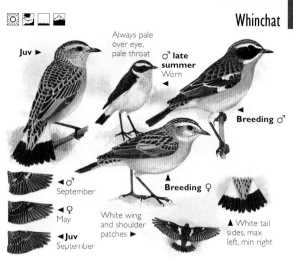

Juv ▶

Always pale over eye, pale throat

♂ **late summer** Worn ◀

Breeding ♂ ▶

▲ **Breeding** ♀

◀♂ September

◀♀ May

◀ **Juv** September

White wing and shoulder patches ▶

▲ White tail sides, max left, min right

Small, stocky, upright bird of grassy heaths and moors. Bold pale stripes over eye and under dark cheek, pale throat, white sides to tail. Male has blackest cap and cheek, apricot breast, white wing and shoulder patches. Female paler, buffer overall. Immature has weakest head pattern, less defined cheeks. Call *wheet-chat-chat*; sweet warbling song with harder notes and trills.

Stonechat

Upright, stocky, short-tailed

Winter ♀ and juv may have pale over eye, paler throat

Dark tail, paler rump, white on shoulder

♀ **1st winter**

◀ ♀ Dark extreme

◀♂ Worn to contrasted impression

♂ **1st winter**

◀♂ **spring** Bold white on neck and shoulder

♀ ▲

♂ **autumn** Spain ▶

Small, upright, short-tailed bird, perches on bushes, wires. Dark head, pale neck sides, paler rump, all-dark tail. Male has black head and throat, bold white half-collar, rufous breast, big white shoulder patch. Female rustier, browner on head, duller neck side. Immature has paler throat but lacks Whinchat's strong stripe over eye. Call a hard *see tak tak*; song a fast, grating warble.

187

Black-eared & Pied Wheatears

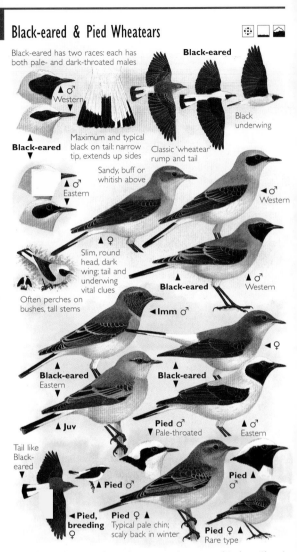

Black-eared has two races: each has both pale- and dark-throated males

Black-eared

▲♂ Western

▲ **Black-eared** ▼

Maximum and typical black on tail: narrow tip, extends up sides

Black underwing

Sandy, buff or whitish above

▲♂ Eastern

Classic 'wheatear' rump and tail

♂► Western

Slim, round head, dark wing; tail and underwing vital clues

♀▲

Often perches on bushes, tall stems

▲♂ Western

▲ **Black-eared**

◄Imm ♂

♀►

▲ **Black-eared** Eastern

▼ **Black-eared**

▼ **Pied** ♂ Pale-throated

♂► Eastern

▲ Juv

Tail like Black-eared

◄**Pied, breeding** ♀

▲ **Pied** ♂

Pied ♀ ▲ Typical pale chin; scaly back in winter

♂

Pied ▲

Pied ♀ ▲ Rare type

Black-eared is slender wheatear with narrow black tailband, curling forwards onto tail sides, bold white rump. Often perches on bushes, tall stems. Male black-throated or with black eye-patch and pale throat. Whitish or deep sandy-buff above, white below, black wings. Female dull brown above, breast washed orange-brown; may have dark throat and cheeks. Call grating *tsree* or *tchak*. Pied is striking wheatear of extreme E Europe. Male greyish-white on crown, buff-white below; face, breast and back black. Tail pattern like Black-eared. Female dull brown, paler belly; breast washed dark brown, often mottled. Autumn birds show pale scaly feather edges on dark brown back, lacy pale edges to wing coverts, more buff on wings and underparts.

Wheatear

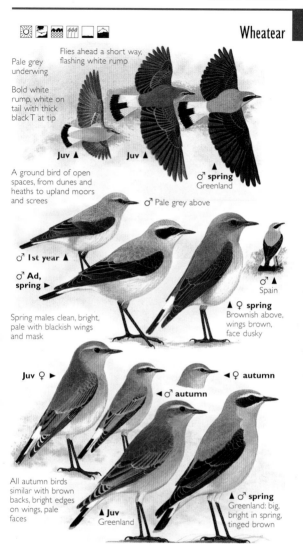

Flies ahead a short way, flashing white rump

Pale grey underwing

Bold white rump, white on tail with thick black T at tip

Juv ▲

Juv ▲

♂ spring Greenland

A ground bird of open spaces, from dunes and heaths to upland moors and screes

♂ Pale grey above

♂ 1st year ▲

♂ Ad, spring ►

♂ ▲ Spain

▲ ♀ spring Brownish above, wings brown, face dusky

Spring males clean, bright, pale with blackish wings and mask

Juv ♀ ►

◄ ♀ autumn

◄ ♂ autumn

All autumn birds similar with brown backs, bright edges on wings, pale faces

▲ Juv Greenland

▲ ♂ spring Greenland: big, bright in spring, tinged brown

Widespread wheatear of open ground, moors, sandy heaths, dunes, often on coast or beside lakes and reservoirs on migration. Big white rump, black T-shape on tail with broad black band at tip. Spring male grey above (Greenland race tinged brown), wings brown-black, underside pale buff (Greenland birds richer peachy-buff). White stripe over black patch through eye. Female sandy-brown above, buff below, eye patch brown, wings brown. All birds browner in autumn, sandy-buff below, wings dark with broad golden-buff feather edges. Stands rather upright, leans forward when feeding on open ground or perched on post or rock. Calls include sharp whistle, *heet*, and hard, clicking *tak*. Song, often in song flight, a fast, rattly warble.

189

Black Wheatear

Striking white rump; broad black tail tip with central T-stem

Pale outer upperwing and underwing

Browner than ♂

Large, thickset, blackish wheatear with big splash of white on rump, vent and tail

Big, dark wheatear, obvious blackish overall except for big white rump, vent and tail base creating eyecatching flash of white in flight. Broad black tailband. Female browner-black than male. Stands upright or horizontal, with up-down tail movement, on rocks, cliffs. Whistled *peeup*, clicking *chet chet* and rattling notes; song a rather quick, low chattery warble.

Isabelline Wheatear

Pale with squarish white rump and thick black band across tail, short T-stem, obvious in flight

Pale stripe tapers behind eye; thick bill

Back and wing uniform in tone

♂ ▶

Dark alula on plain wing

Long wings, short tail

Juv ♀

White underwing coverts

Pale, large, upright wheatear. Relatively small, square, dull white rump, broad black tailband with short central T-stem obvious in flight. Back and wings dull pale brown, show little contrast except for darker alula; underwing very pale. White stripe over eye duller, narrower behind eye (broader, whiter behind eye on Wheatear), dark line from bill through eye.

Rock Thrush

Striking rufous tail; pale patch on back

◄ ♀ spring

Juv, ► autumn

♂

♀

Small, chunky thrush of high meadows, rocks, cliffs

◄ ♂ summer
Dark wings, blue head, red tail

◄ ♂ autumn

▲ ♀ summer

Small, short-tailed thrush with dark-centred rufous tail, of high meadows, rocky slopes, quarries. Male has bright blue head, brown back with variable central white patch, orange underparts. Female dark brown, closely scaled buff above; orange-buff, barred brown below. Call *chak*; song is thrush-like soft, rich warble, often given in song flight.

Blue Rock Thrush

◄ ♀ summer

Wings of ♀ brownish, tail blue-grey

Often shy, flies off over ridge or across gorge, looks very dark

▲ Juv

Long bill

◄ ♂ summer

▲ ♀ summer

▼ ♂ Juv

Large, long-tailed thrush of cliffs, gorges, rocky coasts

Intense blue shows only in good view

Long-tailed, dark thrush of rocks, gorges, coastal cliffs. Male deep blue, head brighter (strong blue in close view, dark at distance). Female dark brown above, dark orange-buff below with close brown bars. Tail and wings dark, no rufous. Often perches on skyline, long bill evident. Call *chook*; song a strong, wild thrush warble, between Rock Thrush and Blackbird.

Blackbird

♀ has yellow bill in summer

♂ yellow bill, eye-ring ►

Dark thrush, short-winged, long-tailed; tail frequently raised and slowly lowered

▲ ♀ Dark brown, with streaked throat

♂ 1st winter ▲ Dull bill, brown wings

Juv ▲ Variable rusty or gingery brown, pale spots above, dark bars or spots below, always darker than Song Thrush

♀ 1st winter ▲ Throat often whitish, streaked; mottled below

◄ ♀ Paler-throated bird

♂

Ring Ouzel ▼

Blackbird ►

▲ Outer wing of ♂ looks paler in flight; tail long, full

♀

Often cocks tail

Common, widespread, dark thrush of woods, fields, gardens, parks. Male striking black (especially in green spring woodland) with vivid orange-yellow bill and eye-ring. In flight outer wing and underwing paler. Female dark brown, bill dark or yellow; throat paler, streaked, underside subtly spotted but never very strong pattern, ground colour always darker, duller than 'spotted' thrushes. Juvenile similar or more rufous, head rustier, back and wing coverts spotted with rusty-buff. Immature male dull black, wings browner, dark bill and eye-ring. Call soft, vibrant, shrill *srreee*; loud, hysterical, rapid rattle of alarm. Frequent *chook*, ringing *pink pink* especially at dusk. Song soft, fluent, musical warbling phrases with scratchy endings.

Fieldfare

Grey rump, black tail unlike any other thrush

Stout yellow bill, dark mask

Striking white underwing, white vent

Ads

Distinctive grey-brown-grey-black above, orange-buff breast, white belly

Breast and flanks blacker in spring

♀

♂ Shorter tail ▶

Big, sociable, noisy thrush, roams fields and moors in winter flocks. Striking white underwing. Grey head, brown back, grey rump, black tail create unique upperpart pattern. Black on face, white throat and belly, flanks spotted black (especially in spring), breast yellow-buff to deep orange-buff. Calls soft, nasal *whee-ee* and loud, chuckling, throaty *chak chak chak*.

Ring Ouzel

Long, sharp wings with pale area above

♀ **1st winter** Breastband obscure; pale scaling overall ▼

White or pale crescent across upper chest

♂ spring ▲

♂ winter ▶

♂ spring ▲

♀ spring ▶

♀ S Europe

♂ S Europe

Juv Pale wing panel; ▶ bars on rufous flanks

Shy Blackbird-like thrush of moors, crags, screes. Male black on body, bold white crescent on chest, wings markedly paler. Female grey-brown, with paler, scaly feather edges overall; dull chest crescent. Alpine/Pyrenees males have broad white scaling beneath. Mistle Thrush shape in flight with long, pointed, pale wings. Hard *tuk*; song loud, wild, repeated short phrases.

193

Song Thrush

1st winter ▲

Juv ▶

Ad ▶

Small, neat, pale, spotted thrush. V-shaped spots more or less aligned. Whiter belly than Mistle Thrush

1st winter Pale spots on wings

Darker birds in NW ◀

Underwing pale orange

Usually flies low

Small, pale, spotted thrush of woods, fields, gardens; flies low. Upperside plain olive-brown to warm brown, face pattern weak. Underside yellow-buff, white on belly, with close, neat, black-brown V-shaped spots all over, more or less aligned on browner flanks. Call sharp *sip*; song loud, repeated phrases, less flowing than Blackbird, many notes strident, others with great purity.

Redwing

Often flies high, in flocks

Underwing strong dull red

♀   ♂

Striped head ▼

▲ Eyecatching white rear flank spot

Flank reddish, vent white; lines of streaks on breast

Black and yellow bill

Ad ♀ ▶

♂ **1st winter** ▲ Pale spots on wings

Dark, neat thrush, bold face pattern. Dark grey-brown above, strong pale stripe over eye and beneath dark cheek. Underside silvery, dark streaks aligned in neat lines; flanks and underwing dull rusty-red. Tail short, square, giving slightly lark-like profile in flight. Flight call distinctive penetrating *seeei*, often at night. Warbling song has repetitive, short, descending phrases.

Mistle Thrush

Long, square tail, long wings, pale rump

Juv has obvious pale head in flight

Fast, strong, bounding flight

Pale, greyish with pale edges to wing feathers; much bigger, longer-tailed than Song Thrush

White underwing

Typically flies far off, high up if disturbed

Variable white sides to tail ▼

Breast spots round or crescent-shaped

◄ Smaller, greyer in Corsica & Sardinia

◄ N Europe

More uniformly buff below than Song Thrush

Powerful, upright, leaping hops across ground

Juv Striking pale drop-► shaped spots above dark bars on rump; pale head

Big, long-tailed, long-winged thrush, pale with bold round spots, pale-streaked wings, white underwing. Bigger than Blackbird, bolder than Song Thrush, with stronger leaping hops; tends to fly higher, farther if disturbed, often well above tree top height. Upperside pale grey-brown, wing feathers edged pale buff. Rump slightly paler, warmer buff-brown. Tail has white sides. Underside creamy-buff with broad, round black spots, concentrated over darker chest sides. Juvenile boldly marked with drop-shaped spots above. White underwing like Fieldfare but wings longer, more pointed. Call distinctive dry, rasping, angry rattle, *trr-trr-trrrrr-zrrr*. Song loud, wild, with longer phrases than Song Thrush but greater repetition than Blackbird.

195

Savi's Warbler

Pale, warm brown, whiter throat; buff-brown belly and undertail

▲ ♂

♂

Round tail

Dark type ►

♀

Pale Medium Dark

Round-edged wing: short coverts, short tertials compared with River Warbler (bottom)

Long undertail coverts

◄ ♀ has shorter tail

◄ Savi's

◄ River Warbler

A typical *Locustella* warbler with spiky bill, flat head, whitish curved edge to wing, long thick rear body tapering to broad-tipped tail. A reedbed bird located by song. Plain warm brown, whiter on throat, rusty-buff undertail. Sharp, metallic call; song a prolonged, loud, fast, droning, buzzy trill, notes far less distinct or ticking than Grasshopper Warbler's.

River Warbler

White-edged wing, round tail, long undertail coverts all typical *Locustella* traits

Plain back

♂

◄ Streaked throat

♀ has shorter tail ▼

♂

♀

Dark brown, more or less streaked across chest

Long undertail ► coverts: pale and dark extremes

◄ Pale ad

◄ 1st winter
Greyer, darker

♂

Broad, round, dark tail

Elusive *Locustella* warbler of wet vegetation and thickets near rivers and marshes. Like Savi's Warbler but darker, duller, with long undertail coverts with series of crescentic whitish tips. Hint of faint dark moustache and variable streaking on throat and chest. Song has fast, rhythmic, chuffing quality, a prolonged *sche-sche-sche-sche-sche-sche-sche-sche.*

Grasshopper Warbler

Softly streaked above, greyish to yellowish below

▲ ♂

Sings at dusk or in muggy, warm weather, bill wide open, often in full view

▲ ♂

Creeps mouse-like through grass, elusive except when singing

◀ Streaks on back strongest in rear view

◀ ♂

Long undertail coverts, slim, flattish head, thin bill, round tail reveal generic relationships

♀ ▶

▲ Juv Few streaks on flank; dark streaks and pale edges above firmer than on adult

Long, diffuse ▶ streaks on undertail coverts

Flies up underfoot, travels short distance in low, undulating flight, dives out of sight into smallest bush

♂ ▶

▲ Ad ♀ autumn

Most widespread *Locustella* warbler, found in grassy places with tangled low growth. Very secretive but may sing from exposed perch on sultry evenings or during day. Slim, flat head and thin bill. Rounded wing edge, long tail and elongated undertail coverts less extreme than Savi's or River Warblers, but still give characteristic impression, unlike Sedge Warbler. Brown above, some greyer, some yellower, with subtle streaking darkest on tertials. Underside yellow-buff, unstreaked or with hint of streaking around upper chest; undertail coverts have long, soft dark streaks. Call sharp *psit*. Song a remarkable, prolonged, even reeling, mechanical and metallic: a series of hard ticking notes at close range, merging into finer, higher-sounding trill at distance.

Aquatic Warbler

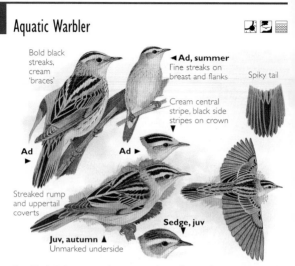

Bold black streaks, cream 'braces'

◄ **Ad, summer**
Fine streaks on breast and flanks

Spiky tail

Cream central stripe, black side stripes on crown ▼

Ad ►

Ad ►

Streaked rump and uppertail coverts

Juv, autumn ▲
Unmarked underside

Sedge, juv ▼

Small, bright, strongly-patterned warbler of wetlands, reeds. Yellow-buff with blackish streaks. Buff central crown stripe and stripe above eye, pale cream stripes on back, streaked rump. Underside buff, finely streaked on adult. Immature unmarked peachy-buff below. Tail spiky-tipped. Lacks dark line from eye to bill. Clicking call. Fast song mixes whistles and churrs.

Sedge Warbler

Juv, autumn ►
Fine streaks on chest, paler crown

Juv ▼

Silvery-white stripe over eye

Pale sandy-rufous rump obvious in flight

♂ summer ►
Plain rusty or sandy rump, soft streaks on back

Whitish or silvery underparts, buff flanks

◄ **Ad**

Round dark tail, unmarked uppertail coverts

Common wetland warbler with dark cap (paler central stripe on juvenile) and whitish stripe over eye, widening to rear; dark line from eye to bill. Back streaked; rump pale, unmarked sandy-buff. Underside unmarked on adult, faintly streaked on chest of juvenile. Call slurred *crrrrr*. Song fast, irascible, energetic, varied, chattering warble with sweet notes and thin trills.

Moustached Warbler

Rusty back, chest and flanks, blackish cap, dark cheeks, bold white stripe over eye and white throat

Often cocks tail, tips up and clambers down into reeds

Ads

Short wings, rusty rump

Short wing

Juv Duller throat ▶

◀ **Sedge**

Like dark, contrasted Sedge Warbler, with more solidly dark cap, broad, wedge-shaped, whiter stripe over eye, darker cheek edged with fine blackish moustache, striking white throat against more orange chest. Back warm brown with blackish streaks, rump pale; wingtip projection shorter. Call throaty *chrek*. Song a fast, soft chatter with distinctive clear, rising whistled notes.

Cetti's Warbler

Dark, reddish warbler with grey underside, dark round tail; thin whitish stripe over eye

Secretive, hard to see but easy to hear; not shy if approached with care, sometimes gives close view

Dark undertail

Dark, elusive warbler of thickly overgrown watersides, ditches, wet thickets. Frequent outburst of song distinctive, but often moves off before being seen, singing again nearby. Dark rusty-brown, pale stripe over eye, greyish below; dark bars under broad, round tail. Call loud, metallic *plit*. Song sudden, abrupt, full-throated *chwee! chuwee… chwe-we-we-we-we-we-wee*.

Reed Warbler

Juv, autumn ▶
More rufous than adult,
juv fades to sandy colour
by autumn

A plain-backed, long-
tailed, spiky-beaked
warbler of reedbeds

Ad, autumn ▶
Worn, sandy-brown,
rump brighter

Weak head pattern,
white throat, long bill

Ad, spring ▶
Greyish-olive tinge
above, rump brighter

Legs darker, greyer than
Marsh Warbler

Sings from reed or
willow stem, dumpy
when relaxed

Moves expertly through
vertical stems, willows,
using strong feet

Quick flight
skimming
reed tops

◀ May show
whitish from
bill to eye

Reed Short wing,
seven primary tips
▼

Reed Warbler tail usually
squarer than Marsh

Marsh Long,
eight tips ▼

Typical plain brown *Acrocephalus* warbler of dense reeds with rhythmic, evenly-paced song. *Acrocephalus* character important: long pointed bill, flattish head (more peaked when singing), long body with flattish back, long slightly rounded tail. Undertail coverts longer than *Hippolais* warblers (Olivaceous, Melodious) but not such a long, thick, obvious feature as on *Locustella* warblers (River, Savi's). Shuffles through reeds, sidles up stems, sings near top. Warm brown above, weak face pattern with hint of eye-ring, dark line between eye and bill. Underside pale. Rump warmer, especially autumn juvenile. Call short *chrk*. Song a conversational, rhythmic repetition of soft churrs and warbles, *chrrt chrrt chrrt chet chet chet jik jik, chur chur chirrup chirrup chirrup.*

Marsh Warbler

Juv, autumn ▶

A plain-backed, round-tailed warbler of dense, tall, wet waterside vegetation and damp bushy places

Juv most rufous, most like Reed; legs paler, claws pale (Reed's dark)

Typically duller, more olive, less rufous than Reed Warbler, but autumn birds very alike

Ads, spring
Pale flanks lack rufous ▼▶

Cold, earthy brown, some more olive, whiter on throat

Marsh

Reed

Bill slightly wider than Reed

◀Juv, autumn

Rounded when ▲ relaxed, rounder head than Reed

◀Ad

Taut, tightly-feathered ▲ when alert; head flattens, angular nape

Ad
Subtly narrower wings than Reed

Wing shapes
Red: Marsh
Black: Reed

One of a difficult group, very like Reed Warbler and Blyth's Reed Warbler (latter has shorter wingtip). Slightly duller, more olive than Reed in spring, greyer above, rump hardly warmer than back; primaries longer with crisper pale tips, tertials have firmer pale edges. Underside dull yellowish-white. Legs paler, browner (grey on Reed), especially on autumn juvenile (yellowish-pink), but juvenile is brighter, slightly more rusty than adult and extremely like Reed. Bill slightly shorter, blunter, head slightly rounder than Reed's. Breeds in more mixed, rank, often very tall waterside vegetation. Song typically much more varied, fast, excitable, with much mimicry of local and African species (frequently Swallow, Blue Tit, Chaffinch).

Great Reed Warbler

Strong bill, bold head pattern

Crashes into reeds; noisy when singing, but can be elusive

Thrush-like shape and action in flight

Dark legs

Long wingtip, long tail

Very large, pale warbler of tall reeds

A big warbler of tall reeds, almost Song Thrush-sized. Looks like Reed Warbler, but has stronger pale stripe over eye, dark eyestripe and bigger, stout, dark-edged bill. Pale sandy-brown tail often held slightly fanned; crown peaked while singing. Song loud, harsh, frog-like, repetitive, with insistent rhythm, *grrrk grrrk grrrk, cirik cirik cirik jik jik jerk jerk jerk carra carra carra.*

Blyth's Reed Warbler

Plain wings, short tips

Broad bill

Yellow gape

◀ ♂ Longer tail than ♀

Small, plain warbler of bushy places; tail often slightly raised

▲ Juv, autumn
Pale eyestripe bulges between eye and bill

Broader wings than Marsh

Flight feathers edged pale

◀ ♀

◀ Ad, autumn
Dull olive-brown above, pale bill, legs grey or brown

Undertail

Secretive bird of scrub and thickets, not reeds or wetlands. Remarkably like Reed and Marsh Warblers. Grey-brown above with warmer rump. Long, pale bill, ridge and tip darker. Dark line through eye and pale, slightly blob-like stripe above it between eye and bill. Short wingtips, dark legs. Call short, ticking *zak* or *zek*; sings at night, rich notes repeated 3–10 times.

Icterine Warbler

Ad, spring ▶
Dull whitish type

Pale, dagger bill, bold eye in plain face

Square tail, short undertail coverts unlike *Acrocephalus*

Long wing projection

Legs brown or bluish

◀Juv

◀Ad, spring
Green and yellow type

Broad, sharp bill

Pale wing panel

Juv May have stronger head pattern but no obvious dark eyestripe

Pale yellow on breast

Rather large, long-billed warbler. Greenish above, pale yellow below, with pale face. Dagger bill, pink-orange at base; grey legs. Usually obvious pale wing panel. Long wingtip projection equals tertial length. Autumn juvenile paler, dull, yellowish-white below, wing panel streaked whitish. Call *di-de-tuit*. Song a prolonged, even, low chattering; fast, with frequent shrill notes.

Olive-tree Warbler

♀ Shorter tertials than ♂

Very big warbler

Strong dagger bill

Long tail, long wing projection

♂ Tertials longer than on ♀

Dull, greyish, whiter below

Wingtip still long

◀♀

♂ Longer tail than ♀

Pale wing panel

White edge and tip to tail

Very big, long-bodied, long-winged warbler of oakwoods, olive and almond groves in SE Europe. Stout, striking bill, broad whitish wing panel, grey upperside, blacker wingtips and tail. Immature more buffish. Tail sides pale. Hops clumsily through foliage, then flies heavily to crash into next tree. Song has Reed warbler rhythm but coarse, harsh notes.

203

Wood Warbler

Juv ►
White primary tips, tertial edges

Long wingtips

♀ ▲
Brown wings edged yellow-green

♀ ►
Clear green above

Strong yellow stripe over dark green band through eye

♂ ►
Long wings

♂ ►
Shorter body of ♂ reduces tail projection

Bright yellow throat, white belly

Beautiful woodland warbler, in oak or beech, and over dark, bare ground. Quite bright green above, with broad yellow stripe over eye, pale yellow throat and chest, white underside. Long brown wings with yellow feather edges. Call almost monosyllabic *swee*. Song sharp, high, ticking notes merging into fast, silvery trill: *t-t-ti-tit-titititrrrrrrr* interspersed with sad *pew pew pew pew*.

Bonelli's Warbler

Greyish head, back, greener rump, wings; tertials edged whiter

♂ Western ◄ ►

♀ Western ◄

Pale, greyish warbler with weak line over eye, no real eyestripe, silvery-white underside

Double 'step' on closed wing ►

Eastern ▲ ►

Duller than Wood Warbler, greyer head, only weak, thin, pale line over eye, almost no eyestripe. Rump yellower-green, wings edged yellow-green, tertials edged dull whitish. Underside clean, silvery-white. Call bright *hu-wit*. Song quick, soft, dribbling or bubbling trill, *pl-l-l-l-l-l-l-l-l-lrrrrr*, less ticking than Wood, less hard than Cirl Bunting. Eastern Bonelli's call is a flat *chip*.

Greenish Warbler

Short wing ▼

Slim, pale warbler with whitish underside, fine pale wingbar (very rarely a hint of a second), long pale stripes over eye meeting over bill

Round wings

Lower mandible all pale

Juv ▲ Sept

Grey-brown legs

◄ Ads ▼ August

Rear flanks clean, whitish, unsullied

Typically rounded, but can look long, slim

Small, slim, large-headed, olive-green warbler with white underside. Long, pale yellowish stripe over eye, very thin pale wingbar (very rarely a hint of a second). Bill small, thin, pale with dark ridge. Pale stripes over eyes meet over bill (unlike Arctic Warbler). Call bright, full *chi-li*. Song a quick, high, cheery warble with a Wren-like pattern.

Arctic Warbler

Very active, with stronger, stouter, more aggressive look than Greenish

Stocky, thick bill, long pale stripe over broad dark eyestripe falling short of bill, pale wingbar, upper bar wears off

Greenish

Long wing

▲ ♀ shorter tail, dumpier than ♂ ▼

▲ Short-billed bird

Lower mandible dark at tip

Long wings

Rear flanks often sullied greyish

▲ Typical long-billed bird

More thickset than Greenish Warbler, with thicker bill. Often has second thin pale wingbar which wears off one or both wings. Olive above, thin pale wingbar, dirty whitish or dusky below. Bold dark stripe through eye and long, broad, pale stripe above, not reaching bill. Dark spot at tip of lower bill. Legs usually paler pinkish-brown than Greenish. Distinct hard, metallic *zik*.

Chiffchaff

Ads, spring
Dull olive, yellowish below

Small, round-headed, short-winged warbler, very thin, blackish legs

Frequent downward dip of tail

Sometimes hovers

◄ Iberian birds (top) longer-winged than others

◄ Ad, winter
Fine bill, thin eyestripe, white crescent under eye

Iberian
Duller type ►

Iberian, spring ▲
Probably separate species

Ad ►
Intermediate form between N and S European forms, migrant or wintering in W Europe

Ad ►
N Europe: dull, greyish-brown

Ad C & S Europe ►

◄ Ad Siberian, autumn Lacks green and yellow, often thin, curved, pale wingbar

◄Siberian

Common in woodland, but migrants occur in many habitats; a few winter in W Europe, many in S Europe. Small, round-headed, small-billed warbler with thin blackish legs. Drab olive-green above, yellowish below; juveniles yellower beneath. Pale stripe over eye (stronger on juvenile). Distinctive thin white eye-ring, obvious beneath eye. Birds from N and E Europe duller, browner; Siberian birds greyer, whitish over eye and on underparts, faint pale wingbar. Primary projection shorter than on Willow Warbler. Tail frequently dipped downwards: an easy identification clue. Call more monosyllabic than Willow, *hweet*; in autumn a shrill *sip* from young birds. Song a simple series of single, bright notes, *chif chaf chif chaf chip chap chip chip chif chaf.*

Willow Warbler

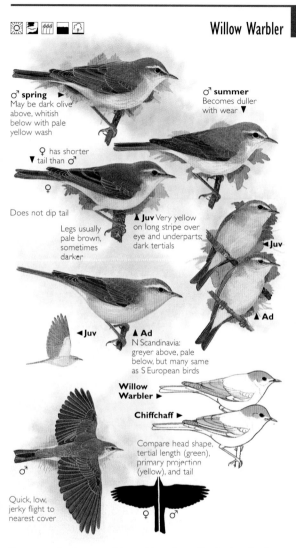

♂ **spring** ▶
May be dark olive
above, whitish
below with pale
yellow wash

♂ **summer**
Becomes duller
with wear ▼

♀ has shorter
▼ tail than ♂

♀

Does not dip tail

Legs usually
pale brown,
sometimes
darker

▲ **Juv** Very yellow
on long stripe over
eye and underparts;
dark tertials

◀ **Juv**

◀ **Juv**

▲ **Ad**

▲ **Ad**
N Scandinavia:
greyer above, pale
below, but many same
as S European birds

**Willow
Warbler** ▶

Chiffchaff ▶

Compare head shape,
tertial length (green),
primary projection
(yellow), and tail

♂

Quick, low,
jerky flight to
nearest cover

♀   ♂

Common, slender, greenish warbler of woodland edge, bushes,
parks. Typically pale-legged, rather flat-headed, and long-
winged, with a distinctive, sweet, descending song. Pale greyish-
green to olive-green above, with pale stripe over eye, longer and
yellower on juvenile. Pale eye-ring does not show well, as it does
on Chiffchaff. Whitish below, flushed pale yellow on breast,
brighter yellow overall on juvenile. Legs pale brown, rarely dark.
Primary projection a little longer than Chiffchaff's. NW
European birds greyer or browner, less green. Does not dip tail
like Chiffchaff as it feeds. Call a disyllabic, sweet *hoo-eet*. Song an
unmistakable, simple cadence, starting quietly, quickly, then
strengthening, descending, finishing with flourish.

Melodious Warbler

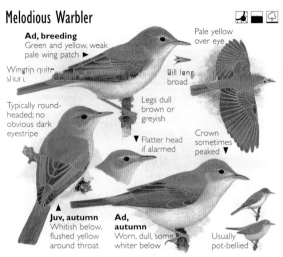

Ad, breeding
Green and yellow, weak
pale wing patch ▶

Pale yellow
over eye

Wingtip quite
short

Bill long,
broad

Typically round-
headed; no
obvious dark
eyestripe

Legs dull
brown or
greyish

▼ Flatter head
if alarmed

Crown
sometimes
peaked ▼

Juv, autumn
Whitish below,
flushed yellow
around throat

Ad, autumn
Worn, dull, some
whiter below

Usually
pot-bellied

A *Hippolais* warbler with a square-tailed, round-headed, pale-
faced, spike-billed character recalling Icterine; shorter wingtip.
Bigger than Willow, stouter brown-grey legs, stronger orange-
pink bill. Greenish above, weak or absent wing panel. Pale lemon
yellow below (juvenile paler, buffer). Call sparrowy, chattering
notes. Song even, quick, rambling chatter of warbles and rattles.

Paddyfield Warbler

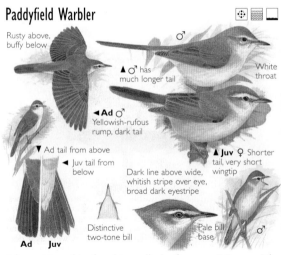

Rusty above,
buffy below

♂

White
throat

▲ ♂ has
much longer tail

◀ **Ad ♂**
Yellowish-rufous
rump, dark tail

▲ **Juv ♀** Shorter
tail, very short
wingtip

▼ Ad tail from above

◀ Juv tail from
below

Dark line above wide,
whitish stripe over eye,
broad dark eyestripe

Distinctive
two-tone bill

Pale bill
base

♂

Ad   Juv

A brownish warbler found in reedbeds of extreme E Europe. Like
rather bright, pale Reed Warbler, but with broader pale line over
eye edged with dusky sides of crown and darker eyestripe; bill
has darker tip. Very short wingtips, long rounded tail. Summer
adult has markedly rusty rump, pale eye. Song like Marsh but
less powerful: a fast outpouring of rich warbles and mimicry.

Western & Eastern Olivaceous Warblers

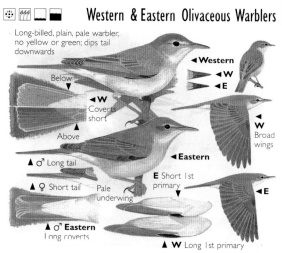

Long-billed, plain, pale warbler, no yellow or green; dips tail downwards

Western
◄ W
◄ E
W Broad wings
Below
◄ W Coverts short
Above
▲ ♂ Long tail
▲ ♀ Short tail
Pale underwing
◄ Eastern
E Short 1st primary
◄ E
▲ ♂ Eastern Long coverts
▲ W Long 1st primary

Pale, plain grey-buff warbler, paler below, with flat head, long dagger bill, and frequent downward bob of tail. Shorter undertail coverts than Reed or Marsh Warbler. Longish, square tail; short wings. Pale orange bill, faint hint of moustache. Eastern birds smaller-billed. Call a hard *tsak*; song has repetitive, cyclical pattern: a soft, fast, chattering, rising and falling warble.

Booted & Sykes's Warblers

Small, spike-billed, square-tailed, sandy-brown

▲ ♀
▲ ♂
Pale-edged tail, pale bill, dark-edged line over eye, upward tail flick
Booted Short, round wings
◄ B
◄ S
Sykes's Long, broad wings
Dark underwing
◄ Booted
◄ Sykes's Shorter coverts
B ►
S ►

Two very similar, difficult warblers, smaller than Olivaceous, slightly more like *Acrocephalus* or *Phylloscopus* warblers. Dark-tipped, pale, spiky bill. Slight dark line through eye and strong pale stripe above it, with soft darker edge to crown. Booted has short wingtip, longer on Sykes's. Outer tail feathers edged pale. Does not flick tail downwards like Olivaceous Warbler.

209

Whitethroat

Rises from bush, hedge or overhead wire in song flight

Juv Ad

Ad ♂ ►
♀ has shorter tail

Ad ♂ spring
Grey head, white throat, rusty wing ▼

Broken white eye-ring or upper eyelid ▼

Long, slim, white-edged tail

Ad ♀ autumn ▼

♀ is browner on head than ♂, more olive on back

Pale legs, unlike Lesser Whitethroat

**◄ ♂
1st summer**
Ad fades to this duller colour in late summer

Juv ▲
Bright, buffy, very rufous on wings

◄ ♀

Ad ♀ summer ▼

Dives out of sight into thick, thorny vegetation

Small, long-tailed, short-billed, white-throated warbler of low bushy or scrubby vegetation, hedgerows. Often perches on high wires. Pale legs and rufous panel on wings, unlike all other European warblers except Spectacled. Male has peaked greyish head, broken white eye-ring, bright white throat, pink-washed breast, dull brown back, white-sided dark tail, and broad rusty feather edges on wings. Female browner on head, buffer on chest. Juvenile bright, with brownish head, rusty wings with dark feather centres. Often cocks and sways tail. In flight tail looks long, slim, almost 'loose'. Calls include buzzy *hai hai hai*, nasal *chaairr*, *wichity wichity*. Song, often given in bouncy song flight, is a fast, buzzy, jerky warble.

Lesser Whitethroat

Plain wings lack rufous; dark legs

Ad ♂ ▶ Easily overlooked in thicket

Ad ♂ ▶ spring

Ad ♀ ▶ spring

Juv Very neat, smart; white eye-ring ▶

Slim, neat, dark, white-sided tail, shorter than Whitethroat's

Ad ♂ spring May be pinker below; eyepatch darker from some angles ▼

Strong contrast between grey cheek and white throat

Juv   Ad

Ad ♀ ▶ spring Head paler than ♂

Dark legs, unlike Whitethroat

Ad ♂ spring

Ad, autumn ▶ September: browner than in spring

Eastern races not reliably identifiable in the field ▼

Juv, autumn ▶ September: grey cap, darker ear coverts, white eye-ring, pale-edged wing feathers

Small, neat, grey warbler of dense thickets and woodland edge, with white throat against dark cheek, white-sided tail, dark legs. Head darker than Whitethroat, with variable dark cheek or mask effect; back duller, darker brown, and wings uniformly dark. Underside pale pinkish. Juvenile has obvious white eye-ring, thin white line from bill to eye, strong contrast with white throat against grey cheeks, and grey-buff wash across chest. Legs dark, never pale as on Whitethroat. Call a sharp, hard *tek*, less thick than Blackcap; sometimes a high, sharp, thin note. Song a short phrase at intervals: a low warble, quickly becoming a short, fast, wooden rattle or trill, *tikatikatikatikatikatika*. Warble is stronger, trill looser in E Europe.

Subalpine Warbler

White moustache, pink throat

◀ ▶ ♂ **spring**

Juv ▶

Long, thin, white-sided tail

♀ ▶ **spring**

♀ **winter**

Reddish eye and eye-ring, yellow-orange legs

♂ ▶ **1st winter**
Peachy breast, browner wing

Juv ▶

Perky, small warbler of low scrub. Male blue-grey with red eye-ring, white moustache, rusty-pink throat and underparts. Female paler, browner, greyish on head, white eye-ring, hint of white moustache, pinkish throat. Autumn birds browner, tertials dark with pale brown edges, like tiny Whitethroat; legs yellowish. Call repeated *tek*; song fast, twittering.

Spectacled Warbler

♂ **spring** Black face, white eye-ring, rufous wing panel ▼

◀ ♂

Juv ▶

♀ ▶ **spring**

White chin, greyish lower throat

Small, short-winged, long-tailed, in very low vegetation

♀ ▶ **1st winter**

♂ ▶ **1st winter**

Rare warbler of very low vegetation, with rufous wings and white throat. Male has grey head, black face, white eye-ring, and deep pink breast, grey in the centre against the white throat. Female duller, browner, with rusty wings and narrow, inconspicuous dark tertial centres (broader on Whitethroat). Legs yellowish. Call a buzzy *drrr*.

Sardinian Warbler

♂ Long, slim tail often raised

Low, dashing flight

White tail corners show as bird swoops up to perch

Juv ►

♂ ► Looks grey with blacker, white-sided tail

♂ spring ►
Typical grey bird with bold black hood, white chin, red eye

♂ spring ►
Browner-backed individual

▲ ♀ spring
Hood browner, back browner

▼ ♀ 1st winter

▲ Juv Brownest, least contrasted on head but still has dark hood, white throat, reddish eye-ring, long thin tail

Juv ►   ◄ Ad

Common, noisy, restless warbler of low bushes, hedges, gardens, and scrubby hillsides in S Europe. Slim, long-tailed, dark-headed, with white throat. Male has black head, bright white throat, red eye-ring, grey body. Female browner, with greyish head, dull white throat, sandy-buff underside with browner flanks; eye reddish-brown with weaker eye-ring. Both have dark tertials with pale fringes, weakly marked wing coverts. Tail blackish with broad white sides; shows white corners at tip when fanned in flight. Flirts and cocks tail as it shuffles through low vegetation. Call hard *tsek* and frequent, hard, dry, quick, rattling chatter *tschrr-trr-trr-trr-trr-trr-trr-trr*. Song similar with whistles interspersed.

Dartford Warbler

Flits low over ground between shrubs

▼ ♂ spring

(♂)

♂ Spain,
May ▼

♀ 1st
▼ winter

Elusive in
dense cover

♀ ▲
spring

Small, dark,
long slim tail
often raised

▲ Juv ♂

▲ ♂
summer

Slim, long-tailed, dark warbler of low bushes and heath. Little contrast between dark grey of head and back, browner wings and deep rufous underside. Red eye-ring, very short bill. Female duller, browner above, paler on throat. Juvenile paler, greyer with brown back and wings. Call short, nasal, churring buzz: *dzrrrr*. Fast, chattering, rather soft song has same buzzy quality.

Marmora's & Balearic Warblers

Skulking, elusive even
in tiniest bush

Marmora's
♂ ►

Marmora's
♂ winter ►

Marmora's has
throaty call note;
Balearic softer

Marmora's
♀ winter ▲

Balearic ♂ ►
Longer tail,
paler below

Marmora's
juv ▼

Marmora's
♂ 1st winter ▲

Like grey Dartford. Balearic has orange bill base, pale orange-brown legs, whiter throat and paler underparts than Marmora's. Male Marmora's is greyer overall, blackish around the eye, with a yellower bill and darker orange legs. Females of both are browner. Juveniles paler and even browner, like young Dartford but whiter on the belly, paler on the flanks, and greyer above.

Rüppell's Warbler

Reddish eye, red-brown eye-ring, orange legs

♂ Juv

♀ Juv

Pale-edged tertials

♀ autumn ▲

◄ ♀

♀ throat white or spotted

Black alula

◄ ♀ spring

Ad ♂ obvious; other plumages more difficult

Juv ▲

▲ ♀

▲ ♂ spring
Black throat, white moustache unique

Large, slim, grey warbler of SE Europe. Male obvious, with black head and throat, white moustache, red eye-ring. Female slightly browner above; head grey with sharp contrast between dark cheek and white moustache; throat pale grey or spotted. Sharp pale edges to wing feathers. Brick-red legs. Long tail with white sides. Call hard *tak*; song is rhythmic, chattering warble.

Fan-tailed Warbler

Tiny, pale, buff warbler, streaked black and cream, of grassy places

◄ Juv
White throat, buffy body

High song flight, bouncing in rhythm with calls

▲ Ad, autumn
Fresh plumage

Round wings, round tail

Ad, breeding ▶
Wears dull and dark in summer

Striped back, clear, pale rump

Flitting flight, low over ground

White tail spots wear smaller (right side)

Tiny, streaked bird of grassy places. Small chunky body, streaked above, pale below; short, broad, white-tipped tail, blackish with white tips below. Strong creamy and black-brown streaks on back, finely streaked crown, pale eye. Song flight distinctive with high, bouncy undulations, each with far-carrying, metallic, slightly vibrant *dzit* in long, unvarying sequence.

Barred Warbler

Pale primary tips, two pale wingbars ▼

1st autumn ▲
Streaks under tail, dark eye, dark-tipped bill

♀ breeding ▲
Yellow eye, faint barring below, pale wingbars

Size, form and barring recall Wryneck

◀ **♂ 1st summer**
Dark eye

♂ breeding ▲
Yellow eye; strong bars

Above Below

A big grey warbler of woodland edge. Long square tail, short stout bill. Male grey above with two white wingbars, pale below closely barred grey, yellow eye in black ring. Female browner, less barred below. Juvenile pale brownish-grey with two buffish wingbars; barred vent; long pale-edged tail, whitish at corners; dark eye. Call a dry rattle, song a rasping warble, often in flight.

Orphean Warbler

Large with dark cheeks, pale throat, buff or pinkish flanks

♂ 1st winter ▲
Longer body/tail than ♀

♀ Breeding ▲
Pale eye, dark cheek, grey crown, long dark tail edged white

1st summer Both sexes have dark eye ▼
♂   ♀

♂ Breeding
Blackish hood blends into grey nape

Above Below

Hefty, grey warbler with dark cap and mask, pale eye, white throat, white-edged blackish tail, faintly barred undertail coverts, dark legs. Male has grey back, whitish underside. Female slightly browner, crown greyer against dark cheeks. Juvenile browner still, cap grey, dark eye. Call *tak*; song clear thrush-like warbling phrases, more flowing and varied in SE Europe.

216

Blackcap

◀ ♂ **Juv**
Duller than
ad ♀ with
darker cap

◀ ♂ **Breeding**
Grey, black cap

Stocky warbler of thickets,
woods, with hard call and
beautiful song

♀ **Breeding**
Red-brown
cap ▶

♀

♂

Stocky warbler of thickets and woods. Male grey with small
black cap; female browner with less contrasted red-brown cap.
Eye not enclosed by cap (unlike black-capped tits). Wings and
tail plain. Call a hard *tak*. Song a discrete phrase (not prolonged
like thrushes): a rich, full-throated, fast warble, usually with slow
start, suddenly bursting into full flow.

Garden Warbler

Pale brown, buffer below,
with thick bill, round
head, grey on neck

◀ ♂ **Breeding**

Plain warbler of
bushes, woods, with
long, full-throated,
warbling song

◀ ♂ Wingtips short
of tail coverts

♀ Wingtips ▲
equal tail coverts

Juv Pale feather ▲
fringes, some
yeller below

◀ ♀

Stocky, round-headed, short-billed, plain warbler of woods and
bushes. Pale, buffish-brown, paler below. Head almost unmarked,
but hint of pale line over eye and weak darker eyestripe; gentle
expression. Subtle grey patch on neck. Plain wings, flight
feathers sharply tipped pale. Call softer than Blackcap, *tsuk*; song
very similar, but more even, often longer, a richly mellow warble.

217

Goldcrest

Thin black crown with pale central stripe

Plain face except dark eye, thin moustache

◀ ♀ Yellow crest stripe

◀ Dummy caption ♀

Tiny, tame, acrobatic bird of thick conifers, thickets, scrub

Pale wingbar edged blackish

◀ ♂ Orange centre of crest fanned open in display

Minute, dumpy, warbler-like bird of evergreens, thickets. Looks pale olive-green, with distinct dark and light wingbars. Pale, plain face with bold dark eye and faint, short moustache. Narrow black crown with thin central yellow stripe (spread in display). Call thin, high, sharp *see-see-see*; song high-pitched, rhythmic, fast *tidl-eee tidl-eee tidl-eee tidl-eee tidl-di-didli*.

Firecrest

Winter ▶
Clean white below

◀ **Juv**

♀ Yellow crest stripe, less vivid than ♂

Bronze or golden sheen over 'shoulder'

◀▶ ♂ Orange-red crest fanned open in display

Wide black cap with bright central stripe, bold white stripe or wedge over eye, thin eyestripe, grey cheek, green back

Like Goldcrest, but greener, paler below. Broader black crown with central orange stripe, wedge-shaped flash of white over eye, black eyestripe, grey cheek, buff around bill, golden 'shoulder' patch. Call fractionally lower than Goldcrest, sometimes shorter *zi-zi* (Goldcrest can make louder, firmer calls). Song simpler, accelerates into firmer finish *zi-zi-zi-zizizizizizit*.

Spotted Flycatcher

Alert on high or low perch, flying out to catch insects

Ad ♂

Long wings and tail

Subdued colours and quiet voice, but flycatching behaviour draws attention

◄ **Juv**

► **Pied**

◄ **Juv** Strongly spotted cream on back, speckled on head

◄ **Ad** Softly streaked on crown, throat and breast

Wing feathers edged pale

Stands upright on very short legs, long tail; does not shuffle through foliage like a warbler

Broad, flat bill with bristles at base ►

Pale, brownish, quiet, unobtrusive bird of open spaces with plentiful perches: woodland edge, parks, gardens, tennis courts, cemeteries. Perches upright on very short legs, with tail and long wingtips pointing down and flicked (not like typical warbler horizontal pose, and does not slip or hop through foliage). Flies out to catch flying insects with distinct 'snap', immediately returning to perch. Brown, slightly streaked cap, big dark eye, plain brown back, wings darker with obvious pale feather edges. Underside silvery-grey-buff with subtle, blurry streaks on chest. Plain grey-brown tail. Dark, quite thick bill. Juvenile spotted pale buff on back. Call quietly distinctive, slightly vibrant, *zee* or *zee-tiktik*; song quiet, scratchy, with well-spaced notes.

Pied Flycatcher

Juv ▶
Small white
wingbar

♂ One or two spots ▼

**♂ ▲
breeding**

**♀ ▲
breeding**

More often
within tree
foliage than
Spotted,
above open
forest floor

◀ ♂ Spanish
Big forehead spot,
big wingbar, grey
rump

♂ breeding
Tiny white spot
at base of
primaries ▶

**◀
♂ 1st summer**
Brown wings

Migrants mainly coastal,
also in gardens, parks

♀ breeding ▶
White tertial edges, thin
wingbar, small primary patch
may show. No upper wingbar

Dark
moustache,
smudgy
chest

**▲
♀ 1st winter**
Variable white in wing
(lower figure shows
primary patch)

**◀ ♂
1st winter**
Blacker wings
than ♀

Rounded flycatcher of open woodland. Flycatches on the wing,
without returning to same perch (unlike Spotted Flycatcher), or
drops to ground. Easily identified over most of range; can be
confused with Collared and Semi-collared on migration or where
species overlap (Baltic, C Europe). Male black above, white
below, one or two white forehead patches, white panel on closed
wing extending along tertials, white-edged tail. Broad white
primary patch, rump greyish-white on Spanish birds. Female
brown and buff-white with more or less dark moustache, wings
have less white. Juveniles spotted above. Autumn birds have
small pale mark at base of primaries, rich brown back and rump.
Calls *tik, whee*; song hesitant *see see see seeti-tree te-titi tree.*

Semi-collared & Collared Flycatchers

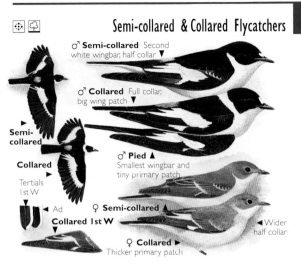

♂ **Semi-collared** Second white wingbar, half collar ▼

♂ **Collared** Full collar, big wing patch ▼

Semi-collared

Collared

Tertials 1st W

Collared 1st W ▼

◀ Ad

♂ **Pied** ▲ Smallest wingbar and tiny primary patch

♀ **Semi-collared** ▲

◀ Wider half collar

♀ **Collared** ▶ Thicker primary patch

Eastern counterparts of Pied Flycatcher. Semi-collared has white throat extending onto neck sides, white-edged tail, large white wing panel, pale rump. Grey-brown female has thin upper wingbar; thin, separated edges to tertials. Collared has full white collar, huge wing patch, whiter rump, plain tail; female has large primary patch, greyish rump, tertial edges merge together.

Red-breasted Flycatcher

Tiny, confiding flycatcher, often perches horizontally with tail raised

♂ **1st summer** ▶

♂ **breeding** ▲ Variable amount of red on throat

Bold white panel each side of tail

Soft brown and buff with pale underside

♀ **breeding** Brownish, dull ▶

▼ **Juv, autumn** Peachy-buff below, pale eye-ring

cocks tail

Small, engaging, with round head, black eye in pale ring, white side panels on black tail. Summer male has grey head, variable red throat. Other plumages duller; brown above, buff-white below with wash of deeper apricot across chest. Flies after insects from perch, flits quickly through foliage, flicks wings and tail. High, sharp song descends from slow start; short, rattled *trrrt*.

Bearded Tit

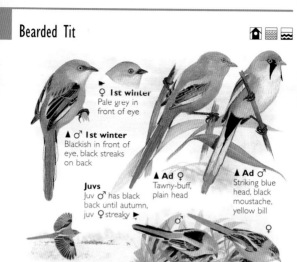

♀ **1st winter**
Pale grey in
front of eye

▲ ♂ **1st winter**
Blackish in front of
eye, black streaks
on back

Juvs
Juv ♂ has black
back until autumn,
juv ♀ streaky ▶

▲ **Ad ♀**
Tawny-buff,
plain head

▲ **Ad ♂**
Striking blue
head, black
moustache,
yellow bill

Small, tawny-coloured bird, easily identified by reedbed habitat, pinging calls and long tail. Whirrs low over reedbeds, hops through reeds. Pale orange-buff with white-edged tail, cream and black streaks on wings, bright waxy-yellow bill. Male has grey-blue head with drooped black moustache. Juvenile has blacker back. Calls metallic, ringing *zing, pwik, ting*.

Penduline Tit

▶ **Ad ♀** Narrower
mask, pale breast

◀ **Imm**
Hint of dusky
mask

◀ **Ad ♂**

▲ **Juv**
Lacks
mask

Quick, flitting,
usually low flight

Nest, incomplete (left)
and finished

Small, rounded, short-tailed bird of reeds, willows, and poplars, along rivers, in marshes. Grey head, black mask, red-brown back, pink-buff underside. Male has broadest mask and deep rusty-red wing panel. Immature pale brown on head, without mask. Sharp, dark bill, black legs, rusty wing. Call distinctive, far-carrying, high, long, faintly descending *peeeeeee*.

Long-tailed Tit

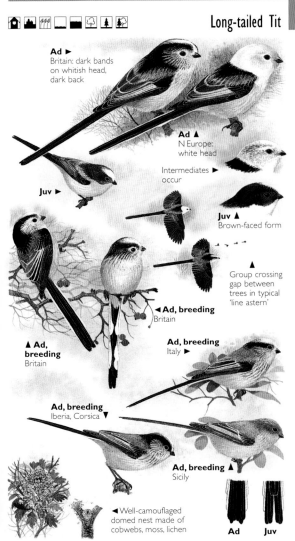

Ad ►
Britain: dark bands
on whitish head,
dark back

Ad ▲
N Europe;
white head

Intermediates ►
occur

Juv ►

Juv ▲
Brown-faced form

▲
Group crossing
gap between
trees in typical
'line astern'

◄ Ad, breeding
Britain

**▲ Ad,
breeding**
Britain

Ad, breeding
Italy ►

Ad, breeding
Iberia, Corsica ▼

Ad, breeding
Sicily ▲

**◄ Well-camouflaged
domed nest made of
cobwebs, moss, lichen**

Ad   **Juv**

Tiny, round-bodied, long-tailed bird of woodland, hedgerows,
thickets. Round head, minute bill, round body and thin tail give
distinctive shape. Typically moves through woods or along
hedgerows in small flocks, crossing gaps one or two at a time.
Looks pale, rather drab, with blackish band over eye extending
onto black back; dark wings, dark pink shoulders and pink flush
on lower body. Juvenile darker, lacks pink. Almost oblivious to
people, often remarkably tame. Acrobatic when feeding;
increasingly comes to garden feeders and may feed on ground
below, tail cocked. Constant calls from flock: abrupt *pit* or *tup*,
rolling *d-r-rrrrr* and sharp, high, colourless *zeee-zeee-zeee*, with
less emphasis than Goldcrest call.

223

Sombre Tit

Sooty cap and bib enclose wide, white wedge-shaped cheek patch

Ad ▲

Bigger than Marsh or Willow Tit, richer brown above

◀**Ad** Quite striking pale edges on wing feathers, but plain tail

Large, thickset, black-capped tit of bushy slopes and rocky areas with scattered trees in SE Europe. Dull black cap and big, brown-black bib isolate white cheeks as long wedge-shapes on each side of face. Back brown, underside paler grey with no hint of brown or buff. Calls include *si-si-si*, grating *zrree-zrree-zrree* and fast *schrip schrip schrip* song.

Siberian & Azure Tits

Siberian Tit
Grey bloom above wears to rusty-brown

Siberian
Pale wing panel, big white cheek, brownish cap

Azure Tit
Unique blue and white with broad white wingbar, hindwing and tail sides

Siberian is big, brown-capped tit with black bib, large white cheek patch, brown back and rusty-brown flanks, found in forests of N Scandinavia. Azure is mainly C Asian, rare in NE Europe, longish-tailed, pale grey-blue and white with white crown, blackish eyestripe, blue hindneck and blue on wings; tail blue in centre, extensively white at sides.

Marsh Tit

♂ has longer tail than ♀

Smooth black cap, small bib, plain brown above, wing panel weak at best; grey-buff below

Northern form ▲ Greyer

No white on nape, no wingbars, no green, blue or yellow

Pit-chew call always best clue

Small, neat, greyish woodland bird. Black cap down to eye level and onto hindneck, whitish cheek; small, quite clean-cut black bib. Grey-brown back, plain wings, grey-buff underside, typically less warm-coloured than Willow Tit. Calls include diagnostic, loud *pit-chew*; scolding *piti-dee-dee-dee-dee*. Song quick, simple *schipa-schipa-schipa-schipa*.

Willow Tit

Willow Tit has longer cap, bigger bib, thicker bill than Marsh Tit

◄ **Willow**

◄ **Marsh**

Broad head, big white cheeks

Typically pale wing panel and rusty-buff flanks useful clues

Northern form Larger, greyer, bigger white cheeks ▲

Very like Marsh Tit, often in damper thickets of willow, hedgerows, tangled undergrowth. Thickset, more bull-necked shape. Faintly rougher, duller black cap, longer white cheek patch; bigger, less sharp bib. Pale panel along closed wing, flanks usually brighter, tawny-buff (but N European birds paler). Buzzing, nasal *airr-airr-airr*, high thin *zi zi*, song *piew piew piew*.

Crested Tit

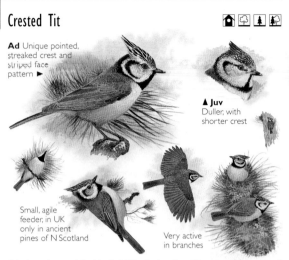

Ad Unique pointed, streaked crest and striped face pattern ▶

▲ **Juv** Duller, with shorter crest

Small, agile feeder, in UK only in ancient pines of N Scotland

Very active in branches

Obvious brownish, black-bibbed tit of conifer woods, or mixed woods with patches of pine and spruce. Unique pointed crest, chequered black and white. Black outline to grey cheek; white neck side, edged black. Brown back, paler underside. Call a characteristic purring, stuttering trill: *p't'rrrr-r'p*. Song fast, mixing calls with sharper notes.

Coal Tit

Grey and buff, with white wingbars, white cheeks and unique white nape patch

White nape

Barely bigger than Goldcrest (lower)

Irish birds yellower on cheek ▶

▲ **Ad** UK and Iberia: more olive above

Tiny black-capped woodland tit with no green, blue, or yellow. Head glossy black with white oblong on nape, big white cheek. Greyish back, two white wingbars, underside clean, bright buff to brownish-buff. Some populations have yellowish cheek, browner back. Call clear, ringing, sad *ty-zee, tyooo, suuu, see see see*. Song fast, rhythmic, bright *sitchu-sitchu-sitchu*.

226

Blue Tit

Ad ♂ spring ▶

Blue cap, ringed with white

White cheek, dark blue bib and collar

Worn ♂ looks like ♀ below ▼

Ad ♀ ▶

▲ Juv Yellower on face

Tiny, common, familiar bird of woods, gardens. Looks pale greenish or yellow. Blue cap ringed white, white cheek, dark bib and neck ring broadening into blue hindneck. Blue wings and tail with white wingbar. Underside pale yellow with short, thin, dark central line. Calls *sisisi, sisi-si-du*; song quick, thin with final trill, *see-see-seedudrrrr*.

Great Tit

Black cap, glossed blue, bold white cheek, black bib and central stripe beneath

♂

♀

♂ Broad band

Many are a creamier, paler yellow below

▲ Juv

▲ ♂ Longer body than ♀

Largest common tit, with bold blue-black head and round white cheek. Black chin extends as broad stripe down middle of yellow underside (widest on male, narrower on female). Green back, grey-blue wings with white bar; grey-blue tail edged white. Calls varied, confusing, include *pink pink*, *chi-wity*, scolding *che-che-che*. Song a ringing *tea-cher tea-cher* or *ti-ti-cher*.

227

Treecreeper

Thin, curved bill

Restricted to trees (rarely walls, rocks)

Northern birds paler, greyer ▼

Long, narrow, pale wing stripe in flight

Richly mottled brown, silky white below

Shuffles, spirals up trees, hangs under branches

Zigzag notches on primaries (see Short-toed)

Primary tips: bigger on Short-toed (right) ◄

Woodland bird, rarely away from tree trunks and branches; creeps and spirals mouse-like over bark. Mottled brown above, white below, flared pale stripe over eye, brighter rump. Thin, slightly downcurved bill. In flight shows long, narrow, pale wingbar. Call thin, whistling *srreeee*; song a sweet, lilting phrase with a flourish at the end, like quick, short Willow Warbler.

Short-toed Treecreeper

Very like Treecreeper, but fractionally duller; typically white throat set against dull underside; slightly rounder; tail more angled in to tree

Fractionally longer bill

Song most useful, consistent clue; but varies

Lacks zigzag effect (see Treecreeper)

◄ More complete pale edge to alula

Compare fore edge of wingbar ◄

Bigger pale tertial tips ►

Treecreeper

Larger, whiter ► primary tips

Short-toed Treecreeper

Exceedingly like Treecreeper: a little duller, earthy brown; white throat tends to contrast with dull underparts; browner flanks. Sharper white tips to primaries. More even, diagonal pale bar across closed wing (less stepped). Sometimes looks slightly rounder, with tail more angled in as support. Call firmer, clear *siut*; song distinctive, short, separated notes *seet-seet-seet-seteroi-tit*.

Nuthatch

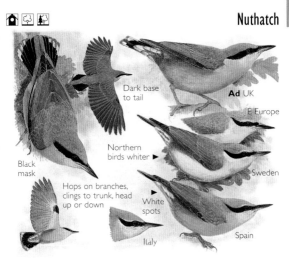

Ad UK

E Europe

Sweden

Spain

Italy

Dark base to tail

Northern birds whiter ▶

White spots ▶

Black mask

Hops on branches, clings to trunk, head up or down

Woodland bird, preferring big trees. Big head, stout bill, wedge-shaped body with short, square tail, not used as prop. Grey above, buff below, black stripe through eye. Flanks richer orange-buff. Tail dark at sides with white corners. Loud, varied calls include fluty whistle, *swee swee swee swee*, sharp *zit*, and fast, whistled, ringing trill on even note.

Corsican & Rock Nuthatches

Corsican ♂ ▼

Corsican ♀ ▼

White stripe over eye

Corsican juv ▲

No white on tail

Rock Plain tail; white face below long black stripe ▶

◀ **Rock** Big, pale, very noisy; on rocks, ruins

No black

Corsican is small, pale nuthatch, only on Corsica: dark cap, white stripe over eye, dark eyestripe. Rock is big, bold, pale nuthatch, on crags, ruins, boulders in SE Europe: very white face below long black stripe through eye, white to pale buff underside, plain grey tail. Rock's loud calls ring around valleys and cliffs: clear whistles, trills, often accelerating while descending in pitch.

Wallcreeper

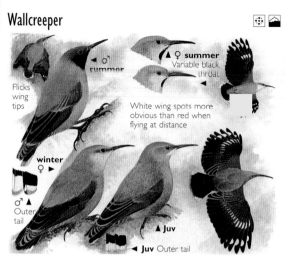

♂ summer

♀ summer
Variable black throat

Flicks wing tips

White wing spots more obvious than red when flying at distance

winter ♀ ▶

♂ ▲ Outer tail

▲ Juv

◀ Juv Outer tail

Stunning bird of cliffs, gorges, quarries, and large buildings in winter. Good views reveal strong red on broad, white-spotted wings. In winter has white throat; in summer black throat, most intense and extensive on male. Short, square tail. Fine, curved bill. Weak, flitting, butterfly-like flight, in short bounds between feeding places on rock face. High, thin, whistled song.

Lesser Grey Shrike

♀ summer

◀ ♂ summer
Broad forehead band

Thick bill and long wingtip useful clues in all plumages

Pink breast

Broad wingbar

Juv ◀

Lesser Grey
Long wingtip

1st winter
(Sept–Oct) ▲
Grey forehead, thick bill

Great Grey ▲

Upright, long-tailed, long-winged shrike. Pale grey, black, and white, with broad black mask across forehead, large white wing patch. Underside flushed pink. Immature barred above, forehead grey, mask from bill through eye. Stout bill. Wingtips extend to base of tail. Drops to ground or chases after prey; hovers over nesting area in song flight. Call a harsh *tcha-tcha*.

Great & Southern Grey Shrikes

Large black, white, and grey shrike with slim bill, short wings, long tail

Great Grey Shrike

Ad ♀ Some slightly barred below ▶

Juv ▶

Ad Single or 'double' wing patch ▼ ▶

Steppe Grey Shrike Rare vagrant with pale forehead, narrow wings, large white patch; long wingtip vital clue ▼

Pale Ukraine race, more white above ▶

▲ Single (top) or 'double' wing patch

▲ Seven primary tips (four in close group)

Eight primary tips (partly hidden if tucked up tight) ◀

1st winter Pale in front of eye, pale bill

Southern Grey, 1st winter ▶

Steppe Grey ▶ Huge primary patch

Upper tail coverts beyond wingtips

Southern Grey

Southern Grey ▲ Darker than Great Grey, pinker below, longer body, shorter wings, longer tail

Southern ▶ White only on outer wing

Large, long-tailed, short-winged shrikes; wingtips fall short of base of tail which is often swung sideways. Can be elusive, but often seen on exposed perches on trees, bushes, wires. Chase small birds or flutter down to ground for prey. Great Grey Shrike pale grey above, white below. White line above black mask, white bar on wings; black tail, broadly edged white. Female faintly barred below. Juvenile duller, tinged buff, more barred beneath, paler mask, bill pale at base. Southern Grey Shrike in France and Iberia a little darker above, darker grey-pink below, less white over black mask except from eye to above bill: variable across SW Europe, N Africa, Middle East. Steppe Grey Shrike (rare vagrant) paler, with pale bill, longer wingtip, mask only behind eye.

231

Woodchat Shrike

◄Ad ♂
Black forehead
and mask

♀

Ad ♀
▼

♀

Juv ►

**◄W Med
islands, no
wing patch**

◄Ad Underside
of tail

Juv ►
Underside
of tail

Juv Pale ▲
rump, upper
tail coverts

Black-centred
rufous tertials

◄1st winter

Relatively rounded shrike, with long tail, bold black and white
plumage, rufous crown. Male has boldest black mask, richest
rufous cap. Large white shoulder patch, white rump, white on
outer wing (except on Balearic birds) give striking pied effect in
flight. Juvenile grey-brown, barred; scapulars whitish with dark
crescents, buffish wingbar. Usually quiet.

Masked Shrike

◄Ad ♂
Wears whiter
below by autumn

White forehead

Bold white
wing patch

Juv
◄
Ad ♂

Long, slim,
dark tail

◄Ad ♀

Juv
Underside
of tail ►

Juv has pale-centred,
greyish tertials ▲

◄Juv
Greyer above than
Woodchat Shrike

Slim, rare shrike of SE Europe, black and white with big white
forehead extending back over eye, apricot-buff flanks. Long,
slim, black tail with white sides. Juvenile like slim, greyer young
Woodchat Shrike but with whiter wing patch, darker bars on
grey back, blackish tail (less brown) edged white (not buff),
slimmer bill. Call a dry rattle, song a rough warble.

Red-backed Shrike

◄Ad ♂
Grey head,
black mask
▼

Ad ♀ ◄
Grey-headed
type

White sides
to black tail

◄ Juv Variable
duller to redder-
brown above
and on tail

▲ Juv Rufous,
barred on back,
scapulars rusty,
tail plain

♀ rusty to
duller brown,
head greyish
or browner;
darker cheek
patch, barred
breast **►**

Ad ♀
Brown-headed
type
◄

Ad ♂ ►
Grey head and rump,
black and white tail unique
for shrike (Kestrel much
bigger; Linnet, Penduline Tit
much smaller)

Small, handsome, brown-backed shrike of upland meadows, heaths, bushy places. Sits rather inconspicuously on sides of bushes, in hedges or on low fence wires. Bill quite stout, head rounded, wingtips and tail long. Male obvious, blue-grey on head with bold black mask, rusty-brown back, grey rump, black tail with white sides, pink below. Female browner, head dull grey-brown with dark cheek patch, underside greyish with fine brown crescentic bars. Dark brown tail. Juvenile brown above with dark bars, some more barred than others, scapulars as back (not whiter as on greyer young Woodchat Shrike); underside whitish, barred grey, tail dark to rusty brown. Call harsh *tche*; song weak, warbling, squeaky chatter.

Rose-coloured Starling

Juv ◀
Pale rump

Ad ♀ Newly
moulted; buff
tips wear off ▶

Breeding
Glossy black
and rose
pink

Juv remains in first
plumage into winter

Juv has
short
yellow
bill

Juv ▲
Pale, wings and
tail darker

Migrant starling in E Europe, vagrant in W; migrants often fly
by in tight groups. Adult pale rose-pink, with glossy black
crested head, black wings, vent, and tail. Bill stout, short, pink.
Winter and immature birds dull, pink-washed brown. Juvenile
(until winter) pale grey-brown, wings darker with pale feather
edges, rump markedly paler; bill short, yellowish, but legs pink.

Spotless Starling

Ad, late summer
Dull, worn ▶

Wings have dark
red-brown tinge in
flight in strong light

Summer ♂ has long,
pointed body feathers

♂ spring
Glossy, oily
look ▶

▼ throat

Winter ◀
Tiny pale spots;
pointed throat
feathers. ♀ may
retain spots in
spring

Juv ◀
Darker than
Starling, but
paler throat

Common starling of Iberia, extreme S France. Adult intensely
dark with dull purple sheen, browner wings in flight. Spotted
with small, greyish dots in winter. Female greyer than male, with
dark feather edges. Yellow bill, with blue (male) or pinkish
(female) base in spring; legs deep pink. Juvenile dark with paler
throat. Loud, ringing song with long, whistled, piercing notes.

Starling

Swirling flocks circle to evade foraging hawk

Sharp face, triangular wings, short tail and quick, straight or undulating flight

Catches flying insects at height, slightly clumsily

◄ Pale underwing contrasts with body

Juv ►
Brown, dark mask, black spike bill

♂ summer ►
Blackest plumage

◄ ♀ **winter**
Spots merge together on pale face; bright wing edges

Waves wings as it sings

Short tail

Bill dark in winter

♂ winter ►

♀ **summer**

Spring

♂ Sum

♀ Sum

Probes soil as it shuffles forward

Common, sociable, noisy, quarrelsome bird of woods, parks, gardens, farmland, city centres. Very dark, with sharp bill, flat head, stout body, short tail. Wings triangular in flight, sharply pointed; flocks look like smoky swarms at distance. Adult blackish, glossed green and purple in summer, yellow bill, orange legs. In winter spotted with pale V-shaped feather tips overall, often merging into whitish face and chin; bolder, rounder spots on lower body, scaly undertail. Wing feathers edged bright rufous-buff. Juvenile mousy-brown, dark mask and dark, pointed bill; occasional variant paler than Rose-coloured, but less body/wing/rump contrast. Call loud, raucous *schweer*, sharp *chit* in alarm; song a series of rattles and whistles.

235

Golden Oriole

Ad ♂ ►

Juv recalls Green Woodpecker but flight thrush-like

Ad ♂
Clear view reveals stunning yellow ►

Ad ♀ ►
Lacks black mask of ♂

Juv ►
Greenest plumage, streaked below

Yellow tail corners

▲ **2nd year ♀**
♂ has wider yellow primary patch

◄ Juv ▼

Secretive bird of leafy woods, riverside trees, plantations. Thrush-like but slim. Male eyecatching yellow and black, with pink bill. Bright female similar without black near bill, most are greener with yellow rump, dark wings, pale underside. Juvenile more streaked. Flight quick with deep wingbeats. Song loud, fluty, brief yodel, *ee-lo-we* or *weedl-o*; call low, harsh *shaaak*.

Nutcracker

◄ Ad

◄ Ad Striking white vent and tip to tail, spots under wing

Perches on treetop; drops to ground like a stone

Primary tips thin on ad (left), wider on juv (right) ►

Obvious white on tail

▲ Thick-billed

▲ Thin-billed

▲ **Ad** Big white spots, dark cap, blue-black wings

Unique Jackdaw-sized spotted crow of mountain conifer forest. Dark brown cap, glossy blackish wings. Brown body with teardrop white spots; eyecatching white vent. Tail has black base, white tip. Stout, pointed, black bill (slimmer on Siberian birds that rarely move west in large numbers). In flight looks long-headed, short-tailed. Call a rattling *krrrrr*, but mostly silent.

Jay

▲ Slow, laboured, rowing flight action

Big white rump

◄ Blue evenly barred on ad, irregularly on juv

Black and white more striking than blue

◄ Ad Body pink or greyer depending on race

A rather small, shy, woodland crow with striking white rump and wing patches. Mostly pale buff-pink. Pale, streaked crown, black moustache and thick dark bill. Large, barred, bright blue patch on wing, but white midwing panel in front of black secondaries more obvious. White rump, all-black tail. Call loud, harsh, tearing *shraik*; also mewing *piyew*.

Siberian Jay

Rufous above and below on tail and wing coverts

Dark cap and face, stubby, thick bill

▲ Juv Darker

▲ Ads Silver-grey, brown and rusty pattern unique ►

▲ Ad

Small, darkish jay of far northern forests, often around forest camps. Dark brown cap and dark face, greyish back, rusty-orange wing patch, rump and sides of tail. Short, quite small bill. Perches rather upright, often with body feathers fluffed out. Flight swift, agile through trees. Mostly silent, but flocks give short, harsh, Jay-like screaming notes.

237

Magpie

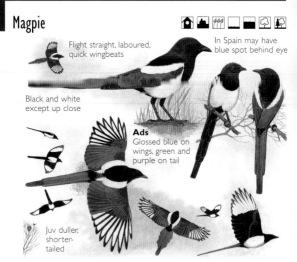

Flight straight, laboured, quick wingbeats

In Spain may have blue spot behind eye

Black and white except up close

Ads
Glossed blue on wings, green and purple on tail

Juv duller, shorter-tailed

Common bird of farmland, woodland edge, suburbs, parks. Long, tapered tail, strikingly black and white plumage. Head, back, and breast dull black; shoulders and underside white. Wings glossed steely-blue, but tips largely white when spread. Vent and rump black, tail glossed green and purple. Flight quick with deep, fast, even wingbeats. Loud *tchak tchak tchak*.

Azure-winged Magpie

Ad ▲
Soft blue wings and tail, black cap

Smooth, direct flight with regular wingbeats

Juv ▲

Blue wears paler, more purplish

◄ Juv
Speckled cap

Slender, neat magpie of Iberian pinewoods. Often social, active, agile when feeding around tree trunks and in canopy. Glossy black cap down to cheeks; white neck and throat. Body dull greyish-beige, paler below, wings and tail pale greyish-blue. No great contrast in tone between wing, tail, and body colours. Nasal, rising *brreee*; rattling *krrrrrr*.

Chough

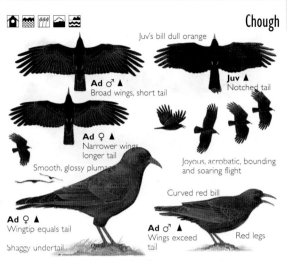

Ad ♂ ▲
Broad wings, short tail

Juv's bill dull orange

Juv ▲
Notched tail

Ad ♀ ▲
Narrower wings
longer tail

Smooth, glossy plumage

Joyous, acrobatic, bounding
and soaring flight

Curved red bill

Ad ♀ ▲
Wingtip equals tail

Ad ♂ ▲
Wings exceed
tail

Red legs

Shaggy undertail

Excitable, agile, noisy crow of cliffs, high peaks, and pastures. All glossy black, with bluish sheen on wings. Red bill, slightly decurved; red legs. In flight, tail square, short; wings long, square, with deeply-fingered tips; coverts show darker than flight feathers below. Bounding flight with deep undulations and dives. Loud, ringing, explosive *chee-ow!* or *peeyah.*

Alpine Chough

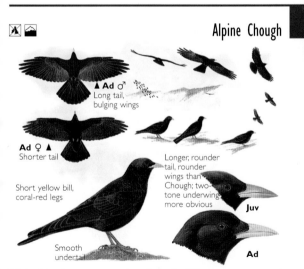

▲ Ad ♂
Long tail,
bulging wings

Ad ♀ ▲
Shorter tail

Short yellow bill,
coral-red legs

Longer, rounder
tail, rounder
wings than
Chough; two-
tone underwing
more obvious

Juv

Smooth
undertail

Ad

High-altitude crow, around peaks and cliffs, on close-cropped mountain pastures, often with Chough. Shiny black. Slightly curved, stout, yellow bill; red legs. On ground, tail looks long; in flight, tail rather rounded, wings rounder than Chough's, less deeply fingered; dark coverts obvious. Flock calls in chorus, with loud, shrill *shriiiii*, penetrating *zieee*, deeper *krru.*

239

Jackdaw

Flight steady, direct, or fast and dashing in tight groups

Greyish body, blacker wings, but little gloss

Acrobatic around cliffs, ruins, big buildings

Smaller than Carrion or Hooded Crow; more pigeon-like form with swept-back, more tapered wings

Distinct black cap, pale eye

Short head, longish tail; rounder than Chough

Juv ▲
Dull, darker nape, duller eye

Ad ▲
N Europe: paler patch at base of grey nape; wears duller, darker, like southern birds

Daurian Jackdaw ▲
Rare vagrant in N Europe

Rook   Jackdaw   Rook
Jackdaw

Small, greyish, black-capped crow with short bill, rounded head, rather rounded wings, pale eye. Short, stout bill. Dark face, black crown. Cheeks, nape, and hindneck pale grey (with a paler band at lower edge in N Europe). Rest of body and wings very dark, dull grey, blacker on wings. Black legs. Rounder-winged, longer-tailed than Chough, more pigeon-like flight shape. Flocks chase around rooftops and chimneys, soar over treetops, dive about cliffs and quarries, and join Rooks feeding in fields. Stands upright, but crouches when feeding. Flight quick, direct, with deep wingbeats. Frequent sharp, nasal *jak*, *chiak*, *kya* and similar notes; often calls in mixed flock with Rooks, sounding generally higher, more ringing in character.

Raven

Long head and neck, long wedge- or diamond-shaped tail

Carrion Crow
To same scale as Raven above left

▲ Bulging inner wing

Spreads primaries to make loud rasping sound at times

Inner primary moult exaggerates angularity

Deep, regular wingbeats; also often soars

Usually obvious in flight but hard to tell from crow on ground at distance

Very large, arched bill

May fly with head and throat feathers raised, creating big-headed effect

▲ Ad
Very big, all black

Pointed throat feathers may be raised in 'beard' ▼

Carrion Crow
To same scale

Biggest crow, found on high moors, cliffs from sea level to highest peaks, lowland forests, and upland farmland. All black plumage. Long, thick, powerful bill, upper edge arched more than Carrion Crow. Feathers of throat long, often tight and smooth but can be ragged and loose, even in flight when head then looks very bulky and heavy. Head protrudes in flight more than Carrion Crow; tail longer, more rounded (more like Rook) or wedge-shaped (distinctive diamond shape when fanned). Long, deeply-fingered wings, often angled back. Strong flight, with regular beats, frequent soars; often rolls onto back briefly. Calls with loud, echoing, deep *prruk prruk* and ringing *tonk tonk*; soft rattling and whistling subsong.

241

Carrion Crow

Steady, strong flight, rarely soars

Squarest wings and tail among common crows

All black at all ages and seasons

Short, square tail, fingered wingtips

Thick bill, flat head

Tightly-feathered thighs

Rook   Crow

Big, flat-headed, all-black crow with strong bill. Has thicker bill than Rook, less pointed. Plumage generally neater, tighter-looking. In flight wings are more square, more even in width, and broader-based. Flies with steady, regular wingbeats, not gliding or soaring so much as Rook. Tail squarer than Raven's. Call a harsh, grating croak, *crarr crarr crarr.*

Hooded Crow

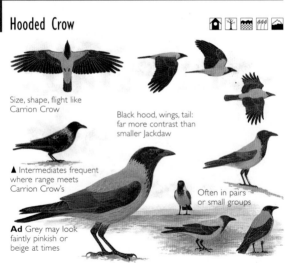

Size, shape, flight like Carrion Crow

Black hood, wings, tail: far more contrast than smaller Jackdaw

▲ Intermediates frequent where range meets Carrion Crow's

Often in pairs or small groups

Ad Grey may look faintly pinkish or beige at times

Equivalent of Carrion Crow in Ireland, Isle of Man, N Scotland, N, E, and SE Europe. Exactly like Carrion Crow except hindneck, back, and lower body pale grey, more or less tinged brownish in some lights. Where range overlaps with Carrion Crow, some hybrids have much less grey, more extensive black breast. Calls like Carrion Crow: harsh, raucous *crarr crarr crarr.*

242

Rook

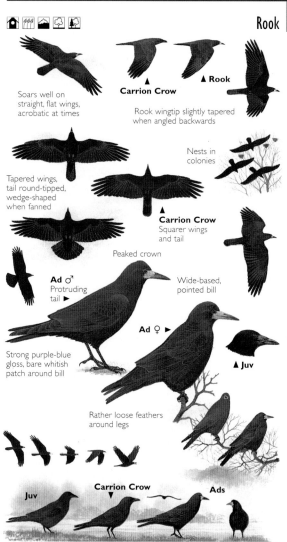

Soars well on straight, flat wings, acrobatic at times

▲ **Carrion Crow**   ▲ **Rook**

Rook wingtip slightly tapered when angled backwards

Tapered wings, tail round-tipped, wedge-shaped when fanned

Nests in colonies

▲ **Carrion Crow**
Squarer wings and tail

Peaked crown

Ad ♂
Protruding tail ▶

Wide-based, pointed bill

Ad ♀ ▶

Strong purple-blue gloss, bare whitish patch around bill

▲ **Juv**

Rather loose feathers around legs

Juv   **Carrion Crow** ▼   **Ads**

Large, black crow of farmland, woods, spinneys, town parks. All glossy purple-black except for bare, parchment-white face. Bill longer, slimmer, more pointed than Carrion Crow's; forehead tends to be steeper, crown more peaked, even on juvenile which has all-black face. Underbody plumage a little looser, more ragged than Carrion Crow's, with 'baggy trousers' effect. More consistently social (but Carrion Crow may feed and often roosts in big flocks); nests in tree-top colonies (Carrion Crow nests are solitary). Rather rounded tail, narrow wingtips. Often soars, especially above rookery. Calls vary: deep, even *kaah kaah kaah* in loud, pleasing chorus from colony; strangled, slightly ringing, almost trumpet-like notes frequent.

243

House Sparrow

Common, social, noisy bird of gardens, parks, fields. Male streaked brown above, plain grey below. Grey crown broadly edged deep rusty-red, grey cheeks, and bold black bib (biggest in summer). Female paler, yellower-brown, streaked pale above, pale buff below; broad pale stripe behind eye. Various short, cheery, cheeping, chirruping calls, prolonged into song.

Tree Sparrow

Small, neat, smart sparrow, sexes alike. Cap rich chocolate brown with no grey, unlike House Sparrow. Thin white collar, white cheeks with bold, square, black spot. Neat black bib against grey-buff underside. Broad pale wingbar. Feeds on ground with tail often raised. Dumpier, rounder than House Sparrow, smaller than Spanish. Distinctive hard *tek tek* call.

Spanish Sparrow

♂ winter Pale feather edges obscure pattern ►

Heavy bill

▼ summer

♀ As House Sparrow; some faintly streaked below, with bolder marks above ►

♂ summer ▲ Striking white cheeks, black streaks above and below

♂ summer ► Deep rufous cap with no grey, white over eye; heavy streaks

Striking sparrow of SE Europe, local in S, often in large flocks and colonies. Male in summer has rich brown crown, bold white cheeks, black bib extending into broad black streaks all over silvery underside. Black reduced in winter, paler streaks above. White lines over eye. Female very like female House Sparrow, bill a little thicker; sometimes with faint pale streaks below.

Italian Sparrow

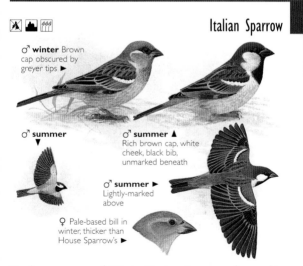

♂ winter Brown cap obscured by greyer tips ►

♂ summer ▼

♂ summer ▲ Rich brown cap, white cheek, black bib, unmarked beneath

♂ summer ► Lightly-marked above

♀ Pale-based bill in winter, thicker than House Sparrow's ►

Handsome sparrow of N Italy, Corsica. Appears to be a stable hybrid between House Sparrow and Spanish Sparrow. Male has brown cap, white cheek, but bib like House Sparrow without extension onto plain grey underparts. Lacks dark cheek spot of Tree Sparrow. In winter cap obscured by buffish streaks; black bib much reduced. Female like House Sparrow.

245

Rock Sparrow

Ad ►

Juv ►

Ad ►

Tail spots vary individually

Above

Below

White tail spots; yellow breast spot, hard to see

Streaked body; striped head

Pale-looking, streaky sparrow of rocks, gorges, sandy and gravelly cuttings, and eroded valleys. Crown striped black and buff, bill large and pale (most obvious features at long range). In flight broad tail shows big pale spots across tip. Back streaked; underside pale with long, broad, dark streaks. Call a loud, twanging, nasal *see-waaii, swui*.

Trumpeter Finch

Ad ♀ ►

◄ Juv

Pinkish or sandy on wing

Imm ♂ ►
October

Juv ►

Ad ♂ ►

Pinkish or bright pink rump

Thick bill, beady eye in plain head

Ad ♂ ▲

Juv ▲
November

Pale, stubby-billed, pinkish-grey finch of desert and rocky areas. Male has orange-red bill and forehead, blue-grey head, paler throat. Body brownish above, pinkish below; wings pinkish with black streaks. Rump pinkest area. Female and winter male greyer, with pinkish-buff bill, greyish breast, pinkish belly, but overall pale and with little contrast. Call loud, nasal *aap*.

Hawfinch

Fast flight, dashing off over tree tops in sweeping bounds

Ad, winter
Pale buffish bill ▶

Big, stocky, bull-necked, short-tailed finch with heavy bill

White tail tip usually striking

Long, broad wings with white band

Juv ▶

◀**Ad ♀ summer**
Like ♂ except grey on secondaries

Ad ♂ summer

Rich browns, orange-buff, black and white

Rests high in treetops

♀

Unique billhook primary shape ◀

Feeds on ground in winter, flies straight up if disturbed

♀

Large, elusive, shy woodland finch. Often feeds on ground and flies up to top of canopy when disturbed, or perches high on tall tree top. Looks bulky, big-headed, and short-tailed, recalling crossbills. Very deep, triangular bill, blue-grey and black on summer male, otherwise yellow-buff. Orange-buff crown and cheeks, black eye patch and small black bib. Grey neck, dark brown back, buff-pink underside. Blue-black wings with broad whitish diagonal band. Tail pale rufous-buff with broad white tip, most evident in flight. Broad white wingbar obvious in fast, direct flight. Juvenile paler, yellower below with short dark bars. Call sharp, Robin-like *tik* or *tikit*, slightly more grating than Robin; song quiet, unexceptional.

247

Brambling

♂ autumn
Long white rump
orange forewing ►

♀ autumn ▼
White rump

♂ summer
Black head and
back ▼

♀ White belly
contrasts with
darker breast,
unlike Chaffinch ►

Orange to
yellowish breast,
white belly

♂ spring Pale grey ▲
edges to feathers obscure black
on upperparts, quickly wear off

♀ summer Back
may wear to plain
brown ►

▲ **♂ winter**
Yellow bill

♀ winter Pale nape,
dark band on side
of neck ►

▼ Back feather has broad
pale tip in autumn, narrow
in spring, none by summer

◄ Wing covert
Orange tip fades to white

Small, neat, longish-tailed finch, very like Chaffinch in shape and
plumage pattern. Summer male has black head and bill, black
back, pale orange wing patch, orange breast, white belly, black
and white wings, long white rump (obvious in flight). In winter
much of black is obscured by rufous-buff feather edges, which
wear away in spring; resembles Chaffinch, but with yellow bill;
orange-buff breastband much more contrasted against white
belly. Female like winter male but duller, with greyish crown
edged dark brown, and buffish cheeks surrounded by grey; nape
has pale grey central patch and dark sides; yellow bill with dark
tip. Call harder than Chaffinch in flight, *tep*; nasal, twangy
zwaink. Song is loud, deep, short buzz, *dzzairr*.

Chaffinch

Bold white shoulder, wingbar and outer tail feathers, greenish rump

♂

♂

♀

♂

♂

♀

♀

♂ spring ▲
Pale tips wear off to reveal blue cap, deep brown back, pink breast

♀ spring ▲
Olive, becomes greyer during summer. White wingbars may be hidden under scapulars

Juv ▲
Buff rump

♂ ▲ winter

♀ winter

♀ ► autumn

Common, often tame, long-tailed finch of woods, parks, gardens, fields, and hedges, with distinctive bold white wingbars and tail sides. Summer male has blue-grey cap against pink cheeks, blackish mark around eye, blue bill. Soft, muted orange-pink breast. Brown back, green rump, dark wings with pale yellowish feather edges. Bold white median covert bar, narrower but longer lower wingbar. On winter male much of blue-grey and pink is obscured by pale buff tips. Female has same wing and tail pattern (lower wingbar yellower) but is dull, pale, greyish-olive, paler greyish on belly, less white than Brambling. Flight call single, simple, soft *chup*, frequent loud *pink*, *pilip*, *hueet*. Song a loud, bright, fast rattling phrase with terminal flourish.

249

Greenfinch

Yellow on base of tail most obvious feature when flying away

Yellow on wings most obvious from side

Ad ♂ breeding ◄

Ad ♀ ▲ breeding

Winter pair ▲

♂ has more yellow on wings and tail than ♀ at same age or season

Chunky finch with deeply notched tail, long wings, thick, pale bill

Dark in front of eye gives frowning expression

Breeding ♂

Breeding ♀ ▲

♂ ▲ winter

♀ winter ▲

In winter ♂ unmarked below, ♀ softly streaked, juv most streaked

♂ . ♀
Outer primaries

Juv ♀
Brownest plumage ▲

Broad-bodied, large-headed finch of woodland, parks, gardens, fields. Dull to bright green, yellow in wings and tail. Deep, triangular, pale pinkish bill. Summer male rich green with flash of yellow on wing and yellow patch each side of tail (the most obvious yellow when flying away); dark patch in front of eye. In winter duller, greyer-green. Female averages duller, a little less yellow on wing, in winter subtly streaked greyish. Immature browner, less yellow but still has thin stripe along edge of closed wing, faintly streaked above, diffuse streaking below; dusky moustache, thick pale bill, short pale legs. Call bright, metallic *jupjupjup*. Song loud, musical series of rich trills, varying in speed, pitch, and quality, interspersed with deep, buzzy *dzeeeeer*.

Siskin

Breeding ♂

Breeding ♂

Breeding ♀

Small, lively, sharp-billed, fork-tailed finch with black and yellow wingbars, yellowish sides to tail

Juv ♂
Lacks yellow in tail

Breeding ♂ ▲

♂ 1st winter ▼

Ad ♀ breeding

Juv ♀ ▲

♂

Ad ♂ yellowest on rump, with broadest yellow wingbar ►

♀ winter

♀

Juv ♀ ▲

Small, delicate, fine-billed, fork-tailed woodland finch that feeds in trees and also at garden feeders, especially in spring. Flocks fly quickly, in coordinated manoeuvres, often mixed with redpolls. Male pale yellow-green with softly streaked back, black cap and bib, bright greenish-yellow face and breast, white belly with fine black streaks. Black wings with broad yellow band. Yellow rump, black tail with yellow side panels. Pale, sharply pointed triangular bill. Female greyer, less yellow, dull below; wings black with narrower, paler yellow bar. Juvenile grey, streaked dark, with narrow wingbar. Calls bright, pure, ringing whistles: *tsy-zee* or *tiu*; also deep, short buzzy rattle. Song lively, varied twittering and trills, with calls intermixed.

251

Serin

Bright yellow on head, chest, rump

◄ Juv ♂

Ad ♀ ▶

◄ Ad ♂

Ad ♂ ▲

♀ ▶

Pale buff wingbars

Juv ▶

♂ ▶

Juv ♂ ▲

Streaked below

Tiny fork-tailed finch of parks, gardens, orchards, with stumpy bill and yellow rump. Male yellow on forehead and face, streaked above; thin yellow wingbars. White below with black streaks. Female paler, dull on head, more streaked, pale yellow rump. Juvenile browner, buff wingbar, rump streaked buff. Call and song fast, sharp, rippling twitter, like glass splintering.

Citril Finch

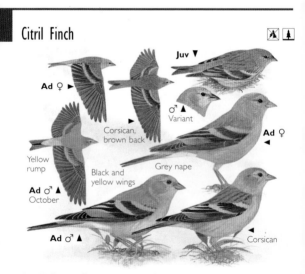

Juv ▼

Ad ♀ ▶

♂ ▲ Variant

Ad ♀ ◄

Corsican, brown back

Yellow rump

Black and yellow wings

Grey nape

Ad ♂ ▲ October

Ad ♂ ▲

Corsican ◄

Small finch of high altitude forest and meadow edge. Green, yellow, and pale grey, rump yellow-green. Male has green-yellow face and grey nape, neck, and chest; underside unmarked dull green. Black wings with two broad green-yellow bars; tail all dark. Female greyer, faintly streaked above; broad wingbars. Call short *teh*; song short, varied trills and rattles.

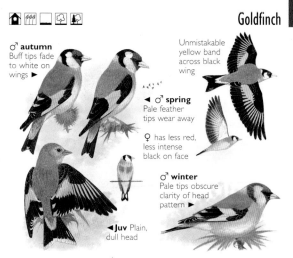

Goldfinch

♂ **autumn**
Buff tips fade to white on wings ►

Unmistakable yellow band across black wing

◄ ♂ **spring**
Pale feather tips wear away

♀ has less red, less intense black on face

♂ **winter**
Pale tips obscure clarity of head pattern ►

◄ **Juv** Plain, dull head

Small, lightweight, acrobatic finch of weedy ground, with broad yellow band across black wing. Bouncing flight. Adult has red face, white sides to head, black nape band. Body tawny, pale below; wingtips black with buff or white spots. Juvenile lacks head pattern; wings duller black and yellow. Calls liquid, lilting, slurred *swililip*, *swilit*, *tililip*, mixed into trilling song.

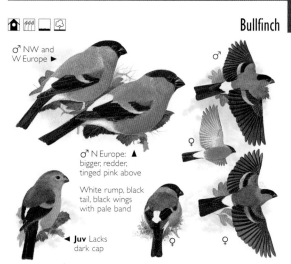

Bullfinch

♂ NW and W Europe ►

♂

♀

♂ N Europe: ▲
bigger, redder, tinged pink above

White rump, black tail, black wings with pale band

◄ **Juv** Lacks dark cap

♀

♀

Heavy, rather sluggish finch of hedges, thickets, orchards, with bold white rump, black wings and tail. Broad white bar across closed wing. Male has black cap and bib, grey back, deep red-pink underside. Female same pattern, but brownish above, pale brownish-buff below. Juvenile lacks black cap and bib. Call a simple, single, piping whistle, *pooow*; creaky song.

253

Mealy Redpoll

Ad ♀ Large-billed form ►

1st yr ♂ ◄

Large, pale redpoll with broad, square wings; streaked beneath tail and on whitish rump; white wingbar

Ad ♂ ▲ Typical small bill

Ad ♀ ▲

◄ Juv Oct

Juv ♂ ►

▲ Juv August

Hoary

Mealy

◄ Juv ♂

Juv ♂ Hoary

Large redpoll, greyish above, whiter below, with white wingbars and variably whitish rump. Undertail coverts white with dark streaks. Darker birds can be confused with smaller, browner Lesser Redpoll, whitest with whiter-rumped Arctic, but larger-billed than either, and quite strongly streaked along flanks. Summer male strongly red-pink on chest. Calls as Lesser Redpoll.

Arctic, Hoary, & Greenland Redpolls

Juv ♀ Hoary ▼

Juv ♂ Hoary

Ad ♂ Arctic ►

White undertail

Broader wings than Hoary

♂ Arctic ▲

◄ Ad ♂ Arctic

Very long wings, very white below

◄ Juv ♂ Greenland ►

Streaks under tail

Heavy, bright, black flank stripes

Large redpolls with broad heads, thick necks, and tiny bills. White on rump, white undertail coverts, tiny white 'shorts' on thighs. Arctic bright tawny-buff around head, Hoary greyer. Flanks very lightly streaked. Juvenile has least white on rump, adult male has big white rump, pale pink chest. Greenland Redpoll big, dark, heavily striped on flanks, recalling Twite.

Lesser Redpoll

♂ ▶ winter

♂ **spring** Red-pink ▲ on breast and rump

♂

◀ Juv ♀

♀ autumn

◀ ♀ winter

Juv ▲

♀ spring ▲

Small, slim, quick finch of tree tops and bushes, with red crown, black bib. Forms tight, coordinated flocks. Small, sharp, pale bill, elongated body, deeply forked tail. Tawny-brown with dark red crown, broad buff wingbar. Whiter below, streaked. Spring male has extensive red-pink on chest. Metallic, rhythmic, stuttering *chuchuchuchuchuch*. Fast, reeling trill in song flight.

Scarlet Rosefinch

Juvs

Thick, deep bill

◀ ♂ Bright red varies in extent

Two pale wingbars

Juv ▶

Beady eye in plain face

♀ ▲

♀ and juv greenish-grey and grey-buff, with fine streaks on chest, pale wingbars

◀ ♀

Juv ▲

♂

Thick-billed, round-headed finch with bold dark eye in plain face, plain tail. Male red on head, chest, and rump; white below. Female brown, softly streaked darker; two narrow buff wingbars. Juvenile olive-brown with bolder buff wingbars, otherwise nondescript except for round bill, bold eye. Call hoarse, rising *sweeh*. Song short, rhythmic, whistling phrase.

Linnet

♂ summer ▶
Amount of red on head and chest varies

▲ ♀ summer
Greyish head with pale crescentic mark above and below eye, pale cheek spot

♂ autumn
Fresh feathers with dull tips obscure bright colours ▶

♀ winter ▶

White feather edges give distinctive white streaks on wing and tail ▼

Juv ▶

Juv ▶
Most streaked, least white in wing

♀ ▶
Gingery with fine dark streaks

♂ ▲
Plain rusty brown on back

White on tail

Lively, slim, fork-tailed finch, feeds on ground rather than in trees or shrubs, not acrobatic. Usually around low bushes, heaths, and hedgerows beside open ground. Wings and tail streaked with white, creating broad pale panel on open wing and white patch each side of tail. Grey bill. Male has grey head, red forehead and breast, with more extensive red-pink in summer. Plain chestnut-brown back, blackish wing with white panel. Female has ginger-brown appearance, with faintly streaked brown back, tawny chest with fine streaks, greyish-brown head with subtle pale mark above and below eye, pale cheek spot. Call light, twittering chatter, *tet-et-et* or *tich-ich-ich*; frequent *hooeet*. Song musical, varied, rattling warble.

Twite

Scandinavian: very buff ►

♀ **summer** ►

Streaky, buff to sandy brown with clear tawny throat; streaks on wing like Linnet

♀

White in wing and tail as Linnet; general plumage, buff wingbar recall Redpoll

Tail darker than Linnet

♂ ▲
autumn
Pink rump, brighter in spring

Juv ♂ ►

Juv ▲

♀ **autumn** ►

Small, unobtrusive finch, flocks on ground or in short vegetation. Tawny-brown, streaked dark. Buff wingbar recalls Redpoll, white streaks in wing and tail like Linnet. Male has deep pink rump, grey bill; winter birds have less pink, females none, and yellow bill. Throat unmarked rich tawny-buff. Call nasal, twangy *twaai-it*; song incorporates call in twittering warble.

Pine Grosbeak

♂ ▲
1st winter

♂ ►
Raspberry red and grey

♀ ►

Big, round-billed, round-headed finch with long tail, thin pale wingbars

♀

♀ **1st winter** ▲
Bronzy-green head, grey body

♀ **winter** ▲

Very large, heavy finch of far northern forests. Small-headed but with stout bill. White wingbars and edges to tertials. Male raspberry-red and grey, female bronzy-green and grey, immature male more orange. Long-tailed in flight; acrobatic when feeding on outer twigs of trees. Bill thick, rounded but not crossed. Call fluty *pluit*, quick *pu-ji-jililip*.

Parrot Crossbill

Ad ♀ ▲
Greenish; dark wings; yellow rump

◄ Juv
Streaky grey-brown

◄ ♀ bill
(♂ in outline)

Big, thick, angled bill

Ad ♂ ▲
Dull red with brown-black wings and tail; often has greyer nape and flanks

Parrot Crossbill (right) broader bill and head than Common (left)

Biggest crossbill, northern, in mature pines. Heavily built and thickset, often has bulky 'mane' around hindneck; flattish crown, small eye. Bill very thick, angled on lower mandible, hooked but blunt, scarcely crossed. Male pink-red with browner wings. Female greenish, greyer on nape. Call a variable, deep, hard *tchup tchup tchup* or *tlup*, less metallic than Common Crossbill.

Two-barred Crossbill

►Ad ♂

◄ Juv

◄ Imm ♂

◄Common
Variant with wingbars

♂ has yellow-buff underwing coverts (grey on Common)

Bold wingbars, V or notched tertial tips

◄ ♂

Neat crossbill of larch woods, pines. Slim bill with long, curved point. Two broad, curved, white wingbars; bold white tertial tips when fresh. Male red-pink, brighter than Common Crossbill, blacker wings with pure white marks. Female greenish, streaked, with yellower rump. Juvenile has much thinner wingbars, inviting confusion with barred variant of Common Crossbill.

Common & Scottish Crossbill

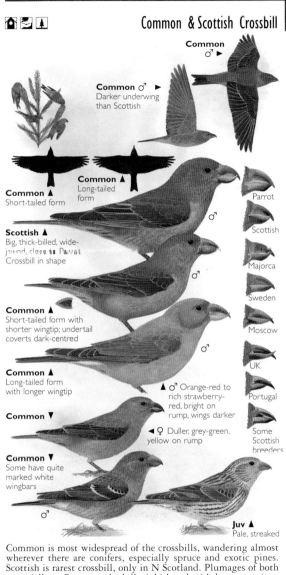

Common ♂ ►

Common ♂ ►
Darker underwing than Scottish

Common ▲
Short-tailed form

Common ▲
Long-tailed form

Parrot

Scottish

Scottish ▲
Big, thick-billed, wide-jawed, close to Parrot Crossbill in shape

Majorca

Sweden

Common ▲
Short-tailed form with shorter wingtip; undertail coverts dark-centred

Moscow

UK

Common ▲
Long-tailed form with longer wingtip

Portugal

♂ Orange-red to rich strawberry-red, bright on rump, wings darker

Common ▼

◄ ♀ Duller, grey-green, yellow on rump

Some Scottish breeders

Common ▼
Some have quite marked white wingbars

Juv ▲
Pale, streaked

Common is most widespread of the crossbills, wandering almost wherever there are conifers, especially spruce and exotic pines. Scottish is rarest crossbill, only in N Scotland. Plumages of both essentially as Parrot: male dull pinkish-red with browner wings and intense red-pink rump, female greener with yellower rump. Wings typically plain brown, may have narrow white bars. Juvenile closely streaked. Crown often peaked; bill very variable, short to long and deep, with long, decurved tip and obvious crossed mandibles. Scottish has thicker bill, muscular cheeks. Loud, far-carrying *jip-jip-jip* or *glip-glip-glip* distinctively 'crossbill' (young Greenfinch close, Parrot Crossbill very similar but deeper). Song a varied warbling with low buzzy notes.

Corn Bunting

♀ has narrower wing, shorter body than ♂

♂ **autumn**
Fresh feathers ▶

♀ **summer** ▼ Worn

Briefly flies with legs lowered at times

Tawny-brown and buff overall, narrowly streaked, no very strong pattern

Sings with head up and back; tail flicked

Head pattern stronger on some

Large, wide bill with S-shaped cutting edge

◀ **Juv**
Brighter buff

♀

♂

No white on tail

Worn duller, ▶ dark, by June

Widespread, locally common bunting of extensive arable land, grasslands, warm bushy slopes with small cornfields. Perches on ground, low hummocks, fences, wires. A big, pale bunting with a plain tail that has no white on sides. Long, forked tail hangs down from perch in untidy fashion. Sexes alike, with no bright colour: pale buff-brown, streaked dark above, rump paler, pale below with dark streaks often coalescing as breast spot. Thick, pale buff bill with dark ridge. Pale eye-ring. Some birds show hint of dark band each side of crown, dark lower edge to cheek, stronger dark moustache, and small pale cheek spot. Call loud, full *plip*; song dry, ticking rattle speeding up into spluttery, splintering-glass jingle: *ti-ti-titikikik-trrrreeeeess*.

Ortolan Bunting

♂ 1st winter ▶

Flat head, sharp bill, eye-ring, pale streak under cheek give distinctive expression

Ad ♀ ▶

Pale greenish and yellowish on head, pale rufous below

◀ Breeding ♂

◀ Breeding ♀

Ad ♂ ▼▲

Undertail mostly white

◀ ♀ and imm have white outer tail

♀ and imm have sharp, pink bill, whitish eye-ring

♀ 1st winter ▲

♂ 1st winter ▶

♀ has shorter tail than ♂

Widespread bunting, locally frequent on bushy slopes and higher upland meadows. Neat, pale, slim-bodied, with pointed, pink bill and whitish eye-ring giving curious, gentle expression. Summer male has greenish-grey head, yellow moustache and throat. Greenish breastband, not contrasting much with pale rusty-orange underside. Streaked brown above, buff-brown rump. Female more streaked, head streaky greenish-grey with paler, more diffuse yellow; paler pink bill. Underside echoes male pattern but duller, finely streaked on chest. Immature more buff-brown overall, pale yellowish eye-ring, orange-pink bill; pale cheek spot and yellowish throat useful. Call a metallic *plip*; simple, whistled song with lower ending: *sreesreesree sree siu siu siu.*

Yellowhammer

Sharp-faced, long-tailed, yellow or yellowish with white-sided black tail, bright chestnut rump

Ad ♂
Bright rufous rump ▼

Ad ♂ Head stripes and breastband vary ▼ ►

♂ brightest in spring

Ad ♀ ►
Rufous rump

♀ spring ▼

♂ 1st winter ▼

▲ ♀ winter

Ad ♀ ▼ breeding

Juv ♀ ▼

Ad Tail

Some are more streaked than others ►

Ad ♂ ▼

Long-bodied, long-tailed, sharp-faced bunting of open farmland, bushy hillsides, heaths, and commons. Males variable, but always show distinctive combination of extensively bright yellow head, ginger-brown breastband, black-streaked back, and rufous rump. Long black tail, edged white. Variable amount of black or greenish marking on head, usually dark lines on upper and lower edge of cheek. Streaked flanks. Female paler, with yellow suffused with green especially on cheek, stripes beside crown, and across streaky breast. Pale yellow below, clear rufous rump. Immature buffier, less yellow. Call metallic, explosive *tswik*, clicking *pit pitipit*. Song ringing, quick, rattling trill or slightly slower with long note at or near end: *ti-ti-ti-ti-ti-ti-ti-titiip-eeee*.

Cirl Bunting

◄ Juv

♂ winter ◄

Olive rump

♂

Brown with hard dark streaks, rump dull olive

♀

♂ mixed greenish, yellow, chestnut and black

♀ ► spring

▲ Outer tail

♀ ▲

♂ ◄ summer

Male recalls Yellowhammer but with greenish crown, black throat, broad black and yellow face stripes, greenish breastband edged rusty-red, harder red-brown back, olive-brown rump. Female has more striped head, duller rump than Yellowhammer. Call elusive, high *sip*. Song simple rattle, hard and fast, or softer, more dribbling *tritritritritritritritri* recalling Bonelli's Warbler.

Cretzschmar's Bunting

◄ ♂ summer

♂ spring
►

♀ Sept ►

♀ pink-rufous, streaked across chest, pink bill

♂ ◄ spring
Streaked

♂ grey on head and chest, throat and belly rusty; pattern as Ortolan

◄ ♂ summer
Dark streaks and pale edges wear off

Very like Ortolan Bunting, but restricted to SE Europe. Male has blue-grey hood, not greenish, with rusty-orange moustache and throat, not yellow; deeper rusty-brown below. Female similar but duller, paler, and finely streaked. Juvenile rusty-brown, greyer on nape and chest, finely streaked; white eye-ring, pinkish bill, lacks yellow on throat of young Ortolan.

Black-headed Bunting

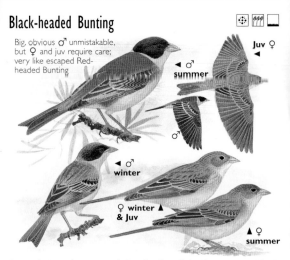

Big, obvious ♂ unmistakable, but ♀ and juv require care; very like escaped Red-headed Bunting

Juv ♀

◄ summer

♂

◄ winter

♀ winter & Juv

♀ summer

Big, obvious bunting of farmland and bushy countryside in SE Europe. Male striking yellow with black hood, rufous back, thin white wingbar, big bluish bill. Female paler, duller, with grey hood. Immature similar to female, finely streaked on cap and back; unstreaked buffish below, yellower undertail. Call *chup* or *zrit*. Song slow, accelerating, descending, whistling phrase.

Yellow-breasted Bunting

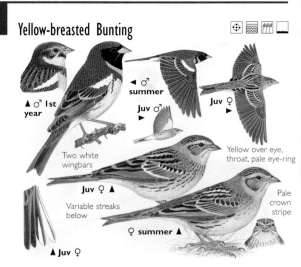

▲ ♂ 1st year

◄ ♂ summer

Juv ♂ ►

Juv ♀

Two white wingbars

Yellow over eye, throat, pale eye-ring

Juv ♀ ▲

Variable streaks below

♀ summer ▲

Pale crown stripe

▲ Juv ♀

NE European breeder, rare on migration in W Europe. Spring male rufous with black face, bright yellow below with thin black breastband; bold white shoulder patch. Female streaked grey-buff and black above, head boldly striped blackish with pale crown stripe, pale ear spot; underside pale yellow with dark flank streaks. Juvenile similar, less yellow. Two white wingbars.

Little Bunting

Small, compact; dull rump, dull forewing lacks rufous ▶

◀ Tail pattern

Dark cheek stripes fall short of bill; rusty crown stripe, bright face

◀ ♂ summer

Ad, April Plain, greyish at first ▶

▲ **Reed Bunting**

▲ ♂ **winter** Pale eye-ring important clue

Juv ▲

Small, neat bunting with sharp, straight-edged bill, pale eye-ring, rufous nape, and black on each side of rusty crown. Summer adult has whole face rusty, with black-edged cheeks (not reaching bill). Juvenile duller, but pale cheek spot obvious; wing coverts dull (rufous on larger young Reed Bunting). Pink legs. Fine streaks below. Call unlike Reed Bunting: sharp, clicking *zik*.

Rustic Bunting

♀ **winter** ▶

♂ **summer**

Rufous rump; pale crown, nape spot

♂ **winter** ◀

▼ Tail

Crown often peaked

♂ **winter** ▲

Juv ♀ autumn ▶ Most like Reed: rufous flank streaks, pale cheek spot, pale crown

Rusty-brown and white bunting of wet northern forests. Spring male has black and white striped face, white underside with rufous breastband. Female similar but cheeks duller, brownish with pale spot and black edges. Juvenile duller still, but peaked crown with pale centre, broad stripe over eye, pale cheek spot, rufous rump, white underside streaked dull chestnut. Sharp *zit*.

Reed Bunting

Dark, rufous brown; rump dark brown, little contrast; white

Rufous wing coverts

♀ **summer ►**
Narrower wing than ♂

♂ **winter ►**

Dark, no obvious wingbar; whitish below

Breeding ♂ ►

♂ **autumn ►**

♂ **spring ►**

Breeding ♂ ►
Very dark above as pale edges wear away

Bold whitish stripe under dark cheek, thick black moustache

Cream and blackish stripes above

♀ **summer ►**

♀ **winter ▼**

♀ Dark crown with little pattern, dark cheeks, pale moustache ►

Juv ▼

Common and widespread bunting: a yardstick for rarer migrants. Longish black tail with broad white sides. Upperparts streaked black, cream and rufous, dull brown rump; underside whitish or pale buff, finely streaked blackish-brown. Weak pale eye-ring, slightly rounded bill, red-brown legs. Lacks sharp clicking call. Spring male has black head, bold white collar, white moustache. In winter black is obscured by rufous-buff edging. Female has grey-brown head, cheeks more rufous, bold black stripe from bill joins streaked breastband. Immature has brown cheeks, dark edges to base of bill; broad pale stripe below cheek most obvious mark on head. Call a full slurred *siu*; very thin, high *see*. Song short, rattling, slowish phrase *srip srip srip sipipip seer*.

Lapland Bunting

♂ winter ►

♀ 1st winter ►

Long-bodied, short-legged, short-tailed terrestrial bunting with strong facial patterns

Breeding ♂ ►

♀ winter ▼

♀ summer ▼

Pale cheeks with angular black corners

Rufous nape, rufous wing panel edged with thin white bars; black and cream stripes above

Juv ♀ winter ▲

Juv ♂ winter ▲

Juv ▲

Ad   Juv

Rather large, low-slung, short-legged terrestrial bunting, breeds in far N Europe, moves to coasts in winter. Often mixes with Snow Bunting, and behaves like it. Winter plumage recalls Reed, but has broad white-edged rufous panel across wing, pale central crown stripe. Summer male has black cap, face, and breast, pale stripe behind eye curving onto neck, broad rufous nape patch. White below. Female and winter male have rufous-brown face, black marks at corners of cheek, dark stripes each side of crown, streaked black and cream back, complex pattern of dark mottles on breast and chest sides. Juvenile finely streaked below but similar head pattern and wingbars; paler legs. Call hard, dull, fast trill, *di-di-di-di-dik*, often followed by sweet, whistled *teuu*.

Rock Bunting

Grey forewing, rufous rump, white underwing

♂ 1st winter ►

◄ ♀ spring

♂ ◄ winter

♂ ▲ summer

Black, grey, whitish face stripes

♂

Juv ▲

Unobtrusive bunting of stony ground, crags, ruins in S Europe. Rufous above, streaked black except on clear rusty rump; paler rufous-buff below. Male has blue-grey head and chest, with black stripes beside crown, through eye and under cheek, whiter over eye. Female has duller version of head pattern. Call thin, high *si*, frustratingly elusive; high, thin, musical song.

Snow Finch

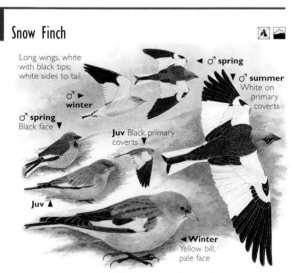

Long wings, white with black tips; white sides to tail

◄ ♂ spring

♂ ► winter

♂ spring
Black face ▼

♂ summer ▼
White on primary coverts

Juv Black primary coverts ▼

Juv ▲

◄ Winter
Yellow bill, pale face

Large, long-winged, boldly patterned finch-like mountain bird of S Europe. Grey-brown above, white below. White wings with black tips; black tail with broad white sides. Back scarcely streaked, unlike Snow Bunting. Bill black in summer, yellowish in winter when black bib is mostly lost. Calls include *zeeeh*, *ti-ti-zu*, chattering notes. Song includes fast trills.

Snow Bunting

Large, long, short-legged terrestrial bunting, small bill, long wings

♀ and juv paler under wingtip than ad ♂ ▼

Most white on ad ♂, least on juv

♀ at all ages has dark-centred median coverts (white bar on ♂) ◄

◄ ♂ winter

♂ Variation ▲

♂ Juv ♀ autumn ►

♀ Variation

Juv ♂ Juv ♂

♀ ► winter

♂ ► spring

♀ summer ▲

♀ winter ▼

Winter birds have yellow bills, much rufous on cheeks, cap, sides of neck

Juv ♀ ▲

Winter/juv birds rich tawny, buff and white, long black wingtips, short black legs

♀ winter ▲

♂ winter ▲

Long-winged, short-legged bunting that breeds on northern tundra, mountains; winters on moors, hills, coasts. Summer male white except for black back, wingtips, bill, and legs. Female browner on back, crown, and cheeks. In winter looks tawny-brown on ground, with rusty-buff cap, cheeks, and chest patches; buffish below. Yellow bill with dark tip, black legs. Juvenile greyish, head plain except for pale eye-ring, subtle paler moustache and chin. Like adult in winter, but upperparts more extensively buff-brown, streaked dark. In flight winter male has white wings tipped black; younger male and female have more black on outer wing, but inner wing variably barred; juvenile has much less white. Calls soft, rippling *tiriririririrp*, full *seuw*.

index